D0438013

GIANTS & HEROES

GIANTS & HEROES

A DAUGHTER'S MEMORIES OF

Y. A. TITTLE

DIANNE TITTLE DE LAET

STEERFORTH PRESS
SOUTH ROYALTON, VERMONT

For information about permission to reproduce selections
from this book, write to: Steerforth Press L.C., P.O. Box 70,
South Royalton, Vermont 05068.

Library of Congress Cataloging-in-Publication Data
de Laet, Dianne Tittle, 1949–
Giants and heroes : a daughter's memories of Y. A. Tittle
Dianne Tittle de Laet.
p.   cm.
Includes bibliographical references (p.   )
ISBN 1–883642–13–2
I. Tittle, Y. A. (Yelberton Abraham), 1926–   . 2. Football players—United
States—Biography. 3. New York Giants (Football team)—History. I. Title.
GV939.T5D4   1995
796.332'092—dc20   95–35474

A portion of the proceeds from the sale of this book is being donated to the
Arete Scholarship Fund. To help with college tuition, this scholarship will
be given annually to a student/athlete at Menlo-Atherton High School who
excels in dedication, spirit, and effort, and who deserves support and recog-
nition.

Manufactured in the United States of America

First Printing

To Blocker

From "The Book Of Games" by Martial

Let Memphis astonished fall silent.
The foreign wonder of the Pyramids no longer commands our
    complete attention.
Let Assyrian architects now refrain from boasting of Babylon.
And the sensitive citizens of Ephesus
can no longer take such pride in their vast precincts of Artemis . . .
                        —no. 1

Is there a nation anywhere so outlandish
as not to furnish a spectator among those in your city,
Caesar?
A Rhodopeian farmer is here, from the banks of Orpheus' river,
    the Haemus,
a Sarmation from the tribes of mares' blood-drinkers,
another whose coastline the farthest ocean lashes;
Arabians and Sabeans have hurried here, and Cicilians saturated in
    their saffron scent . . .
the multiple sound of the voices of your people are different,
    forming one and the same sound . . .
                        —no. 3

As a recent arrival here from distant shores,
watching the sacred games for the first time,
this gift of entertainment bestowed by our Emperor,
don't be fooled . . .
A while before, it was all good dry land
and has only been flooded for a spectacular purpose.
But you don't believe that? Well, watch then,
And see that when the god of war is tired of playing with the water, in
    a twinkling you will be blinking at a land engagement and saying,
"Hey, that was water."
                        —no. 24

            Epigrammata, de Spectaculis Liber[1]

Foreword

The first time I heard Dianne perform with her harp was in the Stanford University Memorial Church just prior to the great California earthquake. She had just finished singing and reciting stories of ancient Greek heroes to the accompaniment of her harp when the earthquake struck. There was a fast exit and upon her return she found her harp undamaged but her seat crushed by a piece of masonry that had fallen from the 90-foot ceiling. The piece of masonry turned out to be part of a mosaic; in fact it was the tip of an angel's wing. This was the first time I had ever heard Dianne perform, and I must say that it was quite an experience for me to sit there thinking that the only Sappho I ever knew played middle-linebacker for the Green Bay Packers, and that Pindar was a mean defensive end for the Chicago Bears. I never would have thought that playing the harp could be so dangerous, and I told her so. She was lucky. We were all lucky that day. But in some way she was lucky the way I have been lucky all my life.

The most precious gift we can receive is the gift of our children. And my daughter is one of four such gifts. As I sat there listening to all this poetry I must admit that I wasn't listening really. I figured that maybe I and Minnette, my wife, did get the wrong baby in the hospital and that our real daughter was perhaps farming somewhere in South Mississippi. I was thinking, however, that we got the best deal.

As I sat there it seemed like only yesterday that a writer from *Sports Illustrated* wrote, "On Halloween evening out Palo Alto way, doorbells on a side street jangled. There on a porch was a little bitty Red Riding Hood hollering 'Trick or Treat!'" And if

Dianne, then four years old, forgot to say thanks, I said it for her. She was our first born. And now we "Trick or Treat" with five grandchildren.

Surely while everyone else was listening to the words of Homer and Euripides, I must have been anticipating the great quake, and that was why my life was passing before my eyes. Or maybe I was just feeling lucky the way old quarterbacks do.

In the summer of 1944 I enrolled at Louisiana State University at age 17 and received my first scholarship. It may not seem like such a big deal these days, but at the time I felt like the luckiest thing on two feet considering the fact that a date consisted of 7 cents for the city bus, 10 cents for a ferryboat ride across the Mississippi River on a moonlit night, 10 cents for a splurge at the coffee shop, and a goodnight kiss (maybe).

The woman on my left, who was also listening to Dianne, did not date me. But she had worn (in the year 1944) a tall red-and-white headpiece when she was the Marshall Maverick's High School head drum major. In 1944, I was the All Star tailback who used to watch her march, leaning backwards and twirling her baton. There was something about that hat that made me know she was the one for me—even though she certainly didn't know it and I had to tell her so in her graduation yearbook. Then again, I had to tell her three years later when she was seriously dating somebody else and I announced our engagement in the December issue of *Sport* magazine. A writer named Fred Digby had said, "Y. A., you have had a fine college career. What comes next?" And I said, "I'm going to graduate in June, marry my high school sweetheart, Minnette DeLoach, and play pro ball." I admit that it wasn't the most romantic proposal in the world, but at least I got rid of the other guy, and I have had the same best friend now for the past 47 years. She was there sitting beside me on the day of the quake. And as I said, I have been lucky.

As a ballplayer the luck started coming my way when I was inspired by my older brother, Jack, who played ball at Marshall, Texas High School and later at Tulane University. By junior high, I realized I had a strong right arm. As far back as I can remember

I was fascinated by a ball spinning in the air. In 1937, when many college teams were scoring touchdowns by throwing forward passes, I was inspired by "Slinging" Sammy Baugh of Texas Christian University. He was my hero. And then the fun began. I enjoyed the game of football when I played it in the sandlots. I enjoyed playing in practice and I enjoyed playing in the games. The fun lasted from Marshall High School in 1938 to December 1964 in Yankee Stadium. During all that time I played with all the great players and had fun. I received many honors, but I never won a championship. In some ways that was my greatest disappointment.

But there I was suddenly listening to my daughter sing of the tough, violent world of her ancient heroes, and it was hard to believe that this ex- Trick-or-Treater up there singing her heart out was the same person who wanted to write a football book. I warned her when the project started that no sports biography would sell without sex stories or at least some "good old juicy revelations" about my coaches or my teammates. Her book has none of that, mainly because I don't know any good old juicy revelations to tell. Mine was the tough and violent world of pro sports, but it was peopled with guys from the good old days like The Goose, Leo the Lion, The Geek, Ski Boots, The King, Lefty, Big Head, Tiger, The Hatchet, Boom Boom, Dookie, Ding Ding, Tuggy, Muscles, Racehorse, Ripper, Stormy, Fatso, Giff, Rosy, Chunkin Charlie, Big Mo. The list goes on but I think that we would all agree that it's not very poetic.

Joe Montana reminded me recently of a conversation we had had several seasons ago when Joe was having some early season setbacks and some of the writers were giving him a tough time. I told him not to worry and explained that in my opinion there are three phases in a quarterback's life. The first phase is good because you are young and new and everyone is booing the older quarterback. The second phase is the worst because you are the older quarterback and the boos are for you. The third phase is the absolute best because that is where the fans and writers marvel at the old broken-down pro who doesn't give up, and they say things like, "Look at that old codger out there—I just love him." I didn't tell Joe that maybe there was a fourth phase, but I think that I am in it now that my daughter is writing on the subject. Let me just say that football has changed a lot. The players today are probably bigger and faster and, in most cases, a lot better. But I think that maybe we, the old-timers, are the best storytellers.

I played with the 49er Million Dollar Backfield; I played with Hall of Famers in New York—Frank Gifford, Rosy Brown and Andy Robustelli. I threw to two of the best receivers—Billy Wilson of the 49ers and Del Shofner of the Giants. Allie Sherman was the best offensive coach, and Coach Cecil Isbell, my coach in Baltimore, convinced me that "I could do it." Frankie Albert was the greatest leader, and coaches Odus Mitchell of Marshall High School and Coach Bernie Moore of L.S.U. were like fathers to me. When I think of these guys they make me smile. Boom Boom, Ding Ding, Dookie and the rest, they make me smile while at the same time they remind me that being a professional football player wasn't always that easy. We quarterbacks used to have to call our own plays and many times the fans would be yelling, and the coaches would be second-guessing us and thinking we were stupid. You knew that the writers always needed something to write about and that after five interceptions and a few losses you would be news. But it was these guys, yes, it was Muscles, Racehorse and Ripper, who could brush all the worries away with the words, "Go For It!"

"Go For It!" is what finally I had to say to her on their account, even though writing a book about football in my opinion made no sense. "Go For It. Shoot The Moon!" As a father, as a friend, and as an old quarterback, that was my only advice to my daughter.

Y. A. Tittle
December 1994

Preface

Hut 1!

In 1982 I was on my way to my parents' home on Caddo Lake to compete in the first annual Y. A. Tittle Triathlon. As we pulled into the driveway of the lake house, music was playing and the lights near the hammock shone through the petals of a dogwood tree. Huline, my father's sister, warmed up some supper as I told her about the dilapidated church I'd seen on Monkhouse Avenue. In the last drop of daylight, the place looked like the No Tell Motel and the sign out front read: "In Love—On Fire—Not Ashamed." Huline was not even slightly surprised, and strange to say it made me happy. Home. I walked down to the lake where lily pads covered Caddo as far as the islands of trees. I checked out the canoe, examined the ropes, the oars, the dusty boxes, the rust, like somebody fumbling through the familiar contents of a grandmother's jewelry box. Then, as the light began to fade I touched a spider's web in the boathouse, and thought: I don't know my father.

All the years I spent watching him, and the years spent learning to love what I observed—but the lines that so clearly mark the boundaries of the playing field are an illusion if one thinks that those same lines contain the dreaming mind and the seeing eye of the quarterback in his moment. The web of his passion and the points of its fragile fastening extended so far back into his childhood as to disappear from the chronology of his life and his own consciousness. One point of connection might have taken place watching my mother parade down Davy Crockett Street as a Princess of the Fall. But whatever they were, he lived a life in which some kind of excellence was achieved. And I naturally wondered how.

Certainly the more I hear about football these days, the more I wonder how he ever made the team. He strove for excellence as if the game were an art form, while around the house he passed himself off as an insurance man. It was only on Sundays that we could see for ourselves a part of who our father was, when he challenged himself to balance his instinctive need for discipline and a standard with the need to play and thereby celebrate. It wasn't unique. In the 1950s, the game seemed made for that. But as to whether he fulfilled his nature with this seventeen year act of brutal devotion, I can only say that the mere doing of it, his wide open embrace of the sport, left upon his character a mark of determination like that of the relentless spider. Patience and impatience were one virtue in him, as he brought to the field not just all that he was, but more than he had ever hoped to be.

But he also demanded from the game in return something I cannot describe. More than throwing, *learning to see* had been his life. And at some point, like a hawk, his eye zeroed in on something else.

Could I respect the distances my father had learned to see? And might it then be possible to discover the endless possibilities for loving that which is beautiful in the world? When I touched the spider's web, I received my inheritance from my father, the athlete.

Hut 2!

My father has lived an entire life like a woman in childbirth—in the moment. To this day, no matter where my father goes, he keeps the green grass of the playing field in his back pocket and on any occasion unfurls it to create an epic adventure around Big Daddy Lipscomb (a favorite), or Yankee Stadium, or somebody playing catch with him in the driveway. Another thing I can tell you about my father is that he is a man who has deep-set eyes. Eyes so deep-set I used to think that wild animals lived in them— hawks, turtles, foxes and hedgehogs. And now when I listen to his stories I think that nothing has changed.

The energy rolls off my father in waves as he speaks of football highlights. First, however, he'll scratch his head as if he doesn't have anything to say. No—first he stands, because he can't talk sitting down, and he moves around a bit as if to pound out a tiny arena. Then it begins. And people listen. Even the people who hate football listen, *"Swing right on two—Hambone Hamblin and Baby Doo!"* There are people stories, family stories, broken bone stories. And to him the past is now, just as fresh as mud and sweat and zigouts.

Today, my father is a spinner of yarns, whose speaking engagements take him all over the country. And while I cannot tell his stories, wherever possible I have followed his rule of thumb when telling one: Lie to tell a truth. As every child is the receiver of the family story, I had no choice but to take the ball and run with it as best I could.

And run I did. . . .

In 1981 I traveled to Greece to compete in the Greek Marathon. It was while sitting at the entrance to the stadium in Olympia that I read about a special branch of choric poetry known as the victory ode and discovered an odd tradition linking sport, music, and poetry in the lyrics of the Western World's first sportswriter. I read while the light began to fail. And to my surprise, I also discovered that where I sat, the infamous Nero himself once sang at the games in a voice "like a crow," but won the singing event nonetheless. As a harpist myself, I could almost imagine Nero. But poetry at the ancient games?

As a curious spectator might, I wondered why, and at what point in the history of the games did poetry quit the race? Did Nero mark the spot? I was also fascinated by the language that once gave utterance to the *arete*, or excellence, of the ancient athlete, because it reminded me of my own experience growing up in the sports world. That too, believe it or not, was poetry to me— painful poetry at times which caused me to gnash my teeth and tear my hair out. Poetry that I did not get most of the time. But poetry nonetheless, that Pindar, dead two thousand years, had found the words for.

As I got up and walked through the stone entrance and into the stadium at Olympia, it was five minutes before closing time. And strange to say, my own memories of childhood, like a rash of chicken pox, began to surface, triggered by the lyrics I had been reading.

I remembered that my father fell in love with spinning objects when he was six years old. And when I was six years old watching him play, a football fan at Kezar Stadium in San Francisco leaned over and asked if I was going to be a cheerleader when I grew up. "No," I replied, "I am going to write a book about Greek mythology and be buried under a cypress tree." Of course, my parents found this incomprehensible. It never dawned on them or me that I could indeed write a book, until I stood there in Olympia, Greece, remembering the expression of the football fan whose thoughtful pause threw wide open the doors of my life. No mythological heroes? There were the fans in Yankee Stadium. In particular, there were the cab drivers in the Mezzanine section, whose faces read like an epic, and whose enthusiasm was enchantment for me.

As a football player, Y. A. Tittle was not only a master of the moment, he was also the only Hall Of Fame quarterback who never won a championship. As his daughter, was it not possible for me to choose the classical "T" formation rather than the contemporary "shotgun" approach to the sports biography, or celebrity memoir as it has come to be known? And could I not be buried under a cypress tree just as easily after writing a book about what it was like growing up in the land of football players?

In the time that it took Tittle to drop back into the pocket and throw, it was a done deal from my perspective. The game had changed so much that my father, while not an ancient Greek, was already a relic from football's bygone era. And then there was the Chicago Bears' championship game of 30-some years ago—the ancestor to today's Super Bowl—I remembered leaving that stadium with a crippled father and a point of comparison, observing from there on out the game's infinite variety of brutality and splendor as it moved from drama to circus, as the emphasis continued to shift from the glorious *we!* to the glorious *me!* over the years, and as the celebration of teamwork all too often paled in comparison to the glorification of an individual dancing in the end zone.

That which once made the brutality endurable for me has vanished, I admit. But what that ingredient was will surface again when I least expect it. And so, it is not for me to criticize the game, but only to note that Jimmy Brown and Jim Taylor never danced, never shimmied or shook in the end zone. As for Y. A. Tittle's receivers, Del Shofner and the rest, they too scored for their teams, not for themselves. And salary was not the issue 30 years ago in New York. The championship was. Our lives would have been different had football been our father's business and not his art form. But I have no regrets. Instead of my book about Greek mythology then, I would write about memories. It could only work as a team effort in which my father and I were willing to cooperate, in which he would have to tell me about his life as a football player, and I would have to listen. I would confess to the sports fan that I knew nothing about football, really. And my father would readily confess that the only Pindar he ever knew played defensive end for the Chicago Bears. The process alone would accomplish a family record.

In Olympia, Greece, it was still five minutes before closing time. And at such a time, should you find yourself alone with the past, beware of a Greek bearing a whistle. Still, there was time for a line from Pindar. I read the words out loud.

> *Gold shines gold when you test it.*
> *Take heart, and what you have ...*[1]

And then the whistle blew.

Hut 3!

The exercise in remembering began. . . . Now, at this stage of the game, I would hope to be forgiven for all of the football blasphemies in these pages. When I saw a play, it might have been a trap. A screen might have been a buttonhook. I apologize to the players for any inaccuracies, and to my parents because I am sharing with the reader glimpses of their lives when they have already lived a lifetime in the public eye. It is also possible that they might not even recognize themselves in these pages. Even for me, they became as remote as ancestors in the writing. The details of their lives no longer seemed so random and accidental, and I took liberties. As if they were broken statues, I moved in to put a finger back or lift a shoulder to what I thought was the proper place.

Where I have added to my father's life motives and feelings that I can only imagine, I have no doubt detracted from his truth and simple elegance as a football player. But I have also tried to tell my own story and capture something of my own journey from daughter to womanhood. And if, in the end, I have accomplished only lies and blasphemies, there is at least this truth: they came to me quite naturally while remembering football dreams.

Dianne Tittle de Laet
Karnack, Texas 1994

ZIGOUT!

READY BREAK!

Wrigley Field
Chicago, Illinois
1963

It is said that Virtue, or Arete, has her dwelling place above high
    rock cliffs
hard to climb; and that she is not to be seen by every eye
but only by one who with sweat and determination
climbs to the peak.

—Simonides, no. 579

Bald Eagle back to pass,
Yankee Stadium.

The Trick

From the *New York Times,* Monday, 30 December 1963:

FANS HEAR BACH BUT CHEER BEARS
by Leonard Koppett

Anyone who thinks he can simply explain American culture in the mid-sixties of the 20th century should contemplate and try his analytic powers on the following scene: At the half, a smartly uniformed, drilled-to-perfection marching band representing Tennessee State University of Nashville, stands on the famous baseball field in Chicago where the chalked 100-yard gridiron of a football field has just barely been squeezed in. . . .

And what does it play? The first section of Bach's Tocatta and Fugue in D Minor. The Bach is followed by a lively dance performed by 11 majorettes. Then the band form the outline of a typewriter, which rings a bell as the carriage comes to the end of each line. Then the football teams—the New York Giants and the Chicago Bears—return to the playing field. The game is resumed and the grim professionals start again to slam into one another and to bounce themselves and their foes off iron-hard ground. And through all this, the 45,801 frozen customers sit and cheer. . . .

This crowd is openly partisan. It booed the Giants collectively, and, when they were introduced, individually. The crowd gave its biggest cheer the first time Y. A. Tittle was tackled attempting a pass and again when Tittle left the field in the second quarter.[1]

Early on, he shut it out. All the boos. All the cheers. There was quiet. And the noise, the world, he left to us sitting in the stands. In his mind, he let there be nothing. It was a void of his own creation perfected at a very young age so that what he willed he could create—sometimes. And sometimes not. But he was playing this game at the age of six, and by thirty-six he was still at it. In

1963, Yelberton Abraham Tittle, professional quarterback for seventeen years, was standing on the 50-yard line getting ready for the handoff.

It was Tittle's last shot at a title. Surrounding him was Wrigley Field. And beyond that were skyscrapers peopled with gray silhouettes in a line. The wind howled. That Tittle heard because he knew that George Halas heard it too. Tittle was the old man's dream demon that afternoon. And this old man who had founded the National Football League, who owned, coached and once played for the Chicago Bears, was a father to the Monsters of the Midway, and the will and mighty enthusiasm of this old ex-sailor was the heart of football itself. Deliberately, Tittle lurked in the old man's skull. Halas did well, thought the quarterback, to thank those hulking gangsters of the sky. He had built the Bears into a team predicated on running the ball and playing great defense. The Monsters of the Midway welcomed the wind.

For three years, ever since Tittle had shown up at the Giant camp too old to be taken seriously, with his tattered body, his old-fashioned high tops and his little-boy pads, he had listened to the siren's song. They had been picked for last, this team of old Giants, but with Tittle at the helm they set out to find the Golden Fleece and came up with three division championships in a row. Three championships, no title, and still the sirens singing, singing of broken bones and all the years.

In junior high, he had broken his nose, his rib and his left arm. At Louisiana State University, he fractured an ankle, rebroke the nose, and was knocked out twice. As a pro, he was knocked out cold three times, broke his back twice, took time out for an elbow operation; after which his cheekbone was fractured in three places, and one of his lungs collapsed. He broke a rib, a hand, and a toe and pulled just about every muscle in his body, including those connected to his armpits and his eyebrows.

But there was also the *trick*. As far back as Tittle went, the trick went with him. As a boy, he never threw but that he imagined first touching the goal in his mind with his forefinger. The trick was his secret, and he worked on it constantly. He could have memorized the *Iliad* in less time than it took his body to memorize the trick, but distances between objects could be made to disappear if you got it right. The trick also made him astonishingly accurate with a football. That's how he nailed the sycamore in the end zone of his mother's rose garden every time and aced a swinging tire 24 times in a row.

Seconds now. The blitz . . .

ZIGOUT!

Dropping back to pass at Wrigley Field, Y. A. Tittle had stepped back in time. In 1943, when asthma sidelined him for the duration of his high school championship, he sat on that bench and felt his insides itch with loneliness, watched his championship go by like wild horses running in a dream. Never again. Retire? Give up? Tell Ahab to go fish in a bucket. By the time he got to Chicago, Tittle had put that ball in the air for the LSU Tigers, the Baltimore Colts, the San Francisco 49ers and the New York Giants; for Coaches Cracker Brown, Odus Mitchell, Slick Martin and Bernie Moore, for Cecil Isbell, Red Shrader, Buck Shaw and Frankie Albert, for Tony Morabito and Allie Sherman. Most every coach he ever had told him he was "the best," a classical passer, even if he ran like a Greek statue.

All until the 49er head coach Red Hickey. When Hickey switched from the T to the shotgun offense he needed a quarterback who could "scramble."

The news broke in 1961: YAT BOOTED OUT OF FRISCO, and the front page headlines were big enough to announce an extraterrestrial's election to political office.

Wrigley Field, Chicago. 2nd Quarter.

I was 13 years old and sitting there in the stands, when the guy in front leaned back and said to the guy on my left, "Without Tittle, the Giants couldn't go from Grand Central to Times Square on the subway." That wasn't very nice. But it did no good pretending my eyes were BB guns and squinting at him, because there was a big problem on the field. The problem was that my father was human and so were all of the Giants. Until that afternoon, maybe up until this second quarter, many fans assumed, as Irwin Shaw wrote, that they were mythological figures who appeared in a weekly rite at the time of the autumnal solstice and performed miracles with a football on the Sabbath. The Giants did have a "Book of Spells." I had seen it myself. It was a play book, filled with funny marks. But now my father's nose was bleeding. And these men in black and orange were piling on top of him.

As if to add to the confusion, the wind was rolling and swirling dust and clouds on the floor of the stadium. As the Giants approached the scrimmage line and my father looked from left to right, I thought of the photograph taken in Pittsburgh which showed Dad kneeling in the end zone and bleeding from the head. It was a baffling photo because it did not illustrate who my father was as an athlete, and because it was misleading to think of his kind of enthusiasm and desire initialed in blood.

But maybe the man in front of me was right. Irwin Shaw had written in a magazine that "Tittle could not throw a football while lying flat on his back," and that "the New York Giants could not win a football game if Tittle was hit hard enough to send him off in search of medical attention."

I'd seen a blitz before, in fact many times. Blitzing described the act of sending everything possible through the line to destroy the quarterback every time he got the ball. Obviously, everything didn't always get through the line. But sometimes it did. And my sense was that the blitz was on and *everything* was coming . . .

I shut my eyes. I recited: *The fox knows many tricks, the hedgehog only one—one good one.*[2] It was a poem I knew, a prayer that touch would remain my father's one good trick. Then I hunkered down to pull with all my might for the New York Giants.

"GO GIANTS GO!"

The Giant defensive captain, Andy Robustelli, watched from the sidelines as Tittle's acrobatic receivers, Del Shofner, Aaron Thomas and Frank Gifford were lining up once more. The offensive unit had become the second highest scoring team in NFL history, averaging 32 points per game, and it was no wonder the oldest of the "greybeard" Giants was confident that the Giants could outclass the Chicago Bears. Already, Robustelli had watched Gifford beat Bennie McRae and score on a zigout pass to the corner, so named from the z-like path of Gifford's favorite pattern. On a subsequent drive, Giant receiver Del Shofner reached for the ball in the icy endzone and it slipped through his hands. Nobody faulted Shofner for the dropped pass. The drive was on. Ahead 7–0, nothing could or would stand in their way this time. For the New York Giants, it had been a long road to a moment. And for Andy Robustelli, this championship in 1963 was to be the last game of his long career.

During his years as a professional, Andy Robustelli had watched TV come over the horizon like a monster hungry for heroes and seen the media take football to center stage. Now, his attention was glued on his teammate, Y. A. Tittle, whose eyes not only measured distance, they had adjusted to those TV lights. In that glare, Tittle had unified the New York Giants team. In 1963, he broke his own league record with 36 touchdown passes, completing 221 out of 367 attempts for 3,145 yards. Tittle had been selected Most Valuable Player in 1957, 1961, and 1963. Awarded pro football's highest honors, he had broken Bobby Layne's all-time NFL passing record and held records for most touchdown passes in one season, most touchdowns in career, most yards, most completions and most attempts. In the 1963 game against the Washington Redskins alone, he threw for 505 yards and seven touchdown passes, refusing to go for the eighth TD—against the wishes of his teammates—for fear it would come across like showboating, for fear it would be in poor taste.

And so it was that Andy Robustelli felt confident that this time the championship was theirs. Like everybody else, the captain of the defensive squad conceded that Chicago's defense was tough. But defense alone was not supposed to make pro football champions, and the Chicago Bears, Monsters of the Midway, were expected to finish no better than second in the league.

Now, however, the Bears were showing their claws. They would first have to interrupt the rhythm that Tittle and his receivers shared. But the bonds of the Giant brotherhood could be strong. Late in the second quarter the oldest of the greybeards sensed a blitz coming. Robustelli knew it before he thought it. And he saw it reflected in Y. A. Tittle's deep-set eyes while halfback Frank Gifford shot downfield on another *zigout!*

Frank Gifford had returned to the Giants after suffering a deep brain concussion in 1960. Tex Maule of *Sports Illustrated* wrote, "Chuck Bednarik's violent, blindside tackle left Frank lying still and almost dead on the cold grounds."[3] But he came back to the Giants. And Frank was there when Tittle showed up at training camp in 1961, looking like a bad omen. One look at this museum piece and Coach Alan Sherman turned to his assistant and said, "My God! He'll get killed! He's got to be kidding!" It got worse when Tittle fumbled the handoff on his first play, in a preseason game against the Rams, and could not move or speak afterwards. He was hit hard. And when he tried to stand, his legs buckled and he could not breathe. Frank thought he might be unfamiliar with the plays and offered to call the next one. But Tittle just shook his head and winced before looking to the sidelines and motioning T —horrible thought—for time out.

Then, Tittle felt like the remains of a rangy old mustang peeping out of an Alpo can. And everyone on the team figured that was his position. It was common knowledge that the Giants' offense and defense did not get along, and Tittle found out soon after his arrival at camp that no one was going to throw a party welcoming him to the team, either. Out of respect to the senior quarterback, Charlie Conerly, nobody would room with him or eat with him. But at least this was hello—when the tackle broke two bones in his back—and before sundown Y. A. was leaning on crutches trying to forget the humiliation he was "too old" to feel.

At camp, Gifford remembered Tittle eventually closing the door to his room so that none of the Giants would see him sitting in there by himself. As the door clicked shut, you had to wonder what he was thinking, when, for the first time in his life, no one expected him to be any good. There could be no embarrassments now, because in Frisco he had already been benched, booed, hung in effigy, and called everything known to man at least a thousand times. Life is never pretty for an injured quarterback.

But as the back and old groin injury healed, the younger rookies rolled their eyes when Tittle rolled out on a bootleg and connected with the other newcomer to the team—his roommate and fellow Texan, a mass of knuckles in uniform, a nimble long-legged skinny-bones, who ran with the speed of a Bedouin camel. Like Tittle, he wasn't pretty. But his hands moved like birds diving for prey, and his arms knew the wingspan of eagles. By the end of the 1961 season, Del Shofner had become the ugly but elegant Greta Garbo of football, and Tittle had been lifted on the toothless winds of a destiny that would carry him into the blow-hole of Chicago.

As Frank Gifford remembered, in 1961:

> the weapon was simple, the results explosive . . . Set as a flanker to the left, Shofner ran a fly—a straight, all-out sprint against the Washington Redskins. . . . He took Tittle's pass on the 10 and scored untouched. . . . Tittle threw three touchdown passes and New York won, 53–0. . . . And the Giants went on to score 170 points that season and win the eastern division championship, in part, because of a suggestion made by one of the clubhouse men who took care of Yankee Stadium. It was Giants equipment man Pete Previte who reasoned that since fast men are put into the lineup in scoring situations in baseball why not try the same thing in football and make use of defensive backs Erich Barnes and Jimmy Patton, both of whom could run the 100 in under 10 seconds?[4]

Winning the 1961 eastern division title was just like being born again according to Frank:

> Pro football, television, advertisers, and a mushrooming sports public met during the '58 through '60 period and the Giants and Tittle were there to pick the first ripe fruit. People saw themselves in Tittle: the agony as game after game got down to the closing minutes before Y. A. pulled them out and, sometimes, failed; his

frustration when a play went badly, and he drop-kicked his helmet 20 feet in front of 62,000 people in Yankee Stadium. . . . In August, Tittle had no one to have dinner with him. And four months later, the Giants gathered in Jim Downey's restaurant in New York to celebrate the winning of the eastern championship. And when all the scheduled speeches and tributes were done, a spontaneous clamor went up around the room for Tittle, and the bald man with jug ears stood up slowly. . . . [5]

In 1961, the Giants offense and defense came together, and players who had once avoided speaking to each other ended the season eating meatball sandwiches together for luck. As the most valuable player in professional football, Tittle was awarded the Jim Thorpe Award, an award voted on by the players themselves. He was also given the Howard Clothes award as the most popular Giant, and over half a million New York fans had voted in that contest. His personal favorite, however, was the "bonus" award where five, ten, even twenty dollars were given to the player who blocked a punt, sacked the quarterback or ran over thirty yards for a touchdown. And on the day Tittle ran for a touchdown his astonished celebration was a spectacle to behold. He threw the football straight up into the air, skipped a few steps, tripped and fell. When the ball came down with a big bounce off the top of his helmet, he threw back his head and laughed. And the fans with a roar forgave.

Then came the end of the season and the final game. On 30 December 1961, the playing field was a sheet of ice when the Giants lost the national championship to Vince Lombardi's Packers at Green Bay's City Stadium. The Packers played flawlessly in that game. Paul Hornung scored 19 points, a championship record, and a sympathetic Packer whispered to Giant Kyle Rote, "Everything right is happening for us, and all that could go wrong is happening to you."[6]

After the game, Tittle missed the team bus and so he hitched a ride to the airport from some noisy Packers fans. "Hop in, Buddy!" "Yahoo!" sounded from the car's steaming interior. "We sure did it, didn't we!" The door opened and someone extended a glass of brandy to the dehydrated quarterback. "No thank you," said Y. A. Tittle as he pulled his fedora down over his eyes and got in. As they inched off to join in the clang and fanfare of the Green Bay victory, Tittle did not let on who he was. What was there to say anyway?

The wind provided Tittle's embarrassment in 1962. It was dark as the Giants emerged from Yankee Stadium after the championship title game, and again the Green Bay Packers fans were ringing cowbells. In 1962, Green Bay's weather had come to New York. And with 40-mile-per-hour winds pitching empty benches onto the field and blowing the ticket stubs up to his knees, "Damn wind," thought Frank Gifford. "You can throw in the rain and you can throw in the snow, but you can't throw in a gale."[7]

But in 1963, great defense and great offense were on the march again, and the greybeards were back. In the opening game of the 1963 season, despite his collapsed lung, Tittle was in no mood to miss his last shot at a championship. And he wasn't the only one. Andy Rosbustelli, Frank Gifford, Sam Huff, Roosevelt Grier and Jim Katkavage put on the uniforms of myth and legend once more.

In 1963 New York City came down with Giants fever and the streets were swept by a plague of joy. Signs cheered on the hometown team in store windows. At a hockey game in Madison Square Garden, the fans chanted for the football Giants between periods. Turn on the radio and the chorus continued. Tittle held one of the largest press conferences to date in a city that had become a football madhouse.

My father received a Christmas package from the men at the local post office with BEAT THE BEARS! written in crayon, and notes of encouragement arrived from the Eastchester Police Department. Nuns at the Immaculate Conception Elementary School prayed for the Giants offense and Sister Marguerite said a rosary for the Presbyterian quarterback every day up to the game. And come November, it didn't even seem like football anymore.

Strangers stopped to clap when my father walked down the street hunched over in the cold like a question mark. At the time, I was disappointed in him because he didn't seem to notice until a very old man rushed out of a kiosk. "YAT?" he said very softly.

Quickly, my father glanced over his shoulder as if to catch a glimpse of what the other man saw. Then he turned back just in time to see the old man take a running leap. Luckily, my father caught him in his arms and for a moment, the old man looked like a bride being carried across a threshold. Somehow, the tears in the old man's eyes and my father's shy look of amazement summed it up. But every once in a while I had to wonder just why a stranger could say another man's name as if he were referring to the hope left at the bottom of Pandora's box, especially when the Giants weren't even winning championships. In 1963 my father was an American mummy wrapped up with so much tape that it was a wonder to us he could step into a cab or make it from the re- frigerator to the sink. But there, in the heart of a great city, it was as if the people and that old man were not clapping for the game as much as they were cheering on themselves.

All those wonderful people, and what stands out in my mind is getting into bed at night with the same wallpaper inches from my face, its countless tiny bouquets flung uniformly from floor to ceil- ing without even one of them asking for a single thing. And I remember announcer Howard Cosell's front doorbell, the twang in his voice like a boomerang, and his daughter whose friendship was like stepping into a palace after the first scary minute. I remember singer Barbra Streisand describing herself as a cross between Sophia Loren and Y. A. Tittle, and actor Jackie Gleason walking over to our table in a restaurant like a man whose force of gravity was stolen from the center of the world. A football fan came over too, and my father autographed his tablemat. The fan looked at Gleason and hesitated. But Mr. Gleason read his face and said, "Me? I'm just a fat tackle, but I'll be happy to sign that napkin!"

But more than anything, I remember that applause. As far back as I can remember, it was something rhythmic and strong like a heartbeat. As a football player's daughter, first I heard it like a heart beating outside in the world, and then, much later, inside myself, I found that my heart was a clapper too. For a time, I even thought the two might be related in some way. They weren't. And for years, I made the mistake of wondering what my own heart was in there clapping for.

As I watched my father play, the hardest thing for me was always one little unsettling word—hero. According to my books, the hero came in disguise. But was the hero really anywhere to be found?

People were fond of calling the athletes I knew heroes. But to me the word *hero* was merely pretty and meaningless at first, like a compliment or a cut flower. Then, over time, it came to imply and assume an imaginary landscape, a complex virtue. And I began to imagine that *hero,* like a bad word or curse, could wake you up and make you wonder. It was the one swear word at the other end of the spectrum, the one positive word of power at the far edge of my speech and my understanding.

The Hit.
Wrigley Field,
1963.

Helmets scratching the frozen ground. Breath billowing . . . Chicago.

As Y. A. Tittle released the ball late in the second quarter at Wrigley Field, his leg fluttered like a moth, and the knee tore loose. Gifford made a U-turn and began a magnificent run in the wrong direction toward his quarterback. And among the players who turned in astonishment to watch the fans cheering an injury was Andy Robustelli, who feared that some of his teammates were going into the seats.

The hit occurred on a blitz when linebacker Larry Morris lost his balance and made contact with Tittle's left knee. Many teammates and Giants fans thought that the tackle was intentional, with the idea of eliminating the quarterback. But Tittle did not. The good news was that the hit was legal. The bad news? The spell of the last three years was broken. As everybody could see, the leg had landed at the wrong angle from the quarterback's body.

As for Tittle, one of the oldest players in the National Football League, it was hard to believe it was over. But for the moment, as the cold sky settled on his chest, Y. A. Tittle could barely remember the pass he'd thrown. Slowly, the game came back, the day and the faces of his teammates. Piece by piece, like a child's puzzle. Deliberately he put body back into a cold soul and felt the wind on his face. Putting aside the fury, the anger, the nerves, he became alert, as if to find that boy inside himself who remembered the way home and who would help him stand and walk and play the game again. Yelberton Abraham Tittle lay there remembering himself and listening to the scream of the crowd. At first it was a note barely heard, then a note sustained, which built to an inhuman pitch. A raw sound, the sound of thousands hoarse with joy. Then he stood and shut it out again. The world, the noise, he left to us sitting in the stands. . . . With the help of Frank Gifford and others, he got to the sidelines.

As it turned out, Tittle suffered severe ligament damage in his left knee. He would, however, return to play in the third quarter, at which time guard Bookie Bolin would suffer a concussion. A fullback, Joe Morrison, would take such a beating that he, too, would be removed from the game along with running back Phil King. Gifford, the man with whom Tittle shared a rhythm, had indeed thought the game "was going to be a runaway. But when Y. A. went down in the second quarter, so did the offense. . . . Though he came back for the second half, playing on guts and Novocain, it just didn't work. George Allen, the Bears' defensive coach that day, knew Y. A. couldn't maneuver and came at us with everyone but the ushers."[8]

Sitting in the end zone, I kept trying to call TIME OUT! but nobody listened. Whether I looked up or down, there were tears. I listened to the Chicago fans shouting, "Kill 'im!" and clenched my teeth. The important thing was that we weren't spectators anymore. My brothers and I went undercover as players. As tackles and wide receivers we took our new positions and were ready to cross the lines, because the Giants needed help. It wasn't a game anymore. It had never been a game in the first place. That only-a-game stuff was like a grown-up's nursery rhyme. That big fat lie was just another moron's joke. And we got it! We finally got it on December 29, in Chicago, Illinois!

Before the game was over, my brother Mike made his way through the stadium to the locker room. He knew our father was injured. But the mood at Wrigley Field was ugly, and my brother's underground journey was filled with frightening echoes and wrong turns in the bowels of the seedy stadium. Finding his way to the locker-room door at last, he was turned back and told to go away and leave Tittle alone. To the boy, the sweaty lineman seemed to tower above him like a Giant from the center of the earth. "Now," he said, "is not a good time to see your father." And the door closed.

Years later, my brother saw a picture of my father's injury presented to his anatomy class as a useful example of what should never happen to a knee. And years later, I remember how that knee came attached to that day and to those Giant years. And I know there is more to my childhood than a bootleg and a blitz.

There is a pass. It happened during the fourth quarter just as Tittle went down. He released the ball and drew a picture of his lifetime, with a pass.

As one of many spectators in the stands that day, I remember a human bullfight. My father considers it the worst game of his life, and I consider it his best. And out of all my years as a spectator, Chicago is the game I find most worth remembering.

Some say that blitz late in the second quarter marked the end of Y. A. Tittle's seventeen-year-long career. But I believe his career had kept him warming up on the sidelines until then. Y. A. Tittle's game had just begun. The Bald Eagle would be back.

ZIG RIGHT Y TARE!

EAST TEXAS

(above)
Marshall
High School
Mavericks,
1941.
Freshman Y. A.
Tittle is # 33.

(right)
Y. A. trying on
his brother's
jersey.

Gold flowers to flame on land in the glory of the trees . . .

—Pindar, *Olympian* 2

Father: *Okay. If we're talking about flashbacks, I have to mention my hero, Sammy Baugh, whom I was trying to emulate in 1936. I was nine years old when we lived outside the city limits of Marshall during the Depression. It was there I used to play football by myself. I would fake a snap to myself, run to the right, and throw a pass. It would be complete if I was Sammy Baugh. Slinging Sammy would play against all the great passers from the Southwest Conference, namely, Bill Patterson from Baylor, and Big Ernie Lane from Rice. But actually he took on every great passer from across the United States, or at least the ones whose names I'd memorized.*

We had bushes, you know, in our yard. Well, we had ten acres. And we must have had at least a hundred or two hundred of these bushes that looked like little round cones and made a good catcher for somebody who didn't have anybody to play catch with. I killed most every one of the shrubs. My father wanted to kill me. But I just couldn't stop. I would go out for hours and throw from this bush to that bush and go over that bush and hit the third bush. When I was 10, this was my game with Sammy Baugh. If he missed two in a row and finally hit one, I'd made sure that Ernie Lane and those other guys missed four in a row.

Daughter: *You mean you played all of the different quarterbacks?*

Father: *Every one. There would be a first down, second down. Completed! Completed! It's a first down! It's a first down on the 25-yard line, and Baugh goes back to pass. It's completed! And again! It's a touchdown for Sammy Baugh! And then Ed Baylor receives the kickoff. He runs it back to the 35-yard line. The QB, he looks to the right. He throws it—It's intercepted!*

And I'd play this game with myself—like idiot's delight. But Slinging Sammy was a winner in my backyard. He hit every bush

a thousand times. Then later on my brother Don was my pass re-
ceiver. Ten cents a week. I mean, I looked at it this way. For 10 cents
a week, you could go to the Strand Theatre. It only cost nine cents to
go to the Strand and see a cowboy movie on Saturday. So Don went
to the movies catching passes for me. And it was good for him too be-
cause he became a pretty good football player later on. But it did
stunt his growth that he ran so much as a little kid. . . .

. . . By the time I got to junior high school, football was organized
and I really didn't play much. My first year I really didn't know
what to do. I think I read too much into it. The next year I quit read-
ing so much into it. Just like I keep telling your son, Michael, "just
get together with the ball."

I played three years in junior high school. Nothing exceptional
there except that football was a way of life. And a lot of the young
guys I played football with, well, I still like to see these people. I
think when we have relationships that young, they become a part of
your life. They're like the soul of your life. To me they are, were. . . .
Anyway, when I went to high school Odus Mitchell came into our
lives. Coach Mitchell made sports fun. He was like a little boy. He
came from West Texas, from Pampa, and he thought these little
Marshall, Texas kids could beat anybody. And we did. Mitchell
coached us in four sports and he himself was an All-District basket-
ball and baseball player. Odus scheduled big teams, the biggest
teams in the state. And boy, when all of a sudden we knocked off
Waco, the state champions from the years before, Marshall, Texas
was on the map and the living daylights had been shocked out of us,
one and all.

Daughter: *And the family.*

Father: . . . *Oh, I always had a finagling family. Even my first*
award, I didn't win. I'm positive it was Huline's con job, and I was so
embarrassed I wouldn't accept it. Here I was, 14 years old, a fresh-
man football player, and we had some top players. Billy Dinkle,
Richard Nutt, Puppy Gilry, Albert Agnor, OK? And they were
much better backs than I was. Besides, my asthma was so bad they

made me sit out and I had to miss the entire championship game. So there we are at the Sullivan Funeral Home's Sportsman's Football Banquet where they're announcing Most Inspirational Player, Most Valuable Lineman. . . . Then out of the blue, "The Sullivan Funeral Home Award goes to Most Valuable Player and Most Valuable Back, Y. A. Tittle!" And that's me, my gosh!

Daughter: *You weren't a back?*

Father: *No, I was a back. But, I mean, I certainly was not the most valuable player. But my sister worked for the Sullivan Funeral Home and there's no telling what Huline threatened them with. If George and Bill Sullivan didn't give her brother the award she most certainly would have quit. And boy, that was my most cherished award, once I got over the shock. I still have that award. No—that award is in the Marshall Historical Society Library, I think.*

As for your Mom, she was like a part of the family, or at least a part of me since eighth grade. There was nobody else in the history of the Strand Theatre in Marshall, Texas, who ever stood up and cheered for the Indians even after they lost!

Daughter: *And Blocker? Tell me about him.*

Father: *Well, as you know, Blocker was my friend. He helped make this home here on Caddo. Every blade of grass, every speck of paint, every nail, every little item around the house, he and I did together. And we were kind of known as the great, well, maybe not so great, fishermen on Caddo Lake. Fishing every morning for bass, out catching white perch and brim.*

I came down for his funeral and it was a most difficult time for me. But I was honored by Odessa (his wife), who allowed me to sit with the family. And I was so impressed with the testimonials, and the manner in which they praised a man. I couldn't even talk. But you cannot convey it. But still, you might figure out a way to praise. Do it in your own words. You praise him. Blocker was a great man and one of my best friends.

Yet in those days when we were young, blacks and whites were not allowed to compete. For that matter, blacks were not even allowed into the high school stadium to watch the ball games. So Blocker and I played marbles. Marbles when we were young. Then we fished when we got old.

Marbles & the Marshall Mavericks

At Grand Saline, the Great Piney Woods begin. On roads like scarlet ribbon I drove at sunset through Waskom, Elysian Fields, and Uncertain, towns like blinks in the road. Carthage. Gilmer. Sign after sign announced that the earth had borne the scratches of humanity for a time, and proclaimed a peace stretching from battlefield to cotton field. The earth grows tulips, feathery pines and wild carrots. There is no such thing as death in those parts—only sleep, sprinkled as if by a mother's hand from the Neches and Angelina Rivers to the bend of the Red River. Things get so restful and lazy under the sway of the trees that they simply forget to play by the rules. It's like this every time I go home. Enter the Piney Woods and from a distance every town looks like a well-kept tombstone, inviting the traveler to come be refreshed in the knowledge of what survives, even on the dark side of the East Texas moon.

It was pleasant as we drove through those small Southern towns to recall the first time I drove with my parents down Victory Drive in Marshall, Texas, so that they could show me the family homestead. I was ten years old and we had gone home for "Y. A. Tittle Day." In 1960 there had been a resolution in the Texas Senate calling for a parade, but all I remember is the banner stretched across Main Street, flapping in the breeze like a small town oracle. It seemed to say: "Look! You, too, can survive and grow up normal! If somebody named Yelberton Abraham Tittle can do it, then so can you!"

After the festivities in town we drove out to the family home on Harper Drive. I sat in the back seat and thought the whole way about all the snakes in those woods and that air so clogged with ancestor spirits there was nothing left to breathe. Naturally, my parents came to life as the humidity got worse, and my father rattled off the genealogies of half the population as if reciting the jersey numbers of his teammates. While he seemed to know every bush, vacant lot and stone like a best friend, it was no fun for me sitting in the back and thinking about Iphigenia and all the other sacrificed maidens in my books. I did my best to strike a low profile, hoping that the ancestors and snakes would forget that I, too, was born there. How could they know I was that same four-pounder framed by my father's throwing hand and surrounded by Racehorse Davies and all the other ballplayers gleefully trying to come up with a name to go with Tittle?

That first trip home, I made the mistake of thinking that people went back to small towns in America to gloat over their escape. Instead, I found that my parents went back to outline a former paradise and connect all the dots by car. First, we stopped, *had* to stop at a place called "Neely Brothers Brown Pig Restaurant," and we had to eat a sandwich called a "BROWN PIG," before heading for a road bump on Bomar Street—the highlight, apparently, of my parent's teenage Friday nights. As they laughed and grew younger by the minute, I aged a thousand years in the span of an hour, and according to the law of those woods, was born again to East Texas.

And so it was that the Piney Woods began to work their magic. As we inched our way down the Old Stage Road, I, who had never really heard silence before, was taken aback by the red soil and the quiet which seemed to be speaking from the treetops. And for a change, I had no choice but to believe the story my parents were telling, because the words themselves were becoming real.

The Woods, "a large rectangular area extending north from the Angelina and Neches Rivers in the southeastern part of the state to the great bend of the Red River in northeastern Texas,"[1] were and still are a powerful testimony to God's imagination. He must have slapped his thigh and laughed out loud to create the birds, beetles, and bugs in those parts, and in no way does one get the feeling eons were spent leaning over a petrie dish. There, He thought of something funny. And as a result, there are swarms of bluebirds, screech owls, and blue herons, every known variety of poisonous snake in the country, and the best white perch fishing in America.

My grandfather, Abe Tittle, had been a rural postman and his wife, Alma, was a quiet woman who loved flowers. She covered a hill with roses after her eldest son, Stafford, died with pneumonia at age twelve. Shortly after Yelberton Abraham was born, the family moved to ten acres just outside Marshall. There, surrounded by the trees, the Tittles had a huge garden, a pond, a meadow the size of a football field, a smokehouse, a wash pot, a butter churn, a barn filled with canned preserves, an old horse, and a milk cow. There were several places on the property to slop hogs (a phrase that fell on my suburban ears like a news flash from the planet Pluto), and overhead, starry nights that made you think angels were up there doodling in the margins for your sake.

Hog Killing Day, which fell on the first cold day of autumn, was described in joyful detail as an event akin to Christmas or Easter. And little hardships were so cherished. Frankly, until then I had never believed a word my father said about his childhood, because if I did, I knew I would have to feel sorry for somebody who didn't know how to feel sorry for himself. He was forever describing ghastly situations in which he had an absolute ball. It was no wonder the grown-up Y. A. Tittle could play an entire football game with a broken hand, and still have fun. It was as if he had been raised in a place with confidence as well as fluoride in the drinking water.

Indeed, that first trip out to the brick home that Abe had built for Alma in her sorrow, I couldn't lay eyes on that big "T" of red stone set in the chimney without the feeling that I had been set up, and that my parents had been set up before me. I knew that the rooms of the house were large and airy before we got there. And that Alma had passed away in the room opening onto the meadow. From there, you could look out and see gum trees and red soil that didn't blacken for a hundred miles or more. I'd heard the sound of crows and heard the back door slam back in 1933 when Uncle Burtis and Colonel Ray had just returned from Caddo Lake. There the long yoyos filled with pike and perch hung down from the lowest branches of the willow trees, the fish mouths in wide open Os and the stiff bodies raised just above the water's surface. The trees, I knew, were wrapped in graceful folds of Spanish moss, and Ray had been hooked twice by those unset yoyos when a light wind was moving through the trees.

That was the drive home which turned the entire landscape of my family life into a giant history book that no one knew how to read. And that's why my parents were turning the pages so fast. On Harper Drive when I was ten, I could almost see the piano crates where people lived during the Depression, and the men looking for work who still took time out to teach the Tittle boys how to take different wooden shapes and whirl them on a string to imitate the sounds of swarmer bees. Mudmarbles, Tin-can Shanny, and Sheep-Board Down were sports that taught the knack of making fun out of nothing and a game out of being alone. And I had to resist the temptation to wave to all those ghosts. Then, as we turned into the actual driveway of the house, I did wave—just in case my grandparents, Abe and Alma Tittle, who had died before I was born, were there to greet me.

1931.

"Tinneha! Bobo! and Blair!"

In the dark, the hoboes disappeared, and all that the boys could hear were the names of railroad towns sounding as exotic as Cairo, Egypt. In 1931 Marshall, Texas was a highlight in the Hobo Travel Guide. As the train slowed down, the hoboes got off and held court in the woods, telling their travels to the country kids who dared approach their fires. While older boys competed for their brides, the young ones sat in the firelight on the edge of the city limits and watched the burning ends of cigarettes, while hearing about the mountains of Appalachia, the cotton fields of Georgia, and the doughnut holes in New Orleans.

Hobo Jungle was a place where the small town ended and the universe began for the lovers who courted nearby at the T&P Railroad's Shop Pond. Patterns of pollination in big cities might resemble the habits of swarmer bees, but Marshall had remained true to the tumbleweed, that giant ingrown tangle which dropped its seed while rolling wherever the wind blew. And so the young ate fresh squirrel and drank coffee from the common pot in Hobo Jungle. For moonlight thrills, teenagers hit the Burleson Dip. For opera, they rang the Wiley College Bell—or the Mavericks from Marshall High School played football. In that landscape, sacrifice still meant something as a deed. And like a country church, where too many people have prayed for the room ever to feel empty, so too many slaves had sweated into the soil when cotton was king, when timber was queen, for the red earth ever to let anyone really forget the blood of all its East Texas children. The mark of Cain was ever-present. It was on everything from drinking fountains to football. But it wasn't on the stories told in Hobo Jungle.

These fires burned only thirty miles from Jefferson, a town where the newspaper logo was still a gryphon identical to the one used to frighten the slaves away from the written word. In that once teeming port where paddle wheelers piled with cotton went to and fro, a black man could only ride a horse or sit with his family in a buggy on Christmas Day, because at no other time could his head be higher than a white man's. If such a crime took place, the master got whipped, according to the law in what had been known as "No man's land," or the East Texas badlands.

But as time passed, J. Gould came to town, wanting to bring the railroad with him. When the townsfolk refused, he replied, "I'll live to see grass growing in the streets of Jefferson!" And so he did. The railroad went to Marshall, instead, bringing with it engine power enough to blow open the doors of commerce. Built on seven hills with a town square and a courthouse with a gleaming copper dome at the center, Marshall began to thrive like the vegetable gardens planted in nearly every yard. The town grew by the light of hobo fires and through the dedicated efforts of teachers like Inez Hughes and Miss Selma Brotsky.

In the 1930s when Y. A. Tittle fell in love with spinning objects, America still lived in her small towns and seemed like the beautiful bride of democracy in a white dress. But for the barbarian heirloom of racism she wore around her neck, she might have walked down the aisle with her head up. As it was, in some places she could barely crawl. But in Marshall, Texas, she was moving, however slowly, and the sun passed overhead daily like a torch to light the hobo fires.

Growing up in this town had its advantages for a boy who was headed for the championship at an early age and cheered in his efforts by the silence of the woods. Behind the Snow White cleaners, Y. A. and his friend, H. L. Blocker, hung out playing mudmarbles until closing time. After dark, he played marbles with his big brother Jack until dinner. It was a no-win situation for Jack, who had to let him win in order to quit and then had to keep on playing after five-year-old Y. A. started crying—until he lost fair and square. Y. A. was either a crybaby or a born winner, and while the athlete strove for balance between body, mind, and soul, Yelberton also had to deal with that baby in spite of every obstacle.

Bronchial asthma was one obstacle for the boy. Born with asthma and a name he couldn't get air enough to say, in Yelberton Abraham the virtues of inspiration, preparation, and perspiration had to be practiced early on so that the allergy to green grass that kept him from doing chores would not keep him from killing time. At an early age, long before there was Texas football or even the English language in his life, Y. A. set out to "kill time" and educate himself in the mysteries of motion. He was killing time while watching the cat as it readied to leap, watching its eye calculate and measure a given distance, and discovering all by himself a world of knowledge in a cat's eyeball. As for the bullfrog, it never noticed if the weather was bad, and never gave up or shut up either. Y. A. learned about stamina from the bullfrog. And from his mother? Alma combing her hair with her wrist turning. Alma flapping the blankets over kids squirming, who was 4/4 time in everything, hummed and sewed and churned the butter—four beats to a measure.

Of course, at night there were fireflies to watch and to chase. And like any other child chasing down a front yard full, Y. A. was in life and in his body all at once; only for him, it meant business. Long before there was Coach Odus Mitchell in his life, he was learning football patterns from the zip and zap of fireflies. Y. A. Tittle was made to order for the game when the quarterbacks called the plays. The next thing you knew, 60% of his plays were audibles called from the line of scrimmage, and the Giants were winning. Behind the statistics, however, was never any great secret and no real genius. Behind it all there was just an observing boy bending the patterns in nature to suit his own design. And no doubt the baby in him made him do it.

Inspiration, preparation, perspiration. Only by a strange alchemy among the three would it be possible for his arm to turn to gold and that baby become a leader. So he practiced. At five years of age, he played marbles with the seriousness of a man working on his doctoral thesis. In church, sitting next to Octavia Granberry, he peacefully executed in his mind the plays he would use later that afternoon at the sandlot. But Yelberton was not obsessed. Like his mother patiently mending a sock, he was only filling in the holes of an appointed destiny.

At six years old, a turning point in my father's life occurred late one afternoon out at Uncle Ray's and Aunt Lenora's Roseborough Farm, where reunions were practically a weekly occurrence. On those "family days," the relatives were greeted at the farm by Uncle Burtis, holding the family photo album, or by Aunt Reba, with skin like a peach and wearing a dress to match—and dying, no matter how she was. Aunt Lenora and Alma laid out the feast, and Uncle Ray Allen, whose leg was shot off during the war, stood and said the blessing with heart and fervor.

Y. A. was only able to sit still at the dinner table because, in his own words, he had been effectively "killing time" for many hours. And there were games played in the country expressly for this purpose. With a clothespin for a trigger and a knot in a piece of rubber "to make it sting a little and for greater accuracy," he and his cousins made rubber guns. Or they made arrows out of house shingles and sometimes slingshots. Or they played "Sheep-Board

Down, capture the flag, red rover, and marbles—'round ring marbles' or 'drop marbles' using a King Edward cigar box in which a small hole was cut and the marbles dropped from belt high. For the ones that went in the ring you got two for one; ones that fell off to the side went to your opponent." Y. A. learned what it was to lie when he had to tell his mother he had ten marbles when in fact he had twenty, because Alma Tittle did not believe in gambling, even when it came to drop marbles.

But that afternoon's family reunion on 22 June 1938, was special because Joe Louis, the "Brown Bomber," was going to fight against Max Schmelling, and the family was going to listen to the match on the radio after supper. It was also special because a fox came out of the woods during the meal and stood opposite the creek, transfixed, it seemed, by the commotion and the flutter of hands. To little Y. A. it was somehow a comfort, even a compliment, that the fox had come. So he watched the fox back. Even after most of the relatives had gone indoors, he remained with his eyes glued to a patch of darkness until his mother came out to hug him, and the concentration of the fox beat him in the end. But having lost in the stare-down, at least he had earned a new respect for the distances between the creek, the fox, and himself, and this carried him indoors just as the fight got underway.

The radio was shaped like a miniature of the fancy wooden doorway which led into church. Gathered around it were the faces of Uncle Burtis, Colonel Ray Allen, and Abraham Tittle, as they listened to the fight in which Joe Louis knocked out Max Schmelling in the first round and triumphed over the forces of darkness. Still dizzy from the stare-down, nine-year-old Y. A. was dazzled, perhaps, by the trembling lips on those faces he'd thought were made of granite and by the communion of their dry, cracked hands. And he imagined perfection for the very first time. With an image of Louis in his mind and a thrill of expectation for himself, he *ran* out the door and announced to the dark woods as if to the fans in New York City, "I'm good!"

And with that, the rippling started—his luck, his career began. Asthmatic, jug-eared, prone to sunburn, and shy, this was one pipsqueak with the heart of the Brown Bomber who was going to the playoffs. And to get there, his parents would just have to get over his allergy to green grass. Practice would begin on the day after the Louis-Schmelling fight. And even that night, when his mind was jam-packed with angels who knew how to play and to have fun, and who didn't mind telling him to go out and do likewise. And that was the task before him.

In 1939, days began early at the Tittle household, with Alma canning preserves or adding cinnamon to a bread pudding, and Abe lighting fires in the bedrooms. Alma was prematurely gray, and Abe was bald and fit. As it turned out, Abe Tittle was a grand master of the bootleg—a play where you pretend to throw one way and then don't. In East Texas terms, he was dumb like a fox, letting on that he was a rural postman when all the while he was becoming a relentless Daniel Boone of commerce. Abe Tittle acquired numerous properites, including four pressing shops. He started the East Texas Candy Company, which became famous for its peanut patties, farmed cotton and corn, sold resoled shoes, taught math at Commerce College, tried to reinvent the razor blade and didn't, owned two grocery stores and personally made cinnamon rolls so good "they would make you talk back to your Mama." He also liked "new things." It was Abe Tittle behind the wheel of the first car in Marshall, Texas. Come time to have a telephone, it was he, himself, who sank the poles for a mile.

I have been told that my grandparents courted out at Caddo Lake. Floating down Star Ditch in Abe's bateau, of course they had no way of knowing that from the air the shallow waterways filled with catfish, blunt red stems and water lilies looked like a Chinese dragon crossed with a Texas scorpion. Nor did they care to know that the maze of ponds, lakes, and bayous interspersed with islands of bald cypress trees was once home to the Caddo Indians, an esteemed tribe whose name for the lake was Tso'to. Renamed Soda Lake by the settlers, it was subsequently called Fairy and then Ferry Lake. But no name was perhaps more appropriate than Caddo, given to mark the beautiful grave of a nation, once 15,000 strong, but which had dwindled to 535 before Texas Independence.

But what difference did it make to them? As Alma reached out and plucked a water lily, she did not know about her ancestry or care that in such a place DeSoto discovered a people who to Ponce de Leon appeared "as civilized as the Aztecs."[2] Most likely, she was content to peek at her glowing face in the lake's reflection when Abe wasn't looking, and pinch her cheeks once more, oblivious to the fact that around those 2,700 acres of eerie watery beauty two Christian nations had fought over the homeland of the heathen while the Caddo acted as peacemakers.

Caddo Lake.

"Tejas!"

The early explorers heard the word "Tejas" repeated so often that they mistakenly assumed it was the name of the land. But the word was Caddoan for "friend," and it was appropriate somehow that Abe and Alma should meet there, in the heart of Texas. Boat rides down the endless maze from Devil's Elbow to Eagle's Nest and Stumpy Slough punctuated their friendship for many seasons, during which Alma kept an eye on Abe's arms reaching out over the water and measured the distance from his hand to hers as from star to star. And then one day, it happened.

They were married in Gilmer, and Abe and Alma's first male child died with typhus. A second son was stillborn. Huline was born in Clayton, Texas, in a house which still stands. Stafford, who was named for the preacher who married Abe and Alma, was twelve when he came down with pneumonia. Then three living sons, Jack, Don, and Yelberton Abraham Tittle. The Tittles built a house on stilts over Caddo Lake, but went there rarely after the stormy night when Abe got stranded and spent a night in Hog's Wallow watching lightning torch the trees. When the moon rose overhead like another lost child, Abe promised God that if he lived to get off that lake he would sell everything to do with it, even the boat. Abe kept his word, though Caddo Lake had been as good to him and Alma as Eden ever was. But with Huline, Jack, Don, and Yelberton Abraham, Abe figured it was time to get to that place after Eden where he could sweat into good ground. No wonder, he thought, the word *sweat* appeared right off in Genesis. Among other things, God knew what it was like to have kids.

So Marshall, Texas it was. In 1940 Marshall was a good place to sweat. Days were long, but the Tittles knew that no matter how tired they were when they went to sleep, they would always be waking up to the same red earth, as flushed as a woman in child-birth, and that for years to come, there would never be anything between lake and town except for the TNT Plant.

Always an earlybird, Y. A. began the day looking out at the horizon, fine as one of Alma's gray hairs, and in his mind, touching it with his forefinger. He had already discovered this trick for making the distance between himself and his goal disappear. But to improve his arm and his ability to measure precise distances mentally, he needed human targets. For this luxury, he paid his brother Don a dime to run out for passes. Don, however, was beginning to whine about life as his brother's yoyo and to insist that his growth was being stunted. So in order to pay Don the extra charge for wear and tear, as well as to strengthen his arms, Y. A., then 12 years old, took a job making ice deliveries.

Usually, there was nothing between Y. A. and the horizon when he awoke, other than the sun which didn't wobble and H. L. Blocker out plowing a field and making himself strong for baseball. Under the latest version of East Texas law, H. L. was Abe Tittle's right-hand man, and they sometimes drove around town together. H. L. could drive Y. A. to football practice; however, he was not allowed to watch practice, and for the privilege of watching a game, he had to hide in the bushes outside the stadium. Many times he did, with fist clenched and fingers crossed for his young friend, even though he himself was one of the better athletes under the sun. H. L. was the pitcher over at the sawmill. At bat, "Crack!" Gazelles dreamed of this man whose grin told the world that he was a participant in life for better or worse. And if he hadn't been born the color of the night on a new moon, he could have made it in the Big Leagues.

To sneak past H. L. was not easy. Y. A. had to leave before daylight and bike over to the ice company where he climbed behind the wheel of the ice truck, stretched his feet to the pedals, and set out toward Lady Bird Taylor's house and her father's general store. Everyone supposed that a ghost named Oonie lived at Lady Bird's. Once a girl of that name was struck while rocking in a chair by a bolt of lightning which shot through the chimney. Oonie was seventeen when it happened. And everybody knew that even after she died, Oonie chased boys—which was why Y. A. felt obliged to hire on Olin Fife, then seventeen. It wasn't that he needed extra help with the ice, he just needed to increase his odds of surviving the corner at Lady Bird's. Next to that big house at the intersection, there was nothing but bugs and blue herons all down the road to Karnack.

So as he drove out to pick up Olin he let his imagination wander back and forth between thoughts of Oonie's hair standing on end, and that most unusual girl, Minnette DeLoach. Then he would begin to practice his concentration trick, so that when he got to Olin's, nine-tenths of his mind would be relaxed and peacefully sleeping in concentration while the other fraction made sure he turned left at the TNT Plant. It wasn't a trance exactly, it was just a kind of football practice he did in his spare time. In this way he practiced feeling the hit relaxed, so that he could avoid injury. Or, if he was injured, it was a way to make sure only one-tenth of himself knew it. With any luck, the other nine-tenths wouldn't catch on until the clock had run out.

So far, there was only one snag to the exercise, and that came from completing his passes so successfully in his imagination that on several occasions he had forgotten to throw at all in real life. He hoped that his football coach had not noticed, but there were times when his enthusiasm got the better of him and he just had to jump, clap, or hug somebody. Coach probably assumed he was firing up the team with his leadership before a crucial play, when in Tittle's mind, the Mavericks had already scored.

Indeed there was a danger in letting imagination and concentration get too mixed up, and perhaps a long country road could teach him only so much. Y. A. wasn't even supposed to be playing football on account of his asthma. And the Lord alone knew what would happen to him, if either H. L. or his father found that he was driving an ice truck!

On the home stretch to Olin's, Y. A. entered H. L.'s own cherished landscape. And everything Y. A. saw there, he saw through his friend's eyes. Whenever H. L. put a finger on a marble of any kind it was like a truth serum. When their heads were down together, H. L. told all and Y. A. could see his home in Leigh, Texas, where the roar of the sporting crowd was nothing as compared to the din of the tree frogs once the sun went down. Now, driving past the outskirts of H. L.'s home town, Y. A. could see his friend taking the canoe and wandering among the charred cores of bald cypress trees after a lightning storm on Caddo Lake. He too, saw a forest reflected in the water, deer swimming between the islands of trees, and snakes dangling from the branches, turtles everywhere lining up on the logs, with their little painted faces in a row tilting toward the sun. The heat. Even that was harmonious with the deafening chant of cicadas and roots that didn't stay put undergound.

Come to find out that what they called "cypress knees" were but the tips of the root system connecting all the trees in an island just under the surface of the water. When the lake was low, they were left exposed as a city, beautiful and scary, and the roots of the trees themselves resembled wise men in mossy robes.

As for Shug, Babe, Sleepy, and Five Cents, H. L. was better than a snake charmer when he told about those guys down at Shady Glade playing cards and telling sports stories which never made the news. These were the men H. L. cherished as pillars holding up his dreams in spite of a downright delapidated East Texas world. What Y. A. wouldn't give to catch a glimpse of them sitting in their chairs surrounded by the cypress trees and cigarette smoke.

Frankly, there might be no end to what H. L. told if he got his hands on one of Y. A.'s cat's eyes or boulders, but that was a temptation to lose that Y. A. simply could not afford. It was enough to know that H. L.'s father could make a bow and arrow and provide for his own; he could feed ten families with a day's catch on the lake or hunt from his house to the outskirts of Marshall and never meet a fence. It was a separate world, and H. L. would never mention his heroes in the context of town. Even Y. A. was forced to shut his mind to the thought of Joe Louis walking on a designated sidewalk or sitting in the balcony section at the Strand Theatre.

Y. A. picked up Olin Fife, and the two of them made short work of their routine deliveries. Afterward, Y. A. dropped Olin off at his house and returned the ice truck to his boss. Now there was a hard working man who pulled a muscle just to say hi. But Y. A. paid no attention. At least not until the day a black man who also worked at the company shooed a cat away from his work place. "Shoo!" he said gently, "Shoo, now."

Y. A. quit his job at the ice company on that day, when he saw a black man being pistol whipped for shooing a cat. And on that day, all of Y. A. Tittle's football tricks, like newly laced shoe-strings, came undone. When Y. A. saw the look in his boss's eyes and watched his body lunge, he was quick to recognize the exact opposite of that human perfection he had imagined while listening to the boxing match, but not quick enough to anticipate the hit, or stop the fall through the trapdoor which opened across all ten-tenths of his mind. In football, the ground is always there. But between man and boy, there was no ground, and no stopping this time for Y. A. Tittle. He could not get home fast enough, as if somehow the road on which he sang "I'll Take You Home Again, Kathleen" had the power to make the falling stop. But his boss's eyes had set off a chain reaction. At home, the clutter of balls and bats was no longer innocent. If his room could have sneered, it would have. So Y. A. Tittle got back into bed and shut his eyes to all the world, expecting that nothing anymore would be of any use.

Then—"Rise and shine!" shouted H. L. Blocker.

And the falling stopped. Little did H. L. know when he glanced up at the house and saw his friend zooming past the chinaberry

tree and barreling down through the tall grass to where H. L. was standing in a sweat, that for Y. A. waking up to him slapping a snake over a piece of barbed wire was the most glorious thing in the world. To H. L. the boy looked like he was seeing a ghost and celebrating every holiday of the year at the same time. But there was something more between Y. A. Tittle and his horizon that morning. And H. L. would never know that for an instant he stood at the dead center of the world in another man's life, or that better than any football dream come true was H. L. Blocker with both feet on the ground.

H. L. Blocker in his beloved Piney Woods, 1988.

Hit 'em in the wishbone, sock 'em in the eye
Our boys will shine tonight
You know it, Mavericks,
You know it Mavericks,
Our boys will shine tonight!

In 1940 my father played ball in open fields where the snakes went slithering through the grass. And when he wasn't playing ball, his brother Jack was showing him the moves and giving advice. "You have to learn the rest of the game too," Jack warned. But forget that. Yelberton only wanted to throw the tar out of the ball. And he did too, better than anyone in Marshall by the time he was in sixth grade. Under Coach Joe Magrill, however, the Junior Marshall Football Mavericks were not a passing team, and Y. A. made newsprint first as a "pretty fair country tackler." He did not see much playing time until his second year, when the Longview coach said, "Watch out for Tittle"—a remark equivalent to winning the Miss America pageant for a Marshall Maverick. Shortly thereafter, Y. A. overheard Coach Magrill telling his math teacher that if he kept trying so hard, one day he might even be better than his brother Jack, by then a football star at Tulane. It was the first time that mere words had touched the boy in his hiding place—like rainfall finding a seed in the dry, hard ground.

In the spring of 1940, Coach Magrill presented my father with his brother Jack's worn out shoulder pads. To Y. A. the scratches in the leather were more marvelous than all of Vulcan's artistry on Achilles' shield. To him, all the luck, the honor, and the good clay soil of Texas were wrapped up in those pads which were scuffed with an ancient code of survival for the modern age. Here, finally, were the hieroglyphs of his brother's advice in a language he could understand.

That year, the question in everybody's mind was whether Y. A. would grow into his ears or his brother's shoulder pads. And when the fall came round again in 1940, the answer was a six foot tall tailback who appeared before the new coach, Cracker Brown. It was Cracker's directive, "throw the ball whenever you get the chance," that took Tittle, like a genie, right out of the bottle. That season, a nameless sportswriter compared Tittle to Sammy Baugh at the same age. And my father inhaled those words whenever his asthma made it tough to breathe. To be compared to Baugh! It was his first real sip of praise, which, like alcohol, must have seemed a little shocking and somewhat dangerous.

Marshall, Texas in the 1940s was also a perfect place for the May Fete celebration held every year on the town square. Just as football was a celebration of the fall and a ritual dominated by the males in the area, this celebration of springtime was an event dominated by the females. And likewise, it was a big event in Marshall, where a typical day just unfolded and you didn't expect much of anything. Not even the cars broke the speed limit in Marshall. And everything was held in check by the usual, which was mostly Starlin and Leadbelly strumming guitars while baby-sitting Irene; old folks making cakes and being visited; and the question: Was Puppy Gilry in love with Patty Pope?

The May Fete was not only a celebration of spring. It also featured a Parade of Months, which gave folks a chance to look back nostalgically over the march of their own lives, and a dance in the evening, when all those months and years came together, bowing down and rising up, dancing in and out.

In 1940 my mother, then age 12, was invited to be the princess of October in the May Fete. This was quite an honor for Minnette DeLoach, and her mother was making a beautiful dress for her to wear—many, many layers of crinoline beneath seven large leaves of fabric in gold, brown, green, and rust. No hoop. But a poofed skirt, with lots of glitter. And more glitter for the crown of leaves she would wear.

On the day of the spring fair itself, my mother marched with the parade around the main square and passed, without even a blink, Bonnie and Clyde's shot up automobile parked in front of the police depot. She did not look to left or right. She did not wave to her friend James Moyers, or smile at the boy she had kissed in exchange for a crucifix just the day before—all because she took her part seriously. It was a great responsibility to be beautiful, and she pouted slightly.

When she passed by Y. A. Tittle, it seems he turned the baseball cap around on his head for no reason. That football fanatic was caught in her gaze like a twig in a lava flow, and didn't he deserve it? The showoff! Didn't he know that she knew he deliberately dropped his pencil at her feet, so that he could stand up and take a look at that scar on her face? Didn't he know that she knew that? Y. A. was named most athletic boy at West End, and it was no wonder she thought about him. His body talk told everything both on and off the football field. Minnette had never seen a boy practically evaporate before, and everything but his eyeballs disappear in the steam. But there he stood in a row of promising young Marshall Mavericks at the May Fete in 1940, flanked by ends James Taylor and Roy Hall, and backs Billy Dinkle, Bobby Furrh, and Bryon Gillroy, to name a few. As usual, Y. A. was the standout. Who else could stand there like last year's Maypole—worse than a bump on a log?

But Y. A. did not know what to make of this month of October —this unusual girl who wrapped herself up in a sheet just to stir up the swarmer bees. Nobody knew what to make of this Cherokee-French firecracker who wore a size-4 shoe. And because he knew nothing, Y. A. cocked his weight from one hip to the other.

Then followed all the long months of summer. Like devils dividing up the planets, Y. A. and H. L. fought even harder over their marble games. And to strengthen their arms they played catch by the hour, until, finally, the leaves began to turn. Autumn came upon the woods like a deep sigh of relief. And Y. A. Tittle, as the tailback in the double wing offense at Marshall High School, was all for it.

The Friday night lights in Maverick Stadium. With no media to speak of other than the radio and local newspaper, small towns were left to their own imaginations. In East Texas, the will to win simply cried up from the soil. So the people gathered for the public dream.

Friday afternoon during football season was a time out from the rules of everyday life. Like so many other East Texas towns— Henderson, Carthage and Karnack, Jonesville, Sulphur Springs, and Waskom—Marshall created its boundaries with the surrounding forest and then filled in the space with steeples, crosswalks, and a laundry load of human habits. Like the other towns, Marshall's was a small, respectable community located at the heart of nowhere, opening like a child's hand in the forest. Against that wild backdrop of the Piney Woods, which was home to some of the happiest alligators and water moccasins in the southern U.S., the human struggle seemed small and the human voice spoke in whispers. And the very existence of such towns was almost touching—except that it was a Daddy's hand in most places, a Daddy's hand which opened in the forest. In Marshall, Texas, a lot depended on who your Daddy was—unless, of course, it was Friday afternoon. Then, it only mattered if you were good at football. Then, you might thank God for being "wonderfully made," and what God knew was talked about on every sidewalk and celebrated when you stood in line at the grocery. In Sunday school one was taught to play fair and square in this world, but only on

Fridays was the lesson enforced. One could not cheat in a football game. Out there under the sky connections didn't count for beans, and nobody's Daddy got you a position. It was perhaps for this reason that the stadiums in every small town in the area were unconsciously revered, marked off, surrounded by walls if necessary, for indeed the green grass of the playing field was an enchanted place.

In 1941 Coach Odus Mitchell came to Marshall from Pampa, Texas, not only to coach, but to prove to a generation of small town boys that there was more than one way for David to beat Goliath. It was a refreshing message for the people of Marshall. Whereas the priest said: "Be Good," Coach Mitchell said: "Have Fun!" Working people listened. And all over the East Texas woods, this "fun" was news.

At the start of the practice season, Coach Mitchell addressed the Marshall High School Mavericks football team: "Gentlemen," he said, "I think it will be better for all of us if I tell you right now that I have not come to Marshall to coach a losing team. . . . There is no such thing as a 'good loser.' I do not want good losers. The world is full of good losers. I want good winners."[3]

As proper Methodist and Baptist sons, the Marshall Mavericks had all been taught to be "good losers." But certainly to the most practiced losers in Harrison County, these words were powerful music. Marshall had not had a winning season since the mid-thirties and had not won a district championship for fifteen years. Odessa, Waco, Amarillo, and Golden Sandys were powerhouses in the state, and these teams Y. A. Tittle did not even dare dream about. Instead, the Mavericks came up against small town teams like Carthage and Pittsburgh. In the years prior to the arrival of Coach Mitchell, they had been tormented continually by the Kilgore Bulldogs, the Gladewater Bears, the Texarkana Tigers, the Tyler Lions, the Lufkin Tigers, and the Loboes of Longview.

Under the football regime of Odus Mitchell, however, there would be no more weak teams and mediocre seasons. Two rules were paramount in Mitchell's revolutionary sports program. One, you believed you were as good as anybody. And two, you had fun.

Odus Mitchell actually believed that his boys could win, and win against anyone. And he felt that making everything fun in the process was key. When twenty-seven years later Y. A. Tittle "still looked forward to practice and hated to see it end," it was the fault of Coach Mitchell, who became the first in a winning streak of coaches for Y. A. What Coach Mitchell did was to leave my father alone and grant him "the freedom to explore." "You are not taught to throw," he said. "God gave you an arm. God gave you the ability to turn your body when you throw, and I am not going to change it. I can't change it. But for every pass you complete in a game, you must complete that pass a thousand times in practice."

Watching Y. A. practice that autumn of 1941, one might think that he had vowed to throw a pass for every leaf that fell. In no time, Tittle could take the snap and tell if a ball was not the proper weight by the squeeze between his thumb and middle finger, by the feel of his own wrist. Then, as the sun went down on the practice field, there was Y. A. still taking the snap from himself and aiming at a stadium lamppost across the field, at a distance of 53 yards. He became so accurate that he could hit the lamppost more than 50% of the time.

In Mitchell's football philosophy, it seems there was no real taste to victory without this corresponding sense of freedom. And that victory was what he wanted his boys to taste. Taste it once and then be hungry for it everywhere in life. Train to be good men and one day you will be. But fundamental to the freedom was discipline and dignity, according to Odus. And so he stressed conditioning and physical training. Practice was not, however, restricted to body contact sessions, and Tittle never left the practice field overly fatigued. Many were the times he went home before a game, played tackle football for a few hours, and then went back to town to play a game that night. Next morning, it was pass and touch.

Odus also asked his players not to cuss, drink, or smoke and he demanded from himself the same commitment. It was his job to prepare the Mavericks physically and their job to prepare themselves mentally. He insisted at all times that his Mavericks practice as they played and play by the rules. Discipline the mind to free the mind. Discipline the body and win. As for those players who practiced with less intensity than they played, even by a step, or those who disregarded training, relaxed their mental discipline but were still great athletes, they did not prosper much under Mitchell's football regime.

Tittle prospered.

He walked home every day after football practice singing and kicking up dirt like it was diamonds. The fact was that as an athlete my father was always practicing. He started on the day he was born and remained at practice right through eating and sleeping clear up to retirement. He did not stop even when Miss Selma, his English teacher, looked directly at him, Albert Agnor, and the other Mavericks before informing the entire class that poetry was the language invented for moments. And it was easy, because he thought that he was devoted to the moment, too, and to the years of practice that went into training for the split second when he could be more than he was. No longer content with killing time, Y. A. was one of many setting out to shoot the moon! And to knock off the Mavericks' arch tormentor and rival—the Lions from Tyler, Texas.

It was dusk when the team bus left town for Tyler in 1941. The sun was setting and the houses sinking into themselves like grandmothers asleep in their chairs. Of course the Mavericks felt the glory of the sunset was for them. And according to the laws of glory, soon everything would become part of the luck. The game was going to be played on the night of a blue moon, and the moon cinched the win.

Straight ahead was Tyler High School with its bright red brick sticking out of the landscape like a sore thumb. Naturally, the Mavericks stepped purposefully out of the bus and walked across a field that in the moonlight looked as fine as needlepoint. Of course the stands were packed. And the Mavericks tromped into the stadium as one would have entered an arena of belief. Coach Mitchell was there reminding everyone that winning wasn't everything but *wanting* to win was. Without that, Miss Inez Hughes would have no history to teach. And whether anybody liked it or not, not only would the Mavericks win with ease, but Tyler High would be transformed into a shrine to the future that night, as both teams taped their wrists and went out to make metaphors.

In a sentence, the Mavericks chewed the heart right out of the Tyler offense. But behind it all was Coach Odus Mitchell's belief in a single word—*we*. Coach Mitchell's passion for the game of football rested, it seemed, on this word, and he devoted his coaching life as much to its expression as to the exploration of its magical meaning.

Coach Mitchell was able to spend more time with other men's sons in any given season than most fathers could afford to spend in a year. His success as a coach came from the example he set as a man with a new idea about human possibilities, and the curiosity he was able to impart to his teenage stallions. They, in turn, were startled by his goodness as a man, without being much aware of his talent as a football coach. Coach Mitchell never "hollered, swore, never even lost his temper." He did on occasion say, "For Cramps Sake!" if the Mavericks lost their will to win, but never if they lost. As for the phrase, it meant simply a return to the *we* until its right magic was seen on the field and felt in the stands. For Mitchell, there was no we without individual merit. And his job, as everybody knew, was to work and rework the definition.

As Marshall High emerged as the new hot shot on the East Texas scene in 1942, Mitchell's positive attitude and highly disciplined structure paid off. Tittle grew into his leadership position, and the Maverick backfield picked up speed with backs Byron Gillroy, Billy Dinkle, and Bobby Furrh, who began to apply their talents and achieve higher levels of performance. Y. A. progressed on a practical level as a young quarterback with respect to his footwork and his field perspective. The T formation had not been invented yet, so the forward passer, called a tailback, took a direct snap from center and he passed and he ran. Tittle was a tailback in the double wing offense. On Mitchell's command, he threw 25 to 30 times a game. He threw from his own end zone and from his own five-yard line. In so doing, he began to see the field as a chessboard and anticipate moves in advance because he had to. When to throw a feather pass. When to throw a bullet. To become a quarterback, there were mechanical steps to take as well as intellectual and emotional steps. What looked as simple as throwing could become as complicated as the strategies of a general, in a war without guilt. To read men in any given situation, to inspire their cooperation and confidence in all circumstances, required not just an arm. It required faith in that creative process churning in one's own gut and a mind quick and decisive.

On a roll in 1942, Odus Mitchell scheduled the biggest towns in the state. And he continued to inspire. The schoolteachers could not believe it. They told the Mavericks they had only won their first few games out of conference, and should just wait until they got to their division. But, "We really did it," my father tells me with a look of amazement, "We won." In the process, Mitchell earned the love saved for a father, and the Marshall Mavericks felt an explosion of confidence in themselves. Against every opponent, Odus turned the game into an exercise of emotion. And my father responded to his style whole hog. No threats. No insults or rudeness. Just respect. Imagined perfection. The way he liked it. And with Odus in charge of the program—an imagined *we*.

In 1943 the headlines in the *Dallas Morning News* read: ALONG THE BANKS OF THE CADDO FROM THE PINEY WOODS OF EAST TEXAS CAME THE CHALLENGING ROAR OF THE MARSHALL MAVERICKS![4]

Though none of the Mavericks had ever been more than two hundred miles from home before, they traveled to Waco, Texas for the opening game of the 1943 season. Not only was Waco favored by 40 points, the Waco Tigers had knocked off the state champs from the year before. As 150 Tigers streamed onto the field in a splash of uniforms and blinding confidence, outnumbering the Mavericks more than 3–1, Coach Mitchell kept repeating, "Gentlemen. They can only use eleven out there at one time. Just remember! Eleven at one time!"

It was lucky that Coach Mitchell had drilled them into excellent condition, otherwise the Maverick team would have dropped dead from disbelief at the end of the game. They won. The score? 20–6! And on that day, my father thinks that he became a real football player. He thinks that the Mavericks became "men as good as anybody, but no better than their best effort." Free to live poor but to dream like demi-gods, free to find victory and taste it again, the Mavericks got back onto the team bus and all the way home, they breathed gold, touched gold, because they were gold. They won that day a victory that was off the scoreboard. Waco was the turning point. And thereafter the Mavericks were in time, in tune, and the team to beat!

In 1943, Y. A.'s senior year, the Mavericks were known as "the passingest team in the state." And all season long Tittle just "shot those fast little wingbacks out there in the flat and hit them with quick passes in what seemed like a track meet with Dinkle, Gillroy and Bobby Furrh."5 Yet, the secret to his great success, it seems, lies nowhere under the heading of football fundamentals or what is properly called *technique*. True, Y. A. Tittle looked forward to practice and hated to see it end. But that was because Mitchell permitted him to roam freely, crisscrossing the blank page in his mind with football schemes and dreams of his own—without ever being second-guessed. This was the great gift to Y. A.'s way of thinking. Never once did coach Mitchell say, "Why did you do that?" after a mistake. The assumption was that he had already suffered for making it and was smart enough to do something about it in a hurry. This "technique" was precisely what Coach Mitchell had in mind for his young tailback when, at the end of the season, the Mavericks won the conference championship, a feat which had not occurred in memory at Marshall High School.

According to the ritual of fall, businesses like Joe Weisman's furniture store closed down early on Friday afternoon for the game against the Tyler Tigers, and shopkeepers and employees alike gathered, some with picnic baskets, beneath the dome on the court-house square. Now dressed in the fitted uniform of drum major and wearing a tall hat, Minnette, at age 13, lifted her baton to the music and led the parade of townsfolk, hundreds of them, into Maverick Stadium.

At the high school, it was usual that year for 10,000 to pack the stands, some standing on buildings, others sitting in trees or on the high embankment. And what my mother saw upon entering the stadium that day were Maverick receivers choking back the dry heaves on the sidelines and players from both sides moving like cosmic acrobats, in dream time, because this was big. This was the district championship! As for my father, he looked sleepy. And indeed, he always felt exhausted before the first hit.

During the entire first half, "What a bore," thought my mother, "who could care less about all those numbers, all those names and weights." It looked like dress up to her, boys dressing up to be men. And while she and Mimi Key, Jerri Jones, and Minnette Harkrider had stuffed silk stockings into brassieres and imagined what it was to be a woman once or twice, these little boys put on shoulder pads and helmets and imagined what it was to be a man every week in the fall. Didn't they get it the first time? Thank goodness, the girls in her Penguin Club didn't have to wear falsies, bring in coaches or have the entire community go overboard with songs and ticket sales.

For her part in the halftime entertainment, my mother wore a tall white and red headpiece. After the band's performance at the half, she removed it and gave her black, shoulder-length hair a toss as she climbed the stadium steps to her seat. Then she turned to watch. The ball, like an enchanted bead of mercury, was every-where at once. Puppy Gilry zig-zagged downfield like a human lightning bolt, and Y. A. Tittle poked out of the grass with his arms unfurled. Feeling herself drawn by the powerful rhythms, Minnette was quick to figure that she didn't live in a part of the world where things made sense anyway. The stands filled to ca-pacity with people who seemed to have materialized in the park-ing lot. To her left were folks with tired eyes, whose shining tots, with ten hairs to a pigtail, wore bows to match the colors of the team.

This was Texas football. Minnette tried to cling to the light of reason but it was no use. Would the Mavericks pull it out? With the kickoff to the Tyler Lions in the fourth quarter, there was a Maverick defender with big bones yet with legs short enough to belong to a Chicashaw. He was not only clumsy and large, he was trying too hard. The sweat poured off his face when he crouched over the line and his eyes were electric moons against his too-earnest face. She tried not to watch, but the boy was a magnet to her eyes. It made no sense.

But Minnette DeLoach began to understand why a touchdown could be a very real goal in a football player's life when suddenly it became the only goal in hers. As the Mavericks gave their all, she would have given her vial of water from the Dead Sea to make *it* happen. And *it* did. Just when she gave up hope, the Tyler quarterback's dead duck of a pass bobbled and flopped. It wasn't a leap exactly, but the Maverick with short legs intercepted and started running. Just like the man in the moon with his mouth in a wide open O.

Minnette held her breath. She blinked. But before she could say a word, the boy had collapsed in the end zone from disbelief and Minnette was out of her skin and into the WE of the world. Marshall a champion? All hands went up, and the drum major added herself to the thrilling incomprehensible oneness by landing a kiss like a fast pitch on the mouth of the nearest face. For their part, the Mavericks landed on that player as if he were a hunk of gold. And the wide-eyed boy was lifted onto the shoulders of his peers, a man, and to Minnette, a shining moon.

> *Our boys will shine tonight!*
> *Our boys will shine tonight!*

In 1943 the Mavericks won the district championship and proceeded up the ladder of playoff games. Then, in a game against Longview, Y. A. Tittle's knee went out. The joint snapped like a harp string, and, a week later, as the Mavericks qualified for the state championship against the Lufkin Tigers, it was unbendable, stiff as a column. It was widely known that Lufkin brought in football players each year from under every rock in creation, while Marshall High was lucky to get the farm boys into the classroom during harvest. Marshall could bring in no ringers, because there was more money invested in vegetable gardens than there was in the bank. But in this championship playoff, at least it could be said that Y. A. Tittle was learning his game.

"It's my last chance, my last shot at these guys. I have to play," he said to Coach Mitchell, pleading for what he mistakenly assumed would be his last chance in the world to get his rear end kicked. And toward the end of the game, Coach Mitchell let him have it. Y. A. was knocked down in every play and then helped to his feet. Still, his attitude was fierce, and he fought that splint as if it and not Lufkin were the other team. In so doing, Y. A. finally paid attention to his brother's words, and discovered the hard way that just as important as the perfect spiral was balance, pure and simple. That more important than mechanics, passion, or will, was the "plant," the leg, the knee as the axis of his game. It was a mistake to go out there. But he was fifteen. It was the championship. It was also a new program, just like Coach Mitchell said—when every heart began to beat like drums, and the harmonies of neglected brotherhood, like rhythms long forgotten, were suddenly remembered.

Y. A. Tittle played football for three years in junior high and three years in high school under Odus Mitchell. He was tailback on the gridiron, shortstop on the baseball field, threw the shot put and discus on the track team, and made All-District in basketball at the forward position. He made a high average in his scholastic work and was on the student council for two years. Thanks to Coach Mitchell, Tittle scored more touchdowns and completed more passes than anyone in Marshall High School history. He lettered in four sports and was named Most Valuable Back for three years in 1941, 1942 and 1943. He received All-District honors in '42 and '43, was chosen to the second All-State team along with quarterback Bobby Layne from Highland Park, and was included on the All-Southern honor roll for 1944.

As the games and seasons had continued to roll during my father's high school years, so, apparently, did the Maverick luck under Coach Odus Mitchell. After every game, Y. A. slept deeply and woke up to the same horizon and to Blocker out in the field with a plow. They seemed like Hector and Achilles, these two, replayed as friends and fellow athletes in a small Southern town. Achilles was the baby, the spoiled one. Hector knew his fatal destiny and fought well. Y. A. and H. L. were locked in a competition equally unqualified, if bloodless, and as for the one who played for the Marshall Mavericks, he learned the full meaning of the famous football *we* from the friend with whom he played marbles and in whom there shone the virtue of never giving up.

And what about Minnette? In 1943, my parents, in their turn, courted at the Shop Pond in Hobo Jungle. Come springtime and the annual May Fete that year, Minnette and the members of her Penguin Club, along with Pickle, Albert, Puppy Gilry, and Y. A. Tittle, marched off into the night to attend the hobo fires. In the firelight there on the edge of the city limits, Minnette watched the face of the quarterback. Y. A.'s face was rugged and rawboned. His mouth was full, his cheekbones high, and his deep-set eyes were the color of Caddo Lake after a thunderstorm. To some he was handsome, to others he was not. But to Minnette DeLoach he was beautiful, because if his face had been a mountain, it would have been one of the most difficult to climb.

In June, Minnette De Loach asked Y. A. to autograph her yearbook, and on the last page he proposed that they get married when they graduated from college. H. L. bought out the Snow White Cleaners from Abe Tittle and built up a decent business. Y. A. hadn't allowed himself much fun off the football field, except kissing a girl named Harriet whom Minnette referred to as Split Tooth. And when everyone went off to cross the rickety "sway" bridge, Y. A. stayed on the sidelines out of respect for both his safety and his knees. Minnette could barely bring herself to forgive him.

He was 17 and about to graduate. She was 16 when he sent her a bracelet in the mail. The chain was very thin and the two hearts with their initials on them were very small. Y. A. was being heavily recruited for football at the time, and it was unpatriotic to think of going anywhere except the University of Texas. But Y. A. wasn't sure. The name of the Texas coach was Dana X. Bible, and the *X* was forbidding, not to mention the *Bible*. So Y. A. cut loose and went down to the lake for a canoe ride. Never before had he done something for no good reason. And that canoe glided into the water like his mother slipping her hand into a glove. The day opened like a party invitation. But to what purpose?

Y. A. paddled the sloughs of Alligator Bayou and Devil's Elbow. He listened to the quiet and watched the mud hens leave a line of wing prints on the water. Then a hawk crossed the air above the cypress. And the wind picked up just as he found his father's house, leaning to one side, just as Abe Tittle would lean on his hip and wait, watching for his children to return after the livelong day. It was a simple green house on stilts, open to the wind at both ends in 1943. An empty room like a tunnel looking through to cypress trees.

BROWN RIGHT COUNTER 34 TRAP!
LSU TIGERS

T Formation
Tigers

No thing, neither tawny fox nor roaring lion
may change the nature born in his blood.

—Pindar, *Olympian* 11

Y. A. "Little Jack"
with hair, LSU 1945.

Father: *We made do in those days, but living was great outside of the city limits. The game of football was in the air. Slinging Sammy was my idol. And I worshipped my brother Jack, who was All-District in high school. It was lucky for me that I never had to wear overalls to school or go barefooted. I never took an egg sandwich to school like half the kids did, because that meant you were poor. And everybody knew who had an egg sandwich. In those days, a lot of youngsters dropped out of school in April to chop cotton, but I was kept from this work. I wasn't even allowed to mow the grass because I had asthma. (I learned how to play that one to the hilt.) In a sense, everyone was poor, but we didn't know it. We were poor, but not that poor. Mother had help. And we had ten acres under cultivation. As kids, we slid on sawdust piles. I couldn't because of my asthma, but everyone else did.*

But out there, everything from Christmastime to football to Hog Killing Day seemed like nothing but a good excuse for coming together out in the country. Hog Killing Day fell on the first day after the freeze. We kept a big black pot in the backyard and there we boiled a pig. My father hung it up on the scaffold upside down and cut it open. You ate everything, remember, feet, ears, you wasted nothing. As kids, we took turns at the sausage grinder and it took an entire day for our family to put up the hams, sausages, and pork chops. Some kids kept the fire under the pot while the others ground the sausage. Aunt Sally and Uncle Top lived up the road, and they helped. Everybody helped, and then you went to help them kill their hog.

At Christmastime, the cooking went on forever and ever, with every kind of pie and cake you could possibly imagine. Once, there were twenty pies lined up in a row. And on one occasion, we had sparklers and firecrackers too. One Christmas, I got a pocketknife.

And it was a big deal. We always had Christmas at Grandmother's with all the cousins. At their house, sugar cane was ground on the property to make sorghum syrup. The mules would go around in a circle. And my daddy would taste it to see if it was right.

When we first moved to the country, there was silence in abundance. For a time, we had no electric lights, we studied by lamplight and used an outhouse. At first we had a wood stove and piped water from the windmill. Later came electricity. We walked down the road to see the lights go on. As kids, that was as big a thrill as Yankee Stadium ever was.

Shortly thereafter, we got a telephone. Central? 30F1. And before I knew it, Daddy was driving around in a Hudson Terraplane car. We prospered in the country, where we had gone after my oldest brother, Stafford, died. Stafford was the smartest of us all, a straight A student.

. . . As for my scholarship with the LSU Tigers, you bet I was thrilled. Not only was I able to save, but I could take a date out on the town. I mean, what more could you ask for?

Daughter: *How much did you get?*

Father: *Ten dollars a month.*
. . . In college, I went to the draft board in Dallas with a bunch of scrawny kids—and was turned down because of my asthmatic condition. I felt so ashamed. The Allies had landed and here I was 4-F. Some big stud I was, walking down South Washington to the Paramount Theatre. All my teammates took off to the service. A squad of 150 guys in the dorm, and two months later there were ten of us left. Here I was, a great big old football star, not in the service. Here I come home, big, strong, and not doing my share. I was haunted by this, I'll admit. But if nothing else, my asthma and even my self-doubt provided me with an inspiration to perform. Don't ask me how it works.

. . . As for my best call? Early in my football career, I was not considered a good signal caller. Mind you, in those days, coaches could not call plays from the sideline, and if a substitute came into the

game, he could not talk to the QB until after one play had been run. If any attempt was made to signal any message to the QB, it was a 15-yard penalty—coaching from the sideline.

However, I must admit our assistant coach had a unique way of communicating with us on certain occasions. I can't say that Coach Moore knew about it, but the assistant certainly knew how to "bend the rules." For instance, the water boy would bring us little jugs of water during time outs. My jug had a different cap from the others. And under the cap there was sometimes a message, like *PUNT*, or *PASS 74X*. In the game against Texas A&M, the score was 6–0. We had been shut out for 59 minutes and not even been close to the A&M goal line. With three time outs left and less than a minute to play, I called time out. And here came the water jug.

I took the cap off and it said, *PUNT*. Punt? You don't punt with less than a minute to play and with the ball at mid-field; otherwise you give up the ball and the ball game. What happened of course was that the assistant forgot to remove the message from the time before. Well, what was I supposed to do? My teammates went crazy in the huddle but the QB was the boss, so we punted. The football bounced out of bounds on the five-yard line, and on the next play A&M fumbled. We called time out, and with one second remaining I threw to Jim Cason for the winning TD pass. LSU 7–A&M 6.

I could not believe my eyes or my ears shortly afterward when Head Coach Moore told the Baton Rouge Morning Advocate *sports writers that it was the gutsiest call he had ever seen at LSU. He said that this young QB knew that since the Tigers had been unable to penetrate A&M territory for 58 minutes, their only hope was to punt and pray for a break . . . That was a lucky one. An unlucky break, however, was right around the corner, and it happened on Halloween night in 1947. It was a cold night, come to think of it. . . .

Let's see. I left home in 1944. . . .

The Tigers vs. Tulane

It was the summer of 1944.

"Hop in, Yat!" said Coach Blair Cherry, the backfield coach from the University of Texas, as he opened his car door in front of the Tittle home. Yelberton had come a long way from the patient sixth-grader who played second string under Coach Magrill.

Now, he had become both the jug-eared wonder with an arm like a bull whip and the blushing recipient of athletic scholarships from almost every school in the Southeastern Conference. Y. A. sent a letter of intent to LSU, the worthy rival of his brother's Alma Mater, Tulane University, only to take heat for what was seen as a glaring lack of patriotism to his home state. As a compromise, he promised to visit the University of Texas for a summer and take in the bright lights of Austin.

The woman wearing the blue dress waved again. Wearing a red bandana and leaning over a scrub board, she straightened and smiled wistfully at the high school graduate for the last time. Taking confidence from her hand, Yelberton turned to Coach Cherry as if to boast about the treasure he knew was buried in the landscape. He wanted to mention that Jean Lafitte used to hide out in those trees when the steamboats traveled from Jefferson, Texas, to New Orleans. But instead, he just thought to himself, here there are wild peacocks and turkeys, squirrel, mink, hogs, fox, opossum and armadillo. There, I'm going to Miss Poole's boarding house to room with the great Bobby Layne.

Finally, Y. A. said, "Sir, if you're hungry, up a ways is Shady Glade and the best chicken fried steak for miles around." He would not fail to say something when they passed Shady Glade, because out in front playing cards and rocking in their chairs like babes in swinging cradles were old Shug, Five Cents, and Baby Boy, all in their eighties. How did they do it? Tittle wondered. How did these men manage to stay so cool, calm and collected against a backdrop so wild?

"Sorry, Y. A. We've got to hurry. Bobby wants to show you around, you know. A hard liver, that Bobby." Coach Cherry flashed him a look. "I think you two will be perfect for each other."

As a country boy, Y. A made a point never to wear overalls to school or eat an egg sandwich, but these were not concerns that Layne could relate to. To the hero from Highland Park, the contents of his roommate's life story were like a jigger of bourbon to be downed in a single shot. Confidence? Confidence roared through the lusty veins of this blond-haired, blued-eyed Bobby Layne. He cussed it. He laughed it. Layne did everything but spit confidence. Failure of any kind did not enter his mind. So why did Yelberton Abraham have to live his life with a fear that went back as far as he could remember? A fear that burrowed deep inside his belly and never went away, except in the arena, where it burned and turned into inspiration—a difficult confidence, rich and strange and passionately fought for.

These two future Hall of Fame athletes first met at Miss Poole's boarding house in Austin. Miss Poole had no sooner finished telling Y. A. how nice and quiet it was at her house than she opened the door to Bobby's room, as if welcoming a renowned scholar to a new wing at the rare book library. Tittle poked his head in the door and said, "Hiya, my name is Y. A. Tittle."

The husky Layne rolled over and even with eyes half-closed, the forward motion that shot from his pupils was startling. "Glad to meet you. My name is Layne . . . Bobby Layne. They got you too, huh?"

That summer of '44, Layne, a great baseball pitcher, hooked up with a semi-pro outfit, while Yelberton, ever practical, took a summer job working at Rooster Andrews' Sporting Goods Store. Days in the summertime were muggy and hot. But the evenings were cool, and that's when Tittle and Layne took off their socks and shoes, and took off—two bare-legged boys with legs like eggbeaters, huffing and puffing, their arms pumping like oil wells. Oblivious of the onlookers, they ran footraces down the middle of the street in front of Miss Poole's boarding house. Layne and Tittle tore up their feet on the road, but that didn't matter. They understood that competition does not only mean to beat another man, but to bring out the best in him. The best against the best. That's how they wanted it to be, and that's how it was on those nights when they put scouts, politics, and contracts aside, and the running was pure, like a heartfelt conversation between them.

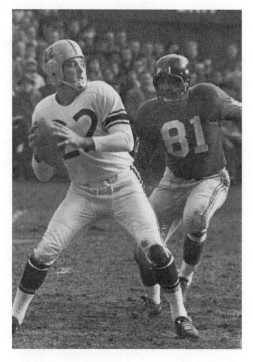

Bobby Lane (*l.*) and Andy Robustelli.

Football great Bobby Layne went on to be a winner at the University of Texas, a winner with the Detroit Lions and a Hall of Fame quarterback. He was "the last quarterback not to wear a face mask and the auto workers of Detroit and the mill workers of Pittsburgh loved him for it. . . . In the early and mid-fifties Otto Graham of Cleveland and Bobby Layne of the Detroit Lions met for the championship four times in six years and three times Detroit won."[1] They won because Bobby did not know how to lose.

Running barefoot in front of Miss Poole's, Layne proved it. And come to find out, Y. A. had as much to learn from Bobby as from the football program under Coach Dana X. Bible. For one thing, just untying your shoes and standing barefoot next to Bobby Layne was "like a trip to Niagara Falls." Like standing next to a force of nature and wondering just how close it was safe to get. Layne taught Tittle to appreciate human energy, never to underestimate the power of a man.

As I understand my father, although Bobby and Y. A. had one thing in common—for both, the game was an instrument fit for music in spite of what the spectator saw—the differences came in the way they tuned themselves for performance. One difference was that Tittle felt he needed every advantage he could possibly get. And no doubt he did. If Layne drank and caroused, he could still get up the next morning and win. My father was a young man who put his body at risk but never his mind, and who would rather break every bone in his body than lose his mental edge. What gifts he had were born from a keen awareness of his own mental and physical limitations, a sense which became increasingly refined, until, as a professional, it might be said that he dignified this sense with occasional exploits on the football field.

Layne, on the other hand, did not believe in the virtue of self-doubt, but in the divine right of his God-given gifts. He did not refine a sense of his own limitations as a way of unleashing his talents, rather he refined his sense of the possibilities, the infinite possibilities. And he was a lucky man, because for him it worked.

Indeed, Layne could party all night and compete all day, while his roommate did the sleeping for him. Layne probably thought my father, from a dry county in the East Texas woods, had been a rooster in his last life. Tittle went to bed early and jumped up at dawn. In high school, he didn't drink Coca-Cola for fear the sugar might shorten his wind. And in college, he drank sparingly. Yet Y. A. appreciated Bobby's zest and vitality, and was in awe of Layne's cool confidence, which more than anything else was in stark contrast to his own ways.

One night in midsummer, Layne was out on the town and Yelberton lay awake trying to come up with at least one luxury he could afford in his life. Oddly enough, heroes were all he could come up with. If Bobby was his own hero, then Yelberton was rich. He had Churchill and Joe Louis. Like counting sheep. . . . He had Slinging Sammy Baugh. . . . And then the telephone rang.

"May I please speak to Y. A. Tittle?"

"Who?" Yelberton replied.

"Y. A. Tittle."

"Who?" my father asked again.

"Tell him Coach Red Swanson is calling from LSU."

Before Coaches Slick Martin and Red Swanson showed up on the following day, Y. A. ate his first store-bought steak and supposedly called Texas football coach, Dana X. Bible. Then he hit the road to Baton Rouge, Louisiana. They made one stop in Victoria, Texas, to pick up Jimmy Cason, who was later to become Tittle's best friend. For 450 miles, however, it seemed that the car upholstery was a continent as foreign as Asia and that neither of them knew the language. They weren't frightened exactly. But for Tittle, it was like running 450 miles in the dark against Bobby Layne. Tittle knew he had to keep going if he wanted to win. For one thing, he had to make up his mind that he would never be caught without that ace up his sleeve—that respect for moments he believed in, private moments of transcendance. As an athlete, it was simply not in the cards for Tittle to become tough or cynical. For another, it was not every day you got to meet somebody with the confidence God gives whole hog to a mosquito. No doubt about it. Thanks to Bobby Layne, Tittle was leaving Texas with the knowledge that the only luxury he could afford was that of believing in heroes even after he realized they were made of clay, feet up to nose. He became a pickpocket after perfection. Piecing together from strangers one who could inspire you to be yourself was a real trick.

Come September, coaches Dana X. Bible and Bernie Moore were not on speaking terms, as Bible felt that Tittle had been stolen from Texas for the price of a breakfast. Yet on a happier note, the temperature was 100 degrees in Baton Rouge, and the finest backfield Bernie Moore ever coached were out there "working like dogs and banging heads."[2] Had the Martians landed on the 50-yard line, the Tiger backfield might not have noticed. Cason was quick and cagey on defense and a "tough little runner." Red Knight from Bossier City was "versatile as a runner and kicker." And tailback Ray Coates was considered "the finest high school player in the state."[3] If Cason was the heart of the LSU Tiger backfield, Coates and Knight its teeth, then Y. A. was its eye. Called "Little Jack Tittle," Yat was the least versatile, but the most capable leader. He poked out of the grass at Tiger Stadium and in his freshman year, wearing his brother's pads, he fulfilled the prophecy of Coach Magrill. College football was not a passing game at the time. But against Tulane, Coach Bernie Moore cut "Little Jack" loose.

According to sportswriter Fred Digby, the freshman quarterback "outdid Sammy Baugh" as he netted 242 yards and completed 14 of 17 passes, including the first 12 in a row. The Tigers prevailed 25–6.[4] And what a day that was in December 1944. The entire Tittle family was present as the Tigers, a roaring underdog with a freshmen backfield, ripped Tulane. There was Jack cemented to his seat with his hands folded into a tiny pulpit of pride, Don grinning on general principle, and Huline stalking the sidelines. Though white-haired, Abe and Alma Tittle were as excited as their children, disbelieving, helpless, and proud.

Alma was now very ill, but the woman who rarely left her roses attended every game she could. It was Alma, after all, who had tipped off Red Swanson when Y. A. couldn't make up his mind between the University of Texas and LSU. Perhaps she knew from growing things where her son ought to stay put, and so she put down her roses to make a phone call in late summer. Alma passed away in the spring of Y. A.'s freshman year in the back room of their home, but she had made it to the Tulane game, the last game of Y. A. Tittle's freshman season.

Far from the crowds of red ants and newborn turtles who once dared cross Y. A.'s minefield of flying objects, Mrs. Tittle watched carefully as her son nailed his heel into the field and loosed a pass that soared like a falcon. Y. A. could no more hear Alma's applause at that moment than he could hear her heart beat. But he had his deep-set eyes from her. Alma had seen three sons die. And for her, the blur of loss was brought into focus only with an occasional moment such as this, when a mere pass left in its wake not a boy but a man with sweat on his face and a scar of sunlight on his helmet.

On the day that Y. A. saw his mother standing for the last time, Alma Tittle saw her son as grown. She rose from her seat and stood there in her blue cotton dress with flowers on it, determined to wear all the joys and sorrows of her life together, like a beautiful necklace. At an outdoor play, her eldest "took his pneumonia." Stafford's face had been radiant as hers as he watched the action. But while that son had hungered for beautiful words, there were no words to match this ferocious vitality, this hunger to participate in the world. In the terrifying game of life, Alma thought, this son was now an enthusiastic participant.

It was not one of the 12 passes in a row which broke quarterback Abe Mickal's record and "outdid" Sammy Baugh that told her this. And it was not the pass to Webb for the second score which so infuriated the Tulane Greenies. It was the pass into the flat followed by a lateral and the final TD against Tulane in which she noticed the almost imperceptible shift in her son's style of play. Alma Tittle had spent hours watching her children learn to walk, and she knew that with that pass into the flat, Y. A. got it. He really got it. And for a QB to get anywhere in the games, rhythm with oneself and harmony with the team were crucial. Merely knowing the steps of movement and balance was not enough. One had to dance, literally. And it was that which Alma Tittle saw. Y. A. had taken his first steps once more. In so doing, her son would become more than a football player, she thought with a slight smile. He would become an athlete one day.

On the day that LSU beat Tulane University, Y. A. Tittle's pro career was born. Until then, LSU had used the single wing formation, and the tailback duties were shared by Y. A. and three others. But the upset against Tulane convinced the LSU coaching staff that they could switch from the single wing to the new T formation. With the T formation, the quarterback became a forward passer and Y. A. "Little Jack" Tittle found full expression for his passion with spinning objects. The passing game.

In the springtime of 1945, practice for the T formation would begin. In the meantime, Tittle was competitive, if nothing else. Competitive at a sustained pitch, competitive at high C. The last game of the season, the romp against the Greenies, was played on a Saturday in mid-December. On Sunday, he and Jimmy Cason made a few phone calls. And on Monday they got a touch football game together for that and every other afternoon until spring. Practice. Practice. Practice. Inspiration 1%. Preparation, perspiration 99%. Tittle practiced the drop-back of five steps and spent so many hours planting his foot in the same spot that he dug four-inch holes in the field.

"I just hope I can get the guys to hit this hard come September,"[5] remarked Coach Moore. And it was no joke. Destiny pegged Cason as a future 49er, Hubert Shurtz, a Pittsburgh Steeler, Dan Sandifer, a Washington Redskin, and Piggy Barnes as a Philadelphia Eagle. No wonder potential recruits dropped like flies in these spring battles. Tittle and Cason would occasionally look into the stands, where their coaches were frantically motioning for them to take it easy on the new guys. It was only natural for every coach to want his recruit to look good. But imploring looks were lost on Jimmy Cason and Y. A. Tittle. In Cason's own words, every time they were urged to take it easy on a recruit it was like "pouring kerosene on a fire." Instead, Tittle and Cason "just killed 'em. Just ate 'em up alive."[6] And although Tittle and Cason were best friends, if they happened to be on opposite teams, either the day ended in a fist fight, in a knock-down drag-out, or they cheated until the sun went down with its last gleam on their shoulders like the hand of a well-meaning ref who is utterly ignored.

In 1945, it seems the success of the campus touch football battles merely set the stage for baseball tryouts. As pitcher, Y. A. Tittle just wanted to strike the batter out. At bat, Cason would have sold his soul for a base hit. Why warm up? Y. A. thought. Why not just "fog" it past him. And that was a mistake. Pain shot from Y. A.'s shoulder to his wrist and the ball bounced to home plate. Tittle had survived the competitive fires of the football league which he and Cason organized, only to injure himself with a baseball pitch.

While Bobby Layne had shown him the beauty of competition, Tittle discovered for himself its dark side and the difference between wanting to win and the will to win. Everybody just *wants*, but the *will to win* runs through the mind like a wild animal. And though it is wild and dangerous, only that animal is worth capturing. It takes skill, patience, and a lifetime of discipline for the real athlete to hunt it down.

With spring practice about to begin, Y. A. Tittle had just caught wind of this startling creature. Fearful that he might be benched during practice for the T formation, he did not mention his shoulder. But after several weeks of practice, the injury could not be ignored. He awoke one morning to find that he could not raise his throwing arm. So, privately, he went to a doctor in Baton Rouge who told him that he had bursitis, as well as a growth on the shoulder bone that had to be removed.

Because a shoulder operation was not in Yelberton Abraham's game plan, for the duration of Y. A.'s college career and his first season as a professional, he entrusted himself to Mother Nature, endured the pain and played scared. This was also the situation in the springtime of 1945, when Y. A. was chosen quarterback with Coach Bernie Moore's announcement: "He can't run worth a darn and he can't block, so we've got to make him the quarterback. Besides, he can throw the ball pretty good."[7] (That was also sobering.) And at first, Tittle did not recognize the T formation as a blessing, because center Melvin Didier's rear end was the only constant. Once that dropped from view, Tittle found himself "moving alone in the opposite direction of the action and his entire perspective changed for the worse."[8]

Springtime brought its challenges. Before the Tulane game, Tittle was by his own account, "a diamond in the rough." Afterward, he was a budding star. A Southern grid scout tabbed him the best passer to come along in a long time. Sportswriters, smitten by the sound of Tittle's name, attached to that "long handle" the hopes for a successful grid season. And he awoke one morning to read in the local paper about his height and weight, his 4-F status, and his ambition to become a history teacher.

The words, "history teacher" struck my father with remorse. In high school, Y. A. had been a good student, inspired by the determined Miss Selma Brotsky and the hardy Miss Hughes, who tackled education as though leading their students in an assault on the forces of chaos itself. But in his freshman year in college, he became an average, even an indifferent student, preoccupied not only by the game but by the trials of his friends who were fighting in the war and by his mother's failing health. Caught up in the patriotism of a just war, Y. A. took out on the football field his guilt over being sidelined when his country was calling. The war was, to his way of thinking, a heroic struggle for freedom, and at the same time his own mother was fighting for her life. Her kidneys were failing. And there, too, he could do nothing but stand by and feel helpless.

After Alma died, Abe Tittle married his wife's sister, Reba Allen, a spinster and a dry, hard seed of a woman who was hopelessly in love with being organized. Reba Allen meant well, but there was never enough detergent to dispel the faint perfume of roses which Alma had left behind. Those would have been lonely days for the young athlete, but he opened the door of home and family to include the floating island of the gridiron, and coaches and teammates present and future. Luckily for Y. A., Coach Bernie Moore, like Odus Mitchell, trusted Tittle's perfectionism and left him to his own standards and his own self-criticism on the field. Y. A. stayed after practice every day to work on his passing, and apparently he was never satisfied. Moore did nothing to interrupt or discourage this dissatisfaction.

As for the T formation, it had been used during the earliest days of football and then resurrected in 1940 by George Halas, the Bears' owner and coach. From the University of Chicago, coaches Ralph Jones and Clark Shaughnessy redesigned it for the Bears, adding "a man-in-motion and a counter play, and giving it deception and speed."[9] Halas whacked the Redskins with the T in 1945, his Bears annihilating the Washington Redskins 73–0 in the NFL championship. And so it was that come spring, Y. A. blinked his eyes at the start of spring practice and found himself staring at Melvin's rear end as Carl Brumbaugh, the former quarterback with the Chicago Bears, shouted out the steps to the T formation.

When Brumbaugh explained what was expected with the T, Y. A. could only scratch his head. "How am I going to get back to pass?" he asked finally. "Oh, you'll get back all right," Brumbaugh replied. "Don't worry about it. I haven't lost a quarterback yet."[10]

Y. A. wasn't the only one who squirmed. To begin with, "nobody in that part of the country had ever taken a direct hand-off from center." It was like changing the constitution. And all those "natural-born single wing men felt kind of silly standing there like *that*. For Tittle, it was strange to be up so close to the line with hands under the center and the defensive middle guard staring you in the eye."[11] Secondly, he stumbled on the drop-back. He had little over two seconds to get set, plant his foot and release the ball, keeping track all the while of where the blockers and receivers were. Suddenly, there was more to the game than spinning objects. With the T, there was the drop-back. To hit that "turn-in" or "sideline pass" in a second or two at most, this single move had to be worked on constantly in order to achieve speed, hit the spot with the right foot and be ready to throw. Timing was everything. The drop-back was just as important as the pass. Maybe even more so.

Y. A. throwing from the T. LSU, 1947.

In 1945 every school in the Southeastern Conference stayed with the single wing, except Georgia and LSU. Inspired by the victory over Tulane, Coach Bernie Moore decided that this formation would enable him to use his four star tailbacks simultaneously rather than alternately. One tailback, then, would become a passer, the two best runners would become right and left half-back, and the fourth tailback would play fullback.

Coach Bernie Moore confessed that he might be "all wet" about the T. Therefore, when LSU first used the formation in a conference game, it must have been heartwarming for him to see the opposition looking as lost as puppies with their eyes still closed. Tittle sent Cason out for a pass and nobody covered him. Though still sloppy with his pivots, Y. A.'s drop-backs had improved because of the countless hours spent planting his foot over and over in the same spot. His best friend, Jimmy Cason, marveled that Tittle's heel was making what looked like gopher holes in the turf. But the T formation had changed Tittle's thinking just as it changed college football after the war. A new era had begun.

Ready Break!

In 1944, the Tigers had finished 2-5-1. But in 1945, there was a turnabout with the T formation and the team "was propelled into the national limelight for the first time since the 1930s."[12] As the Tigers charged through 7–2, 9–1, and 5–3–1 seasons, veteran *Times-Picayune* sports columnist Peter Finney wrote that:

> Y. A. took devilish delight in beating Greenie Wave from Tulane University. His career total against the Greenies was forty-two completions in fifty-six passes and eight touchdowns. . . . The incomparable Tittle left five LSU records: passing yards in a career, 2,717; complete passes in a career, 166; touchdown passes in a career, 21; total offense in a career, 2,619; touchdown passes in a season, eleven in 1946 . . . .[13]

As passer, Y. A. averaged 54 minutes a game, playing halfback on defense and quarterback on offense. At the same time, the dull, deep ache was always there in his shoulder, and he never knew when the shooting pain would strike. If it came, it nagged him early in the week, and sometimes there was an uncomfortable twinge on the night before a game. But on game day, it always disappeared, and Tittle was able to stand his ground against some notable players in 1946, among them, Charlie Trippi of Georgia,

Harry Gilmer of Alabama, Charley Conerly of Old Miss, and Johnny Rausch from Georgia Tech.

As Finney tells it, in the opening game in 1945:

> the Tigers defeated Rice 42–0 and "Slim Jim" Cason made LSU history by scoring three touchdowns in a 13-minute span. . . . The following week, the Tigers accomplished their most dramatic victory of the season before 27,000 at Grant Field in Atlanta, Georgia. . . .Tittle, who played sixty minutes against [Georgia] Tech, had a red hot arm throughout the 1945 season which closed with a smashing 33–0 conquest of Tulane before 52,636 in New Orleans . . . [14]

In 1946, LSU lost only one game, to Georgia Tech, and proceeded to the Cotton Bowl in Dallas, Texas, to meet the Southwest champion Arkansas. There, however, the Tigers ran into some weather. Bad weather, with subfreezing temperatures and the field a sheet of ice. Nonetheless, the Tiger backfield gutted it out with their salty dreams of hope. Finney said:

> the game ended in a scoreless deadlock but with LSU holding a 15–1 advantage in first downs and a 271–54 edge in total yardage. Harry Rabenhorst, who recalled it as the only game in memory in which all of the LSU linemen wore gloves, retains a vivid picture of Bernie Moore on the sidelines. "The cold brought tears to everyone's eyes," said Rabenhorst. "I went up to Bernie one time and, sure enough, the tears had frozen on his cheeks." [15]

To the fans, quarterback Y. A. Tittle seemed like a priest in a grand communion. He appeared able to go out and create for himself and the Tigers endless possibilities for fun in the world. As for Y. A., he braced for that ache in his shoulder, and come hell or bad weather he began to anticipate the hit and whatever else the game had to offer. Rather than simply reacting to circumstances, he learned to anticipate the game's opportunities as well as its dangers. For this, Tittle was grateful, as if for a mystery. He had no way of knowing that he was destined to become "LSU's greatest T-formation passer ever" and leave behind "a fistful of records (most of which lasted until 1972), most of his hair, and a lingering legend." [16] All he knew was that the legend he had earned to date suggested that the road ahead would not be easy for the balding Eagle.

Brown Right Counter 34 Trap!

Bobby Layne was throwing footballs. Frankie Albert was throwing footballs. Johnny Lujack and Chunkin' Charley Conerly of Ole Miss were throwing footballs. And they all wore baggy pants, belted at the waist. It was a cold Halloween Night. According to sportswriter Marty Mule from "The LSU Tiger," on that October night in 1947, "one of the first of the heated LSU-Rebel bouts featured Tittle at quarterback for the Tigers and Charley Conerly at quarterback for Old Miss playing for first place in the SEC standings . . . ."[17]

> Conerly hung a pass up and Tittle, playing left corner on defense, timed his move and intercepted as the Old Miss receiver ran past. The intended receiver reached back, making a seemingly futile grab at Tittle's midriff before falling by the wayside. Between that slight tug in one direction and Tittle's momentum to the other, however, something had to give. It turned out to be Tittle's belt buckle. The end zone was 70 yards away, 40 of which were negotiated by a tippy-toeing Tittle running with one hand holding up his pants, the other cradling the ball.
>
> Barney Poole, Old Miss' all-time great end, recalled decades after their memorable night together. "I was racing down the field after him laughing and laughing. I couldn't help it, it was just the funniest thing I ever saw in football." Poole admitted that "Coach Vaught taught us a lot of football, but he never did teach us where to throw the head when tackling a man losing his pants." Poole, however, finally caught up with him and hemmed Tittle in on the sideline and . . .
>
> "I tried to stiff-arm him," Tittle said.[18]

And that made all the difference. Tittle was tackled on the 18-yard line. He was later quoted as saying, "I was on the 30-yard line. And I've never been so alone in my life." Y. A. Tittle's first real roar of approval from the fans came as his pants fell to his knees and he struggled to the sidelines like someone putting on a girdle while crossing an ice floe. And among the 46,000 in attendance at Tiger

Stadium was Minnette DeLoach with her new boyfriend. Even his teammates Zolly, Piggy, and Alnut were grinning like possums as they backed off.

Didn't anybody care that LSU attempted a field goal and missed, or that Ole Miss won and the Tigers lost their bid for the Sugar Bowl?

This was abuse.

Yet throughout Y. A.'s career, it would remain true that even when he lost, he never lost his will to win. And from this perspective the game against Ole Miss was like a sip of castor oil—it was good for him. It has always been the rare privilege of the athlete to move in mysterious realms of joy and pain. Even to go nowhere as a pro ball player requires a high pain threshold. Y. A. was not only determined, he seemed hell-bent on earning a new pain threshold.

In the game against Vanderbilt played later in 1947, for instance, Tittle was knocked out cold and revived with spirits of ammonia. When the team physician warned against letting Tittle play again that night, Swanson bellowed "AND WHY NOT?" to which the physician replied meekly, "Well, the boy is hardly breathing." In an atmosphere as charged as a battle cry, this tidy piece of logic did not translate. Swanson thundered back, "Hell, you are a doctor . . . MAKE HIM BREATHE." And Tittle got up while the physician and coach were still eyeball to eyeball and guided the team to victory that night: 19–13.

For the next thirty years Tittle would ride the wave of the T formation. But his first encounter with the T taught him that "dropping back from center is the single most important thing for a quarterback to master."[19] Tittle was seventeen when he learned. And thereafter, as quarterback, he would have to throw, not run, thank God. During the war years, he would become a thrower of footballs instead of handgrenades. Yet this young man who was 4-F, who was never expected to play sports, was playing ball among the swamps of Louisiana with enthusiastic determination, and an oxygen tank on the sidelines. For four straight years, the Tigers scored more TDs than any other team in LSU history. And there was Coach Bernie Moore on the sidelines saying, "You're good, boy. I'm leaving LSU when you do."

Academically, Tittle became a history major, endlessly absorbed in the patterns of human will and endeavor even off the field. Miss Selma and Miss Hughes reappeared in his conscience, good teachers who had illuminated for him in high school both the mountain range of knowledge and the deadly swamps of ignorance. And though an hour diagramming sentences with Miss Selma had made football practice seem like eating ice cream, their spirits had remained with him. They increased his odds for victory in the future—and reminded him that he could end his athletic career by stepping into a gopher hole like his brother Jack. So Y. A. went to class, was punctual, and in the end he developed a passion for American history, most likely because he liked people and could never get enough of them trying to move in a forward direction while falling flat on their faces. Perhaps this love was bound to come to one whose life was animated by a passionate commitment to the good try. And if nothing else, Y. A. was passionate about people. He revered the past and possessed infinite patience when listening to the elderly. The green grass of the even playing field haunted and inspired everything from his conversation to his politics.

On campus, he was one jock who refused to join a fraternity, because the reasons one was invited to join did not jibe with his sense of fairness. It wasn't just a quirk of football logic. In the back of his mind, the underdogs and so-called losers like Shug, Baby Boy, and Five Cents from Karnack, Texas, must have swayed like cypress trees. Besides, without an even playing field, how could one compete? And without competition, where was the win? And without that, how did the the best or the beautiful show itself? How did *man* shine? In one of his history lessons, it was either Heraclitus or Herodotus who wrote: *Happiness is the exercise of vital powers along lines of excellence in a life affording them scope.* If that was so, then Y. A. Tittle at nineteen years of age did well to remember how competing in the half-dark against Bobby

Layne brought to the very edge of breath a tradition extending back to the games of pharoahs, ancient Greeks, and the Chinese ruling classes of 2,500 years ago. Or, if not to them, at least to the teams of Persian warriors, often numbering a thousand on a side, who battled over a carved willow root!

As a student, was he supposed to skip the chapter in which the avowed heroes of the Western World took their games more seriously than the Trojan War itself? So Menelaus loses the chariot race in Book 23 of the *Iliad*. He pounds the ground. And in the end, turns out to be an even bigger baby than Jimmy Cason. Didn't scholars find this behavior unsettling even in the slightest? And how did Zeus go from turning himself into a housefly to hurling a thunderbolt? That was college football! The sometime power and majesty of it wasn't supposed to be there, but it was. There was no understanding it, for that would be akin to calling Zeus a housefly when he was a god, or assuming he was only great, when gods and mortals alike knew otherwise.

Yes, the lines of the playing field were there to provide the scope, sometimes. And meanwhile Tittle kept practicing and kept taking every opportunity he could. For one thing, he reminded Minnette DeLoach of his proposal of marriage in her high school yearbook by announcing their engagement in *Sport* magazine upon his graduation from college at twenty-one years of age. She was not a subscriber to *Sport* magazine, but her boyfriend at the time read about it and was not amused. Tittle also took the opportunity to sign his first pro contract with the Cleveland Browns while standing on the grass after his last game in Tiger Stadium. The coach walked out onto the field and asked him to sign for $10,000. At the time, Cleveland was the hottest team in the pros, with the fabled Otto Graham as QB number one. And they were going to pay him to play? There was the same old sweat on his face and scar of sunlight on his helmet. But the contract was brand new.

There was no time to wonder where he might have ended up if LSU had not made the switch to the T formation. The question did not enter his mind as he became increasingly caught up in that cyclone of feeling where all that mattered was the respect of one's peers.

Years later, a day would come in the Rotunda in Dallas, Texas, when Yelberton Abraham Tittle would stand at the mention of his own funny name and be inducted into the Texas Sports Hall Of Fame along with Olympian athletes and fellow Hall of Fame quarterback, Bobby Layne. Miss Poole herself was in attendance. Even I was there to hear for myself:

"Bobby, you know that if I hadn't left Miss Poole's, you'd never have gotten a chance to play."

Layne replied: "Ah shucks, Y. A. It's just lucky for you you left. Or you'd still be sticking to that bench."

But as the eye of the LSU Tiger from 1944 to 1948, all that really mattered to my father was to have given his all and beaten the Greenies. Go in. Pass. Come out. And breathe. Never guessing that his football destiny may have had its roots in his mother's rose garden, Yelberton Abraham Tittle was still working out the steps to the T formation when he graduated from Louisiana State University. Not only did the T put him in a new relationship to the game, it put him in the game. And many years later, it accounted for his movement—his stance, snap, and drop-back when his leg was torn to pieces on a blitz. That would be Y. A. Tittle's greatest dance in 1963, his tragic dance against George Halas and the Chicago Bears. But for the present, there were years of practice before him. For the time, he was still a novice. And it was enough to keep pace with Bobby Layne and to match him stride for stride, just as he did on those humid summer nights in front of Miss Poole's boarding house. Nothing really changed after that. No matter who the opposition was, and no matter how many years went by, Layne would always be invincible, eternal and laughing. For Tittle, the self-doubt never did go away. But then, that was the way he began to like it in 1948. In time, he would like his self-doubt as black as his coffee.

RED RIGHT POWER 29 B LIKE BOY ON 3!

BALTIMORE COLTS

We are things of a day.
The dream of a shadow is man, no more.
But when a brightness comes and God gives it,
there is a shining of light on men and life is sweet . . .

—Pindar, *Pythian* 8

Daughter: *Did you play better than you practiced?*

Father: *No. I always made a point of practicing like I played. That is, I tried at all times to do my best because—who was I, to think I could turn it on when I wished. Some athletes played better if other people were watching. But I played no differently. It was the same in front of the crowds in New York City as it would have been if I was all by myself in the dark.*

Daughter: *Were you afraid of getting hurt? Was Layne ever afraid?*

Father: *Layne and I, we both came up on sand lot football. He had no fear. And no, I had no fear on a football field. But let me add that my basic personality is to be fearful, fearful of high places, driving too fast, snakes, walking on a high ledge or a mountain trail. I'm afraid of fist fights. I never was a fighter. And I am afraid of most things. Basically, I am very conscious, overly conscious of safety, except for one place—the football field.*

Once I was at a sports banquet in Seattle. The guy on my right was the first person to have climbed Mt. Everest, and the guy on my left had just broken the world's speedboat record (his neck was in a brace). During the course of the luncheon, both of these men mentioned how courageous they thought I was to go out there for 17 years and face five or six rushing linemen averaging 250 pounds apiece, who all aimed to tear my head off. I looked over at them and thought, what is courage? Maybe courage is what you are used to. You wouldn't get me driving over the speed limit or standing on the roof of my own house. Those linemen coming my way? I didn't even see them.

Daughter: *Has the game changed?*

Father: *Complicated. For one thing, football has become very complicated. There are situation substitutions on almost every down. Defensive players coming in and out, offensive players coming in and out, all plays are signaled from the sideline to the quarterback. Audibles are frequently called by the quarterback. Sometimes even I get confused!*

Daughter: *Is it really that complicated?*

Father: *Well, most people think it is, and you would expect it to be. Frankly, I think the complications as they are portrayed by the high-priced sports telecasters are overdone. I will give you my personal opinion and some examples.*

In my era, the Green Bay Packers as coached by Vince Lombardi were the most successful team in pro football history at the time. Lombardi won with the application of basic fundamentals and a more or less simplistic game plan. What I mean by this is that the Packers fooled very few people with complicated plays and won games by what I consider to be the basic standards of winning: that is, the best blocking and tackling football team always wins.

Another example would be our New York Giant team in the early sixties. We never had more than seven or eight offensive running plays for any one particular game. Our team combined with great defense became the highest scoring team in the history of pro football in 1963.

Another example would be the Hula Bowl in 1955. I coached the team personally, and we had a limited number of plays. We scored 56 points with a very simple offense put together in one week. Some of the players on that team, however, Doak Walker, McElhenny, me, outside receiver Elroy "Crazy Legs" Hirsh, Leo Nomellini— all future Hall of Fame athletes, and All-Conference players Bill McCall and Matt Hazeltine. My point is that we had the best players, and it didn't take a rocket scientist to design scoring plays.

In my view, most teams win because they have the best chucker at quarterback, the best skinny guy running around right end, two big overweight guys who can block the defensive ends, and an antelope playing wide receiver.

Daughter: *What you're saying is that football is not a science, no matter what anybody tells you. . . . In what other way is the game different?*

Father: *Football today is big business and many players can become independently wealthy after playing only a few years. People might say that in our day owners paid us too little and took advantage of us. To be honest, I have to admit that we took advantage of them. Some of us would have played for nothing . . .*

Beginner's Luck

1948 . . . A man was sitting on the Baltimore team train with his heart pounding in his fingertips. On his way to training camp in Sun Valley, Idaho, Y. A. Tittle was throwing touchdown after touchdown in his mind. He was a man with a contract and a black Champion Studebaker to his name. Y. A. watched as Charlie O'Roarke, Lee Arto, and Hub Bechtol, a three-time All-American, climbed aboard and thought: A pro career? I am on my way now. Then the whistle blew.

At the next stop, a guy named Ernie Blandon walked down the aisle of the train and nudged him. "So you're Tittle?" he said. "I played with your brother Jack at Tulane." Then he grinned. "Guess what?" he said. "Your life is gonna change." It was that simple. With that, he walked on. But Tittle could not get over Blandon's smile. To see him grinning woke Tittle from his reverie like a smack to the funny bone. Yet as he faded back just one more time to pass, the towns outside the window began to remind him of the towns back home, small towns where dawn and dusk were practically the only tourists.

Y. A. Tittle was still thankful and almost incredulous that what he had said to Fred Russell, the writer from *Sport* magazine, had come true.

"Y. A., you have had a fine college career. What comes next?"

"I'm going to graduate in June, marry my high school sweetheart, Minnette DeLoach, and play professional football."

The collective spit and meanness of Art Donovan, Lee Artoe, Big Daddy Lipscomb and Hardy the Hatchet Brown were as snowflakes compared to the fury of his beloved, Minnette, when she found out that she had been proposed to in a sports article. If Tittle could survive that, he knew that he could handle pro football under any circumstances. For the several months before she gave her answer, Y. A. experienced Minnette thundering across his soul like Attila on a rampage—and he had no way of knowing if she wanted his head or his heart.

She wanted both. And in June, they were married. As always, the biggest moments in Y. A. Tittle's life seemed plagued by bad weather, and their wedding night was no exception. As they drove in the Studebaker through a rainstorm to rival the archetypal deluge, the windshield wipers began to make the newlyweds seasick. To settle their stomachs they stopped for root beer, feeling as forlorn as the last male and female of the human species. But then one soft drink led to another. And it occurred to Y. A. Tittle that Joy needs no practice, but Disaster likes warming up on the sidelines.

Minnette DeLoach Tittle on her wedding day, 20 June 1947.

According to my father, their honeymoon night was spent in Natches, Mississippi, getting tanked up on root beer. Considering his previous experience with women, it is no wonder that Y. A. Tittle drank 10 soft drinks. Into his mind came a replay of the rainy night in the woods back in 1943 when the local hot potato, Nellie Jo, had beckoned. If he remembered correctly, on a dirt road near Caddo Lake, he and Nellie Jo removed the back seat from Bobby Furrh's car and carried it deeper into the woods. Setting it down, they "started to court," when, in the dead of night, "the four horsemen of the apocalpyse came riding." Upon finding the car in the road, the horsemen had detoured and come at an easy canter toward Bobby's back seat enthroned in a small clearing. They came, the horses whinnied and reared and trampled Bobby's back seat like a wild mushroom. It took only seconds. But the almost-lovers had rolled off the car seat in opposite directions before the horse hooves pummeled the upholstery, and the riders rode on unaware. Nellie was not about to have her optimism squelched; Y. A., on the other hand, gave up the ghost. And now, prepared for his wedding night to become the sequel, he downed another root beer.

He was not wrong. Disaster struck at the Bentley Hotel when the bride and groom met Y. A.'s former coach unlocking the room next to theirs. In the ensuing conversation about his contract, Y. A. was so nervous he failed to introduce his bride. He realized his mistake when Minette charged into the bathroom as soon as they were inside the room. And that's when Y. A.'s brother, Jack arrived. At 4:00 A.M., it wasn't Jack so much as the champagne he brought which seemed out of character with the night's events.

But eventually, Jack left. The rain did stop and the sun did rise. Having drunk enough to drown in, Minnette and Y. A. settled down to sleep off the root beer and dream of journeys in the high desert and better times to come.

Sun Valley, Idaho was one of those times. For those reporting to Coach Cecil Isbell in 1948, it didn't get much better. Training in Sun Valley was like showing up for boot camp at the Pearly Gates. The Baltimore Colts were the star tourist attraction come July, and the stands were packed with fans applauding their morning and afternoon workouts. As part of the "Help the Weak" program initiated by Admiral Jonas Ingram, the commissioner of the All-America Conference, several prominent AAC stars were turned over to the Colts, who were in the hole $165,000 and had lost 11 of 13 games in 1947. To save the franchise, players Dick Barwegen, Ollie Poole, Pete Berezney and Lee Artoe "added muscle" to the worst team in the league. Cleveland gave up Ernie Blandin, one of the AAC's best tackles, and halfback Mickey Mayne.

While Tittle was on his honeymoon, he too got tossed into the Baltimore camp by Paul Brown, the head coach of Cleveland. Y. A. had signed with the Browns on the playing field after his last college game and been given as a bonus the black Studebaker with white top and red leather upholstery. Overnight, he went from the best team to the worst. But the worst team looked promising under the tutelage of Coach Cecil Isbell, the onetime quarterback from Green Bay. With the Browns, Y. A. would have played backup to the legendary Otto Graham. The Colts, on the other hand, were a team of rookies, and their weakest link was the quarterback position. Coach Isbell was out to get Bobby Layne, Y. A. Tittle, or both.

Isbell lost Bobby Layne to the Chicago Bears and gained a son in Y. A. Tittle. As a coach, Isbell was a creative and empathetic man who endeared himself to his players with warmth and integrity, and to his young quarterbacks, O'Roarke and Tittle, with the words, "There is only one way to play this game. Throw the damn ball!"

More than anyone else, Isbell taught Tittle to depend on himself and thereby how to throw successful passes: "Don't expect help from anyone but your receiver," he used to say. "It is you and him against the defense. He's got to beat his man. Then you have got to hit him with the pass. There are no magic tricks in passing. You make your own gains. And you do it by throwing the hell out of the football."[1]

Isbell's words were blunt, but Y. A. was moved by their poetry. Never one to fade back with "the idea of looking at two or three different receivers and finally throwing to one in the open," Tittle figured that "if you can hit only one man on a pass, you might as well depend on your arm to get the ball out to him and not on a razzle-dazzle pass pattern to suddenly spring a receiver into a hole in the secondary where nobody is covering him and where anybody's mother-in-law could hit him with a pigskin."[2]

Many quarterbacks "hope that a pattern will spring somebody loose." Isbell would say to heck with that. "Depend on your own arm to get the ball to your man." That's rule number one. "Do not rely on pass patterns to miraculously work somebody into the clear." Two. "Do not expect defense to make a mistake." Three. "The receiver's job is to get open. The QB's job is to hit him between the eyes with the football. . . . Completed passes do not just happen. They are made by the passer and by his receiver—man to man. . . . "[3]

1948 was the year to put Isbell's words to the test. "Layne came out of Texas and went to the Bears along with the Notre Dame All-American, Johnny Lujack. Charlie Conerly finished his career at Mississippi and signed with the Giants. Harry Gilmer of Alabama joined Sammy Baugh at Washington."[4] Quarterbacks, good ones, were coming up roses and '48 promised to be a great year for quarterbacks in pro football.

For Y. A. Tittle, it was a year in which he learned that in order to compete he would have to begin to see his good luck as bad luck by most people's standards. Y. A. managed that.

In August, he was unable to participate with the other quarterbacks in the Chicago College All-Star Game—it seems that when my mother called training camp to say that she had blown the top off the Studebaker, my father suffered the first injury of his pro career running to the telephone.

On the road to Sulphur Springs, Minnette, Huline, and Huline's newborn son had found themselves in another of those downpours reminiscent of the Flood. The top blew off the black Studebaker in a lightning's flash and little Tommy's christening dress (Huline's labor of umpteen hours) went to looking like wet onion skin draped over a pollywog. From Sun Valley, Idaho, it was not possible for Y. A. to imagine the magnitude of this situation. But it was under these circumstances that Minnette and Huline rolled into the driveway at Aunt Reba's, where Mr. Tittle had waited anxiously all day for a glimpse of his first grandchild, and under these circumstances that they rolled out and continued on to the hospital for the day's grand finale—an appendix operation. Minnette was operated on that evening, worried about money that night, and called her husband in the morning to tell him about the car.

Because my father only thought in terms of real catastrophes when people called long distance, he was desperate with worry when he pulled his hamstring running to the phone. Clutching his leg, he said, "What? You mean nobody's dead? . . . Don't worry, darlin'," he said. "Just try and take it easy." (There was no way he could blame Minnette for forgetting to latch the top because he too was practically allergic to details.) What worried him was the bill for $240. And his leg.

Later in the day, he told Fitz Lutz, the trainer who was working on the hamstring, "Boy, am I glad I have a contract. But you know, Fitz? No wonder the team lost money last year. With five quarterbacks and all. Don't you think that's too many?"

"Sure is. But you know they're only going to keep two."

Y. A. shook his head. "I don't deserve to be so lucky." he said, "To have a contract, I mean. I guess I'm one of the two."

"They all have contracts out here, baldy. You still have to make the team, you know. You have to make the team to get paid."

Tittle reacted to the news as if the top had just blown off the Studebaker again. While Baltimore practiced on a hard rodeo field surrounded by the most glorious scenery the Texas rookie had ever seen, Y. A. found himself suddenly locked up in that spectacular playpen with a bum leg. With a trainer who kept telling him to take it easy, and a coach he had borrowed money from to pay for his wife's medical bills.

It was time for fate to show its hand. . . . In 1948, Y. A.'s first preseason game as a Colt was played against the Los Angeles Dons in Portland, Oregon, where Tittle watched Charley O'Roarke and Jarring Johnny Kimbro from the bench. Then, with two minutes left and the Colts trailing, he entered the game and threw the greatest pass of his entire career on the first play of his first game as a pro. When his protection broke, he aimed a 25-yard crossing pass to Lamar "Race Horse" Davies. But, because of overexcitement and pure nervous terror, he overthrew Davies and hit Johnny North in the endzone with a 55-yard strike.

Baltimore not only beat the Dons, the headlines proclaimed that Y. A. Tittle's pass was "just about the prettiest pass ever thrown in the state of Oregon." Naturally, Tittle kept his mouth shut and just nodded his head when a week later he won the starting job. Along with Wendell Williams, Billy Hillenbrand, Race Horse Davies, and Johnny North, the Colts were fired up and prepared to buck Baltimore's losing image. During the preseason, they suffered a painful loss to the 49ers, but came back and avenged themselves in their last preseason game in Toledo, Ohio, where they beat Cleveland, the AAC champions from the year before.

After this preseason victory over the Browns, thousands of fans greeted them at the airport in Baltimore. Never before had Tittle seen anything like it, as the players sat in open cars during a ticker tape parade down main street. It was the kind of reception that should be reserved for conquering heroes, but Race Horse and Wendell Williams waved back a cheerful and innocent hello. Out of old habit, it seemed, the people came out to praise. And the Colts, as preseason victors, had merely fumbled into that limelight just as somebody had always fumbled into it. But the hollering, the shouting, the frenzy of human empathy was a shock to someone who had never seen it as Tittle saw it that very first time.

Indeed, the Baltimore fans would remain loyal to the end. So loyal, that even after the team disbanded two years later, a thousand of them would travel to Philadelphia and cheer Tittle as a 49er from behind the San Francisco bench. An assistant coach with the Colts in 1947, Tarzan White, summed up the town's spirit with the remark, "This place is like a big Green Bay."[5] And so it was. The community supported the team with ticket sales, kickoff dinners, and assistance in finding jobs for the football players. With that kind of backing, the Colts, like baby birds teetering on the edge of the nest, took off to meet the eastern champions from the year before, the New York Yankees, at Memorial Stadium on September 5. Isbell had told the newspapers that Tittle would be starting in the league opener, and he had been criticized for not going with the more experienced O'Roarke. Still, Isbell stuck to his instinct, and "his boy" did not let him down.

On September 5, Y. A. Tittle broke four All-America Conference passing records as a rookie and helped defeat the New York Yankees, 45–28. Y. A. himself could not believe what was happening. "He threw five touchdowns and handed off to Billy Hillenbrand for the sixth. . . . He averaged 16.5 yards for every pass attempt and completed 11 of 20 passes for 346 yards" while "the offense gave him great protection against Arnie Weinmeister and the other New York pass rushers," and "the defense knocked Buddy Young, the Yankees' great little halfback out of commission and battered Spec Sanders to a standstill."[6] It was beyond Isbell's wildest expectations.

Just to prove it was no accident, two weeks later, the Colts knocked off the Yankees once again. And come October, the team that had almost lost its franchise led the eastern division by a game. Strange to say, it was a loss to Cleveland rather than a victory that won for the Colts their professional dignity, a loss that Paul Brown called one of the hardest wins of his entire career. It was like the knock-down drag-out fight between Jimmy Cason and Y. A. Tittle played on a grand scale. And as usual, the fans were in their seats and the weather gods were whooping and hollering.

Flood, mud, wind and more mud. As for Otto Graham, Mac Speedy, and Edgar "Special Delivery" Jones—only the whites of their eyes showed through the mud-plaster. With Baltimore in the lead in the final minute, O'Roarke got off a lousy punt to the Colts' 26-yard line. And Otto Graham took it from there. Splashing down the field, the grim players seemed like torture victims playing hot potato. The fans could hardly see what was happening, but on the Baltimore sidelines, the players' faces told the story better than the programs or the scoreboard.

With that 14–10 defeat, the spectators saw that competition, like a gem-cutter, could sometimes bring out the true character of a man. The Colts had talent, but they also showed character in the clash against Cleveland. They redeemed themselves from the losses of their previous season and continued their rise, like a phoenix out of the ashes.

Y. A. finished fourth among the AAC's passers and would face George Ratterman in the championship playoffs against the Buffalo Bills. Baltimore was ready to bust. There was just one caveat. As yet, the Colts had only proved that they could win, and lose. As a franchise, they had yet to prove that they could shoulder the burden of success.

Five days before the playoffs for the title, some of the veterans felt that compensation should be made, since there was no provision in their contracts to cover a playoff. The response from general manager Walt Driskill, and the president of the team, Jake Embry, was that a divisional playoff was a part of the player's regular contract. They hoped proceeds from a championship would take the Colts out of the red. Some of the players, on the other hand, expected fair pay for the extra bruises.

The argument escalated until Embry threatened to forfeit the title to Buffalo and make the announcement to the public. Stung, Baltimore Colts Ernie Blandin and Dick Barwegen informed the front office that half the team was ready to strike. The strike contingent, however, had agreed to abide by a vote of all the players, the majority of whom, like Tittle, were willing to play ball, money or no. There was some resentment when the "no money" element won. But there was little time for it to show itself.

The championship. On December 12, the Baltimore Colts were locked in "a wide-open offensive battle,"[7] every one of them. All season long, Tittle, like everyone else, had worked hard at earning every penny of his contract. Beyond this, he stubbornly chose to ignore everything good that was said about him, and pretended that his wife could starve to death as the result of his every move. It was the beginning of a habit which would worsen with the years. The more his athletic exploits took him into the eye of the crowd, the more he burrowed into a room of cool, dark solitude, training his eye on his own goal. Even at the height of his career, Tittle was constantly afraid he would lose his job and was busy creating a cliff edge for himself, while his fans saw him sitting in the lap of success. But that was how he played his game—according to the dark laws of fear and anxiety. If he won, he was alive, and if he lost he was dead and his children sold into slavery.

But in his first season as a pro, he was still erratic in his abilities to concentrate. Sometimes he could not shut the world out entirely, and chaos poured all over his carefully tended fields of concentration. So it happened on December 12, in the fourth quarter of play when "Ratterman . . . lobbed a short pass to Mutryn who was hit hard by the Colts, and Barwegen coughed up the ball as a result. Picked up by the Colt's tackle, John Mellus took off like hellfire for the end zone but was stopped by the whistle belonging to Ref Whelan. He ruled that the play was an incomplete pass, not a fumble. Buffalo, therefore, kept possession of the ball and scored, six plays later, on Ratterman's pass."[8] And at that, right there in the friendly face of the fan, the real violence of the game suddenly broke loose. If it was tough on the field, it was ever so much more so in the stands when the Walter Mittys turned cut-throat. Tittle was startled by it, and amazed. Never before had he seen this darkness of human rage triggered. Looking up, he saw the fans were fighting among themselves. A fire was lit in the stands. Extra policemen were summoned, but they were unable to protect the officials from the bottle-throwing crowd. It was like an ancient stoning. With a swollen eye and cut mouth, the referee made it to the locker-room under the protection of players who gave him their bodies as shield. But the police could not disperse the crowds surrounding the stadium and chanting, "Let's get Whelan!"

Disguised as a ball player, Ref Whelan boarded the team bus, and the faces and shouts of the mob soon faded into the distance. I try to imagine how my father saw this. I would have my own views of the fans later, but he was only twenty-two, and already the momentum in his own life was building. It was flooded with people and the current was fast. He needed to hurry up and concentrate. The game, the ball, the pass. That was his job.

In 1948 the Colts missed winning the title, but Y. A. received the Rookie of the Year Award. He had accomplished his goal—making good on his first pro contract and doing well by his coach, Cecil Isbell, whose football philosophy he so heartily endorsed. But all was not beautiful in Baltimore. On the day he received the Rookie of the Year Award, he also lost a coin toss to Wendell Williams and won an apartment with no bathroom or shower in it. These facilities were located in a basement with no heat. My parents moved into the place sight unseen and, as I am told, "it was tough in November."

In 1949 the Baltimore Colts agreed to a 30% pay cut on the day before the season opened. The team rationed chewing gum and traveled on buses held together with bailing wire. On payday, cars were left running so that no time would be wasted in getting to the bank. Since more than half the paychecks bounced, the road to the First National Bank was like the Indianapolis Speedway when they were given out. After several players complained, the owners replied by scheduling three exhibition games in six days. The players were told that, "Baseball players play every day." And with that, morale fell catastophically.

In 1949 the winning team from the year before proceeded to break every record for losing. Baltimore lost every game but one, and they lost big. Against the Rams, they lost 70–21. After scoring 70 points, the Rams pulled an onside kick with 15 seconds remaining in an effort to go for another score. In the game of football, this is an insult. Fortunately, the Rams were offsides when they pulled this maneuver, and the game ended with big, fat Art Donovan, the captain of the Baltimore defense, coming unglued.

On the locker-room bench, Donovan shouted hellfire and brimstone.

"We will never forget!" he screamed. "We will sacrifice the season if need be!"

And before he almost swallowed his tongue, he let it be known that the Colts would take their revenge against the Rams in the last game of the season!

The Colts came back, alright—and lost to the Rams by a mere 43 points. How Art Donovan seethed. After the game, he glared around at the slumped shoulders of the losers and finally settled on Tittle, who must have looked like the best opportunity for a victory in sight. Later that evening, Donovan filled the team's shower stall to the brim just before the quarterback's turn to wash up. For Y. A., the season ended when he opened the shower door and was knocked flat—at the hands of his own defense. Down the drain went the idealism of the rookie.

Also in December of that year, shortly before the end-of-season washout, I was born. I came early, I think, to make up for some of the losses of the season. On December 17, the Shamrock Bowl was played in Houston, Texas. The Shamrock Bowl was a night game and not part of the regular season. Back in those days, the quarterbacks were still allowed to call their own plays, and Tittle was trained to go with a hunch. Just about the best hunch he had during the '49 season was to trust his instinct even after the game and do something that made a big difference to me, though it made no sense whatever to his teammates. Although his flight home to Marshall was not scheduled until the next day, and his wife wasn't due for another two months, my father knew he had to get home, and so he did. He hitchhiked to Carthage where he caught another ride to Marshall. And at 4:00 A.M., he gently pulled down the covers to his bed. Thirty minutes later both he and Minnette were sitting bolt upright in blood-soaked sheets. There followed the sort of comedy scene in the face of potential tragedy that my parents are famous for.

While my mother and I were neck in neck in a galloping race to death, Dad went frantically looking for a coat. He would have gone to the center of the earth to find it. A scream: "Which coat?" And then my mother's thin voice—"I only have *one*."

With that, they were off. Tittle never knew what beating a clock was until they got to the hospital. While my mother and I charged down the home stretch, the Rookie of the Year was in the next room shouting, "C'mon! Minnette! C'mon!" He was banging the door down and he was not a happy cheerleader. He was shouting so loud that the nurses felt sorry for him, and my mother was sorry for the other mother she thought was in the next room. He was shouting so that even I might have heard him. And that is how we all made it into the sunshine together on December 18. I was born to commotion.

Within weeks, all three of us were inhaling and exhaling the days as if eternity were on our team. Dad, however, took a little getting used to. While fathers of the day were not famous diaper-changers as a rule, Y. A. developed an overnight attitude. He was more like a professional grandmother than a football player, and his departure from the stereotype got us into trouble with family who arrived from all over the state, with awe in their hearts and dust on their shoes. The females in particular did not expect to find a masked All-American Conference hero holding an eyedropper and feeding what looked like a nose. But Tittle was a pro, and if nothing else, the boos had taught him not to care what other people think.

It is no wonder that I was the season's highlight and the benchmark of my father's pro career up until that time. And yet, one glance at those baby photos which show me looking like Hopalong Cassidy riding a football prove that my parents finished off the '49 season of record losses with a lot of nerve coming from somewhere. With any humility, they might have found a baby blanket and put me under an azalea bush. Nonetheless, I am grateful for being born in the Piney Woods among countless other animals under the stars of my mother's love and my father's intuition.

The new year in 1950 found my father back in Baton Rouge, digging ditches, selling cars, and teaching history part-time at University High School while my mother remained in Marshall for several weeks more. During this time, hunger declared itself on every front, and Minnette responded to it like an athlete. Though weak, she moved through the quiet of the day wasting no motion and thinking no thought but that of victory over the course which stretched before her. As she attended to the needs of a four-pound infant, she was surprised to find that the most insignificant chore was like a candle being lit before a dark altar, and a place which had hitherto been invisible was suddenly revealed. It seemed that just as tenderly as she claimed responsibility for her child, she herself was claimed. And the mothering of the world was a mystery that revealed itself to her as the surface of the world rearranged its magnificent cloak to bare its magnificent shoulder.

Minnette's father, Arthur Young, had passed away in October. She had mourned his untimely death at the age of 44 and had carried that ending as well as a new life within her. With the new year, Minnette was herself again, as she stood at the back door of her parent's house listening to the night brimming with hoots and cricket-chirps and birdcalls. And though she tried to decipher their meaning, she figured it was okay if she couldn't. Years later, I would discover, too, that sometimes after a baby is born you feel that you don't have to hurry any place because you are *there*. So it was that Minnette stood in the doorway holding a plate of crackers, while her countless ancestors were clapping from a thousand stars.

Of course, when the phone rang, it was her husband telling her not to starve. And for the first few minutes of conversation Minnette had trouble listening to her husband's description of a lucky break over at Berksham Air Force base, because she was still so pleased with the night's splendors. But come to find out, Y. A. was also selling life insurance to make ends meet. And a young cadet who happened to be throwing around a football with a bunch of guys took pity on the man running across the field with a briefcase.

"Hey, insurance man!" yelled the cadet. "Can you catch it?" And Tittle said, "Sure can!" And he did.

"Why, that's pretty good for an insurance man," snapped the cadet, "but can you throw it back to me?" And the insurance man said, "Start runnin'." The pass wasn't seven yards in the air before the briefcase flew open, and Y. A. sold a group plan.

At the end of his story, Minnette whispered finally, "Good night." And for the first time since October, she was able to sleep deeply and dream of fires burning toward the sea and waves uncurling with children. In another dream, she was flung into the night, where she crawled across a snowy world toward a fire burning in the distance. Hyenas came. But she stayed the course and opened the door when she came to it. On the other side, she saw nothing changed, only that animal prints of every kind were beside her own. Encouraged that other creatures had gone before, the sadness broke, the snow was love. And her will became real from remembering her hand on the door like a gift from the darkness.

Not in her wildest dreams, however, could my mother have come up with a worse nightmare than the one my father lived in 1950. The best that can be said with respect to Y. A. Tittle's performance was that at least he was not alone. It was a real team effort. Most of the records that year were set against the Colts, and they gave up a total of 462 points during the season. In one game, Detroit's Clyde Box gained 302 yards against Baltimore in a single afternoon. But practically every week, the Colts could be counted on to come up with a new low.

That year, the American Conference merged with the National Football League and the Colts became the unlucky 13th swing team under Clem Crowe, who took over for Walt Driskoll. Clem didn't fare much better than his predecessor. The Colts came up short when the talent was distributed from the defunct Buffalo Bills and New York Yankees, but that didn't really matter until the team discovered that one of Clem's free agents was a guy who had been pumping gas since eighth grade and had never even played high school football before. Then it hit them.

The Colts were Clem's sacrificial victim. All season long the Colts got kicked from one end of the field to the other, and Tittle's cracked elbow sported a knot the size of a fist. The Rookie of the Year from 1948 was offered another pay cut or a release to Chicago. By opting for less pay, Y. A. discovered that talent alone is not enough. Leadership, comradery, and the character of a team count for real points on the scoreboard.

It was at Comisky Park that he noticed. Out on the field were many of the same players from the 1948 Colts, with the addition of a crackerjack from Tulsa, Hardy Brown. For a small guy, Hardy Brown was a human handgrenade. This wild man on defense was a demolition squad, with a tackle like a karate chop. As a teammate, the one worry you had with Hardy was that he might congratulate you. But there was no danger of that for the Colts at Cominsky Park, where "Chicago set a record by scoring 48 points in one half and Jim Hardy of the Cardinals threw six touchdown passes in the game."[9] The Colts had finally arrived at the slaughterhouse. And it was hard to watch, especially for the players Clem found hiding under the blanket when he went looking for substitutions.

But that was football during its gold rush years. The media was nowhere in sight. And in its absence, the game was an invitation for Life to laugh at itself, or, at the very least, sit down and take the load off its feet. The best man won? Not always. The best man always tried. People brought their own images of striving and success to the games—images that were not drug-induced or media-induced, but were often the result of a week on the job and the need for a time out.

It was as if America was still grinding out her concept of the *we*, and this was the beauty of the games. Entertainment played a part, but it wasn't the whole show. Of primary importance was the concept of individuals coming together as a team. The good of the whole, whether it be team, the community, or the society at large, was important not only to read about, hear about, or believe in, it was important to *see*. And the moment of victory wasn't entertaining, it was an epiphany brought home by men built for collision.

This defined a team of fooball players in 1950. Bumblers, fumblers, losers, winners, they were men built for collision. And when one of them happened to be the genius of a given moment, he was cheered not because his talent set him above anyone else, but because in his striving the multitudes could relate to him. As no other people in the world, Americans seemed locked in a struggle to the death with the meaning of the smallest word—the *we*—which was creating the national conscience like an irritating grain of sand.

It was in this atmosphere that the Baltimore team showed a smattering of Americans just how it didn't work. The Colts lost sight of the principle. And onto the stage in place of the leading star came a dog and pony show with bells, whistles, and losers, big time. Small wonder that my father so vividly remembers his first touchdown pass in the NFL. It wasn't thrown until the sixth game of the season on 29 October in Kezar Stadium against San Francisco. Replacing Burke, Y. A. came off the bench and in less than a half threw 18 completions for 230 yards, and a touchdown pass to Harold Crisler.

Because it wasn't a bad day, it was memorable. The team was about to go belly up, and Y. A. was one of 28 to be picked up by NFL teams. He would head for Frisco bearing the reputation of a courageous young quarterback. My mother, of course, was not so sure about the courage. She always said that there was no such thing as a hero up close. And this revelation was brought home in a blinding flash thanks to her husband's performance in the great milk-stealing scandal.

Ever since their engagement had been announced in *Sport* magazine, she had known to be on guard against Y. A.'s little surprises. The contract with the 49ers was another one. But Tittle was so confident that Minnette would not object to the California sunshine that went with it, he stepped into the entry of their apartment house, $13,500 contract in hand and smiling. Minnette was standing on the stairway landing. And there, in the hallway, her husband came face to face with the landlady's son, who had been let out of the the state penitentiary the day before.

"Milk thief! Your wife is a milk thief. She stole my milk!"

My father looked up at my mother's face and saw that it was about to fall off from sheer rage and come clanging to the floor like a tire rim.

"I'm sorry," said the East Texan, "but we don't steal people's milk."

"Milk thief!" the man hissed.

"I think you have made a mistake, sir. In fact, I am sure you have."

"Thief!"

"Excuse me but I think you should take that back," Y. A. Tittle said calmly, "what you just said about my wife."

Minnette perked up.

"Make me," the man said.

"Make you? No sir. I'm asking you."

"Make me."

"I think you should apologize."

"Get upstairs," said the man.

"Me? Get upstairs? You apologize to my wife."

"I said, get upstairs."

"Go ahead then, make me," Y. A. said.

"Well, maybe I can't make you, but I've got something here that will!"

Y. A. thought: Did he mean to say he had a gun? Time to punt!

And before anyone could move, Y. A. Tittle's fist was on his hip in a flick of exasperation.

"Honey," he said, "I'm tired of you stealing people's milk."

On this note, my parents left Baltimore and drove west to California in the Studebaker. I listened to those halting, puny pieces of flat, grown-up speech passing back and forth, sometimes interrupting with a scream or a sob, but most of the time I just kept to myself and my own language. I did my best to fill the car with baby babbling, and this, at some point in the journey, must have reminded them of sorghum syrup. And for my father, sorghum syrup was the cue for the lily pads to bloom back home, and the snakes to climb the trees and dangle in the sunlight. It meant candy in your pocket. Hoop cheese from the store. All those Texas small-town miracles that horses ground out with the sugar cane.

And now, California was dead ahead. And Tinneha, Bobo, and Blair were behind. On the fender of the Studebaker, Tittle had signed his name to a contract with the San Francisco 49ers and become a player in the new National Football League. He even forgot to notice if the contract included a raise, because he was already seeing the printed words as tiny players on the line. Already, there were men in motion like the King, the Geek, and Joe the Jet going deep and down the page. Already, his imagination was dancing to the bootleg between the lines as he wrote with confidence the initials, "Y. A." then "Tittle," deep in the opponent's end zone, on the dotted line.

In October of that year, the men and the field materialized, and it came time to throw. And with wide receiver and ex-basketball star R. C. Owens, Tittle perfected the Alley Oop pass, which was to become his signature. It came about by sheer accident during a lousy practice session in which Tittle became so disgusted with himself he threw the ball straight up into the air as high as he could and stomped off, turning around only when hoots of excitement stopped him in his tracks. Owens apparently had jumped up as high as he could to catch the ball in the end zone. And that was the beginning. The Ally Oop wasn't in the books. It wasn't even in Tittle's mind. By San Francisco fans, it was remembered as a pass like a meteor; for the quarterback, it was the mistake of a lifetime.

Beginner's luck? At least everyone agreed that for sizzle and slapstick in the last ten seconds of a game you went to Kezar Stadium. There was Joe the Jet Perry, Mad Dog Henke, Gordy Soltau and a long-legged Choctaw Indian named Billy Wilson. There was the team captain, Bob St. Clair, who ate raw fish, raw chicken, raw everything (and whose toes were longer than his wife's fingers). There was Leo the Lion and Hurrying Hugh McElhenny, also known as the King. Hardy Brown, of course, was the KO artist and the Billy the Kid of football. There was even Tiger Johnson, Y. A.'s old friend from Camp Tonkawa who had competed against him in high school. They all streamed into the open air to the welcome of the common man. Seagulls lazed overhead and the national anthem rang out.

Tittle was selected to the Pro Bowl game in '53, '54, '57 and '59. In 1957, he took another shot at a championship against Detroit and received the Most Valuable Player Award. But the main thing was that in exchange for doing his best he would never again be called Mister. Y. A. was happy with his contract and the beautiful burden of smiles. He was happy even with his name.

"Y! A! TITTLE!"

To us, the name always seemed like a consolation prize, made worse by the relatives who reminded us that Christ once said "tittle."[10] But at the Niner games in 1957 it didn't sound so bad.

"Tittle! Tittle! Tittle!" And we were there when the sound made a turnaround and *tittle* made a comeback. While Unitas, Luckman and Baugh had names as good in themselves as luck or fate or sky, we had nothing at all until the fans made it sound like another word for the American Dream.

FIFTY ONE . . . Y RIGHT . . . RIP . . . ALLEY OOP!

SAN FRANCISCO 49ERS

Consider: For highest justice attends the saying—Praise the good...
The splendor running in the blood has much weight.
A man can learn and yet see darkly, blow one way,
then another, contending ever on uncertain feet,
his mind unfinished and fed with the scraps of a thousand virtues.

—Pindar, *Nemean* 3

The Million Dollar Backfield:
Y. A. Tittle, Joe Perry,
Hugh McElhenny,
John Henry Johnson;
1957.

When daughter was seven years old:

Daughter: *How do you learn to throw the Alley Oop, Dad?*
Dad: *You don't. You just throw it. You just throw the ball straight up into the air as high as you can, and you hope that somebody catches it.*
Daughter: *But what if the wrong person catches it? What if nobody catches it?*
Dad: *That's the chance to take. That's your tough luck.*
Daughter: *I think it's pretty to watch.*
Dad: *It is.*

Colonel Slick & the Million Dollar Backfield

A man in miniature, my father was no bigger than my thumb, and watching him play was the saddest thing I ever saw. Everybody else had fathers who they thought were ten feet tall. I *knew* my Dad was in a league with the inchworm. He was never big or strong, but always fragile and small as far back as I can remember. Some days he got even smaller. Some days he even got squashed. And worst of all, I never knew how to protect him.

After the offensive huddles popped apart like snapdragons, I'd turn to watch the faces around me. That look of amazement was the most beautiful thing in the world. But while my father was on the field, I kept counting all the numbers on the sidelines in the hope that he wasn't benched yet. By the time I worked up the courage to watch the field, the game was over, or just about.

It seemed to me like the spectators were also divided into teams. There were those who watched simply to watch, and those who watched the game to learn. As a kid, I ended up on the latter team. I really didn't know much about the game, but football taught me everything I knew. I knew that if I put my toe onto a playing field boys instantly froze with the look that said I didn't belong. I knew that when Y. A. Tittle went out onto the grass, he became everybody's favorite son. And with just about every move he made, it seemed like everybody in the world knew my father better than I did.

Between 1951 and 1960, while my father played for the 49ers, I gradually grew to consciousness in San Francisco. I watched my parents, and later the games and the players, making my own

observations, reflecting, and with the help of my journal finally piecing together ideas and interpretations.

1950. The 49ers fell flat on their faces in their NFL debut, winning only three games.[1]

I am the navigator and explorer of my mother's face. Were it not for that large island floating into view, I would have remained forever adrift in a sea of my own aloneness. But as it is, she is there.

1951. In an amazing reversal of form sparked by a great rookie group, the 49ers finished only a half game off the top. Led by Hardy Brown and his famed "shoulder tackle" the club had one of the toughest defensive units in the league.

Mom has two eyes, two ears, a nose and mouth. She has a half-inch scar above her upper lip and a widow's peak.

1952. After a blazing start, the 49ers slumped in mid season. Hugh (The King) McElhenny came off the University of Washington campus to become the "Player of the Year" and the most feared runner in football.

She looks at me and I am sometimes less, sometimes more than I am. I am decorated with cloth.

1953. The 49ers had their best NFL showing posting a 9–3 record, normally good enough for a championship. Detroit, however, was 10–2. Two of the San Francisco losses came with Y. A. Tittle sidelined because of a severe facial injury.

I dream. I am alone in a forest and I am hungry. I find a cabbage of a most unusual color. I must eat it. Suddenly there is a knife in my hand so I begin to cut, so carefully. I cut it in two. And I discover heaven inside of an ordinary cabbage. It is a little room. It is a room inside a room inside a room and it is geometrically perfect.

The bathing beauties of Caddo Lake. Minnette and Dianne, 1952.

1954. Early momentum was broken by injuries to key players such as Y. A. Tittle, Hugh McElhenny, and Joe Perry. Perry gained more than 1,000 yards again, the first man ever to achieve this distinction in consecutive seasons.

I am a wild multi-colored horse who paws the driveway with my hoof.

1955. With Hugh McElhenny hobbled by a foot injury, the 49ers had their second worst season in history under Norm Strader, who succeeded Buck Shaw as head coach.

I wait for dreams. Every night in my bed, I curl my fist into my neck and I wait until they come.

1956. In Frankie Albert's first year at the helm, the 49ers were bogged in last place at midseason with a 1–6 record. They won four and tied one of their last five games for a brilliant stretch drive.

Unlike my mother, my father never dreams—I know. For her, the dream is a journey and a matter of life and death. Dad's unconscious is never such a loud mouth yelling from the sidelines. He would never think to take a blue stone in hand and climb the mouth. Or be lowered by a vine hanging from the sky into a circle of mothers. Not in a million years. He never dreams, or if he does, he dreams awake. His dreams come true. There is no point.

1957. This undoubtedly was one of the most emotional and dramatic seasons in 49er history. Every game was a "cliffhanger," and the Alley Oop pass from Y. A. Tittle to R. C. Owens became a household byword. Emotions reached a peak when the much beloved 49er owner and president, Tony Morabito collapsed and died of a heart attack at the Chicago Bears game on October 27. Trailing 17–7, the 49ers fought back for a great victory. The magnificent Billy Wilson caught a pass from Tittle for the winning touchdown in the fourth quarter.

Tied with Detroit 8–4 when the season ended, the 49ers lost the division playoff game, 31–27.

Dad doesn't dream and all he ever talks about is a "tight ship." When he is away he misses us. So why does he go away? I don't think it's fair that he lives this exciting life away from home and when he comes back he is boring. He never wants us to leave the sidewalk or do anything. We can never allow him to become the quarterback in this house because he will abuse the position. I know because he cheats at ping pong and forgets the score when he isn't ahead. I will never play with him again. He never ever wants to rally. He only wants to win.

In 1957 people whispered when they mentioned Hardy Brown. Women pinched their lips and men shook their heads. I knew, because at age seven I was begining to pay attention to Brown and the Million Dollar Backfield that included Y. A. Tittle. I knew they didn't call my father "Colonel Slick" for nothing, and I could see why they called Hardy "the Hatchet."

In essence, his knockout punch was this: Hardy would move into a person coming at full speed by lowering into a crouch. As the ball carrier tilted his body forward, Hardy drove off his knees, exploded upwards at the last second, and threw that shoulder like a golfer executing a perfect swing. Though his blow was no more than 8–12 inches in extension, he always "hit 'em in the head." And the bigger they were, the harder they fell. It didn't matter if they weighed 275 pounds, his punch was deadly. He broke face mask after face mask, and he knocked out most everyone he ever hit.

Although he weighed only 185 pounds, he took out the entire starting Washington Redskin backfield except for the quarterback. The King of the Killers knocked out 21 men. He came right out of the ground just like Old Faithful and KO'd them all. Hardy didn't need to weigh much because when he hunched over the line, his opponents found themselves wondering if he wasn't a messenger sent from heaven to remind them of their mortality. For some athletes, it took more than a leaf falling on the snow to get them to remember. But the Hatchet got the message across. There wasn't a man in uniform who didn't feel grateful for the little joys in life like blinking and swallowing while the Hatchet was on the field.

For instance, in 1952, New York Giant Jack "the Giant Killer" Stroud was the toughest lineman on the team, with a reputation for having the best built body in the league. At Kezar Stadium, the Hatchet and the Giant Killer met face to face on a sweep, and Stroud went down with a broken jaw. While sipping beer through a straw it's difficult for anyone to think nice thoughts, and apparently Jack Stroud never thought one. What pained him was having to wait four years to get Hardy on the payback. When finally he got the chance, Stroud asked to go in on the kickoff. With the play in motion, he proceeded to ignore the ball carrier and go after Hardy with a vengeance, with a fury that almost made music. Everybody watched to see if the Billy the Kid of football could be mowed down by this locomotive of revenge and human hatred. And to the Million Dollar backfield standing on the sidelines, it was just like the William Tell Overture: on the play, Hardy broke the Giant Killer's other jaw. And within 24 hours, Jack the Giant Killer Stroud was back to sipping.

The Million Dollar Backfield was the nickname given to the 49ers' starting backfield in 1954. Composed of John Henry Johnson, Joe Perry, Hugh McElhenny and Y. A. Tittle, it would become the only backfield in football history where all four players were inducted into pro football's Hall of Fame. But in the '50s, to the thousands of fans in the San Francisco Bay Area, these players simply looked as good as a million bucks. They looked so good that in 1957 everyone was talking about a championship.

Instead of SEE SPOT, and SEE DICK RUN, I practiced reading headlines: TITTLE BREAKS JAW . . . DOES IT ONE MORE TIME ON GUTS. . . . Come December, I was cast as the statue of the Virgin in our school's recreation of "The Juggler of Notre Dame." It was my job to stare at a nail on the ceiling. I did not blink. Did not see the procession of townspeople bringing gifts. Did not see the juggler dance. Not until the juggler of Notre Dame gave his all and left the perfect gift at the feet of the statue, did I do anything except stand on my apple crate, sweating and imagining Hardy The Hatchet giving 100% in the real world. *Ta pow!* The perfect gift. And Hardy Brown, the orphan from Oklahoma, was with me on the countdown when the statue came alive.

Now that we have some money, we have a color TV set of our own. Of course nothing ever quite works the way it is supposed to. And so Mom and Dad spend half their lives heaving large sighs, fiddling with wires, and reading directions. Dad complains constantly that we are becoming a family of functional illiterates, when the truth is that we don't like fake nightingales. I don't know why my parents get upset when these contraptions break. They are not real. Mom and Dad are falling for these gizmos and doodads we cannot touch, just like the emperor fell for the nightingale from Japan.

We have also bought property in the Napa Valley so Dad can have a sports camp for boys. The deal is that I won't be left out, but the truth of the matter is that I will. Whenever there is a game to be won, Dad forgets all about words. He simply can't help it. And I know I won't get to play in any games or build my character. I will just have to be as invisible as an atom and stay out of the way, or catch pollywogs until dinner.

. . . I think I was wrong at first about Sports Camp. It's better than going to Forest Lake, where last year Mom got bit by a spider and got sleeping sickness. Also I have fallen in love with my cousin Jackie, because he spoke to me the other day and asked me if I would like to see the baby alligator he brought all the way from Louisiana. He showed it to me after dinner and I got to touch its tail.

But what about the championship? In 1957 anybody could tell you that Hardy Brown and the San Francisco 49ers had been at it for seven long years. My father made up plays in the huddle like he was flipping hotcakes, but the 49ers never came up with the perfect gift—the championship—for their town or for the one man who wanted it as much as they did, the founding father of the team, Tony Morabito. The son of Italian immigrants, he grew up in San Francisco in the same neighborhood as Joe DiMaggio. But football was Morabito's game, though he struck out three times trying to get a National Football League franchise in San Francisco. Finally, he borrowed $100,000, mortgaged his house, and approached the All-American Conference with his bid. Morabito wasn't interested in a football franchise as a tax shelter. He believed that San Francisco had potential as a great sports town. And though he expected to lose money on a football team in a baseball town, it was worth the gamble, he told them.[2]

Bingo. The team was born. In 1951, a record salary of $20,000 went to the Niner's creative, left-handed quarterback, Frankie Albert. A strong leader and individualist, Albert personalized his calls in the huddle and his style was synonymous with fun. For instance, he knew that All-Pro tackle Leo "Nomo" Nomellini dreamed of being the old-time fullback, Bronco Nagurski. And when the time was right, instead of calling a 31 Trap, Albert called for a "Nomo 31!" And a one or two yard gain by Nomo as fullback was a sight. But if his team needed a morale boost, if Leo needed a boost, so be it. Albert let Leo Nomellini crash the line like a hippo falling through a doorway. He was in the business of heroes, of inspiration, after all. And he let it rip.

That was Albert's style, and Buck Shaw's coaching method fell easily in sync with it. Relaxed and respectful, Shaw never resorted to draconian methods of motivation. If anything, Buck pressured his players by so believing in them as men and professionals that it was tough to let him down.

In 1951 Albert led his team and he bootlegged like Houdini. The bootleg is, of course, the quarterback's version of a magic trick. A play of deception, it is an offensive maneuver whereby the QB fakes a running play to one side and then meanders off to the other side as if he is out of the play. Because the quarterback still has the ball, he then must either run himself or pass to the end, who, after faking his block, goes out for the pass. Frankie Albert was a master of this play.

Among the teammates to be initiated into the mysteries of Frank Albert in 1951 were a good group of rookies, as well as my father, Jimmy Cason, and Tiger Johnson. While Albert frolicked through August, September, October, everybody seemed to thrive on the congenial atmosphere, except for the guy sitting on the bench. Soon to become another master of the bootleg, Y. A. learned its intricacies at the feet of Frank Albert, who because of his small size was well served by the art of deception.

Tittle was sidelined with a muscle pull prior to the 49ers' opening game of the 1951 season. As that injury began to heal, his old bursitis came back on a bumpy train ride to Syracuse, New York, where he had hoped to see some playing time. At the train depot, stabbing pains made it impossible for the quarterback to lift his luggage off the train with his right arm. But this was something that Y. A. would never admit to a soul. In the real world of animals who move in packs or herds, if you're injured, you're out. My father, the athlete, had signed up for this twilight world.

There seemed to be no way out for him this time, until his fate, again in the form of bad weather, came to his rescue for once. A storm tore through Syracuse and the game was canceled. Y. A. seized the opportunity to get treatment on the sly from a doctor with the Syracuse International baseball team, and healed while suffering yet another week in purgatory on the bench.

Number 14 did not have to suffer long. Summoned from the bench at Kezar Stadium in the fourth quarter with the New York Yankees leading 14–12, Tittle liked it when the men's heads came together in the huddle. He liked it as never before. "Can you beat your man to the inside?" he said to Billy Wilson. "I'll try," Wilson said. "Okay then, the snap count is on three. Let's pull this one out."[3]

But the flanker back, Schabarum, ended up receiving the winning touchdown pass instead of Wilson. Uh oh, Tittle thought. Not again. And sure enough, one sportswriter, maybe the same one, called it the "prettiest pass ever thrown in Kezar Stadium." The following week Tittle got into the game a little sooner. And against Detroit he got into the game in time to deny the Detroit Lions the NFL Western Division title by scoring the winning TD on a bootleg. And that's how the 1951 season ended, with Hunchy Hoernschemeyer, the Lions' halfback, calling Tittle every name in the book and with the QB for Detroit, Bobby Layne, giving him the nod.

1952. Next year, 49er Hugh McElhenny became "the King" of broken field running, and Buck Shaw divided Albert's and Tittle's playing time. Bobby Layne's Detroit Lions finished the season 9–3, and two of their losses were played against San Francisco, whose stingy defense gave up only three points. Positioned to sew up their division championship, the Niners had only to beat the Chicago Bears for a second time.

The Niners were in the lead 17–10 in the fourth quarter, when Albert dropped back to punt to the Bears. But Frankie saw, or thought he saw, an opening, and instead of punting, he ran. Too soon, the hole which had opened closed. And Albert bit the dust too deep in 49er territory. Always an individualist, Frankie Albert had trusted his instinct as he did in every moment of practice and play. But this particular gamble cost him. San Francisco lost 20–17, and Albert got eaten for breakfast by fans and sportswriters alike on Monday morning. ALBERT'S FOLLY ON FOURTH DOWN[4] the papers called it. Albert retired at season's end and the Niners bowed to Detroit that year.

In 1953, Tittle became the undisputed quarterback of the 49ers in what was not a boring year. The season opened with a many-headed boxing match against the Philadelphia Eagles. The Eagles' star receiver had words with Charlie Powell, which included fists. The Niners defended their teammate, and the 49er band defended the team. Some brandished clarinets and others used them as weapons.

One of Tony Morabito's dreams came true that year. Football dug its cleats into the West and 90,000 fans packed into the Los Angeles Coliseum to watch McElhenny and Los Angeles Ram Crazy Legs Hirsch go for broke. That was also the year that Joe the Jet Perry become the first 49er player to gain more than 1,000 yards in a season. The 49ers were considered first in terms of thrills and spills that year, but Detroit finished the season one game ahead. It was in the final game against Detroit that my father suffered an excruciating "spill" after scoring on a bootleg. The play was over but he was grabbed and swung in a circle by Jack Christiansen. When Jack finally let him go, Y. A.'s face cracked over Jim David's knee like a raw egg. My father's face broke in three places and forty-four bone chips were removed from his cheekbone. The good news was that he was required to wear special face protection happily ever after. And the face mask, in due time, became part of every football player's standard gear.

People think my father is a superman but he is just a mother hen who sits and worries more than Georgia Baba's grandmother. Everybody else gets to imagine he is great, and we end up with a plain old person.

. . . Dad just walks walks walks around the house wishing it was not an elephant burial ground for things—hairbrushes, toothbrushes, paper clips, pencils, light bulbs, socks. Who needs this stuff anyway? If I didn't have my parents, I would just live in the tree out front and eat the lawn till I died. But my parents really need us. Dad is constantly going away. I could never work at a job where I had to take my clothes off and have everybody tell me I had a bad figure. And that's what happens to Dad. Everybody talks about Y. A. Tittle's form. We don't care about football here. We never talk about it. It's boring.

In 1954 my father was put together again, and the 49ers were considered the hottest team in the league, having won seven straight preseason games. But then the King suffered a broken shoulder. One week, the backup quarterback broke his throwing hand, and my father broke his the week after. The chemistry for victory was there apparently, but two quarterbacks with broken hands did not help matters. The failure to take the title in 1954 was a tremendous blow to the team. To make matters worse, Coach Buck Shaw was released and replaced with a coach who was as rigid as Shaw was relaxed, and who went by the book alone.

Under the leadership of Red Strader, the 49ers finished next to last in 1955. Though he wheeled and dealed for decent beds and meal money on road trips, the fact was that you didn't want to win for Red. Gone was the spontaneity, the creativity, the fun. And the Niners languished. The situation grew even worse when Frankie Albert became coach the next year.

Handwritten annotation on photo: To Well— Did I ever say thanks? Y. G. Tittle 3/30/93 — PASS PROTECTION - 49ers vs Colts 1956

The problem was that Coach Albert wanted to call the plays. And Tittle would rather eat his helmet than give up matching wits with the defense and trying to outthink his opponent. It was just one more little insult he did not need.

49er pass protection, 1956.

Typically, a prearranged game plan allowed quarterbacks flexiblity to make adjustments to the game situations. Often Tittle chose to listen to his players in the huddle, because he found that it fired up the team with a sense of unity and purpose. This, on the other hand was punishment—to stand around "like a monkey on a string"[5] waiting for somebody else to tell him what to do. No quarterback for a thousand miles signed on for that. No quarterback was paid for that. Maybe Paul Brown called the shots in Cleveland, but how many quarterbacks in the NFL played for Cleveland? Besides, according to Coach Isbell, it was up to the man as quarterback to do this. Nobody else. Nobody higher up and certainly nobody off to the left standing in comfortable shoes. Just the man and his moment. Without that, Tittle wondered, what was he doing in this crazy game when he could be out there selling life insurance? What had he broken his face for?

As usual, there was no time for anything but action. Head Coach Albert and his assistant, Coach Red Hickey, sent in plays from the sidelines and no matter how hard Tittle tried to remain a good team player, the 49ers lost six out of their first seven games. After the fifth game, Yat was replaced by quarterback Earl Morrill, and for the first time in his life he did not care.

It was after a walloping loss to the Detroit Lions landed the 49ers in last place that Frankie approached Y. A. in the lockerroom and said, "It's all yours." The entire team responded and won every game thereafter, with the exception of one against the Philadelphia Eagles, whom they tied. Although they finished third in 1956, at least the push was on, the momentum was back. And like Lazarus risen from the dead, their collective imagination overtopped all limits.

"Fifty-one . . . Y right . . . rip . . . Alley Oop!"

1957 was the year of the fourth period comeback. At the beginning of the season, Coach Odus Mitchell called to wish the former Maverick luck and to remind him not to forget the quarterback sneak he had taught him. Y. A. remembered the quarterback sneak alright. He also remembered the Piney Woods *we*. And he promised Coach Mitchell he would do his best.

Dad goes away. Then he comes back. He goes in and out of our lives like an ocean wave. The last time he was home, he walked up the sidewalk and called us by our Texas names, Lima Bean, Catfish, and Gumbo. Mom doesn't particularly care for these East Texas words, especially hogshead cheese *and* chitlin. *I would die if my nickname was Hogshead Cheese. But it isn't. It's Gumbo.*

Dad doesn't talk about things, just walks around with big muscles in his legs and a big bruised toenail. He likes to check things out and make sure the house is safe. Mom and Dad don't go out. If they do go out, we go too. We drive on Bloody Bayshore and go over the Dumbarton Bridge past the big mound of salt and the pink ponds filled with chemicals. When we can see across the bay on a clear day,

I pretend I am seeing Japan. Then we stop off and get an ice cream cone and we go back home to our beagle dog Petey who is usually in my bed with his head on the pillow when he isn't trying to choke himself tied up on the leash. Petey is a beagle, a red dog, and because there is a play called a red dog, *Petey was a present from somebody. People always give us things. Mom is a big reader so we have a wall full of books in the den right next to the trophy room. One of them is called Y. A. Tittle's Sex Life. Somebody gave it to us. It is the biggest book I ever saw and there isn't one word in it.*

Tittle kids dressed up for Sunday school, 1955.

Well, just as soon as we get used to having a father he goes away again. Dad is just like Clark Kent, who leaps tall buildings with a single bound. Dad puts on his uniform, too. He must go off and do football for people otherwise we will have to to live under the bridge and eat spam. If Dad doesn't throw the ball right, I will have to wear dresses that are too small and then people will blame me for wearing them just like they blame Barbara Geisler. But so far so good. We still live in a house and sometimes with a father.

. . . In 1957, Elvis records blared in the locker-room. As the players dressed to "You Ain't Nothing But A Hound Dog," Y. A. was asking himself furiously: Who the hell am I and what am I doing here? He ripped some tape and wrapped his chest and ankles. Then as he put on his jersey, he asked himself why he always felt this total delirium of frustration before a game. Was it fear of losing? No. Fear of losing his job? No. Injury? Never. Fear of what the sportswriters had to say? Certainly not. He couldn't say what fear it was, but if he didn't perform well, he'd be letting down the team.

Game time finally arrived, and the 49ers came out of the locker room and face to face with the Chicago Bears. Coach Tiger Johnson was on the sidelines in ear muffs and overcoat. In 1956, Johnson had been All-Pro center with the 49ers and was now, in

1957, sidelined as a coach in the cold, watching Joe the Jet Perry rip through the middle. Tiger had been Y. A.'s devoted friend since Camp Tonkawa in the fifth grade, where the two of them had met, played, cheated at washers and mumblety-peg, yet never gotten to the bottom of who the other was. And as Tiger stood there in the cold wishing he was bottom-fishing in hell, it was pleasant to return to thoughts of muddy nights in high school football where the will to win seemed to cry up from the soil.

For seven years now, Tittle had been quarterback for the 49ers. And for seven years the Niners had used the Windemere Hotel on the South Side as their base when playing teams in the Chicago area. The 49ers practiced at Stagg Field. At Wrigley Field, the Monsters of the Midway grunted and fumed. Like everybody else, Tiger Johnson loved to hate Chicago. For one thing, Stagg Field was in full view of the telescope that belonged to Papa Bear George Halas. Of course, the Bears' telescope was discovered with the 49er telescope. Wrong plays were practiced in order to trick the spies. Halas shot back with itching powder, and it did not go unnoticed that his name was inscribed on the game ball.

Wasn't he colorful? thought Tiger Johnson. Never a coach to stand on the sidelines like a man in an invisible straitjacket, Halas ran up and down the sidelines, even onto the field when necessary. At that very moment, for instance, he was out there giving Y. A. a healthy shake. "Tell the truth!" Halas screamed, as he twisted knobs into Tittle's jersey. "You tell that ref you threw the ball away!"

"Now lookee here, Mr. Halas, sir," said Y. A. "Dadgum that number 29. I swear I was throwing to him." But where Tittle might fool a ref, it was impossible for him to outfox old Halas. For one thing, thought Tiger, it took one to know one.

Yep, thought Coach Johnson, as he rocked back and forth safe on the sidelines, nobody knew better than he did the meaning of the phrase—*you gotta pay the price*. Why, hadn't he broken a bone for Tittle just about every time he turned around? Take the game in San Antonio in 1956. That night his friendship with Y. A. nearly cost him his life.

Yat truly went berserk that night in San Antonio, Texas, after finding that the Niners were short the first down. And suddenly everything went dark. At the time, Tiger figured that his friend must have turned out the lights in the stadium with willpower. Then, "Tiger!" Johnson heard his name with that little spoonful of Southern sugar thrown in. What looked like a fox was slinking across the darkened field, belly to belly with the land, headed his way. Then Tittle cocked his head and whispered, "Start a ruckus, one yard is all I need." And so, like a good old-fashioned thunderbolt, Johnson let it all hang out. And while everybody screamed, hollered, and kicked the tar out of him, nobody noticed Yat looking down at his toe. Thwump! The ball rolled one, then two yards, before kicking up another three and coming to rest under a bench. The wrong bench. When the lights came back on, there was mass confusion because the ball had disappeared, and the ref didn't know what flag to throw. Johnson managed to roll his eyes toward his friend and see Tittle take off his helmet and look somewhat contrite. Typical, thought Tiger.

Man, but it was cold! In an effort to keep warm at Wrigley Field in 1957, Coach Johnson began to hop up and down on the sidelines. And he was not the only one. Halas was being a real fuss bucket. And now Coach Albert was over there trying to tell Tittle something, when Tiger knew he wasn't listening. Tiger recognized that peculiar cock of the head. To Johnson it was obvious that someone was about to pay the price. And thank goodness, thought Tiger, it wasn't going to be him for once.

Dang Halas! Why did it have to be that the visiting players' bench was close to the fans' section, where they not only chewed tobacco, but they spit on the players all game long? Poor Yat. His jersey was covered with tobacco juice. And to make matters worse, the 49ers were now inside Chicago's 20, which meant that the 49ers did not blink their eyes for fear of the Halas "backfield-in-motion penalty trick."

Rumor had it that George Halas had authoritarian control over anyone in his football kingdom including the referrees, who obeyed by calling penalties against any team in scoring range. But

Tiger had faith in his friend. As always, the touch and timing were there as Yat called an audible on the line of scrimmage. Then, to his amazement, Coach Johnson heard the ref bleat, "B-a-ackfield in motion!" And saw a flag go down on the play.

"That does it!" screeched Coach Johnson. That was the last peep he wanted to hear out of that parsnip. He'd been Y. A. Colonel Slick Tittle's personal bodyguard for seven years as a 49er. On Y. A.'s behalf, his knee had been operated on three times, and on account of Frankie Albert, he couldn't see out of his left eye. Johnson simply was not going to take it any more. He'd be damned before he'd let his buddies be cheated again. The sense of justice welled up in his breast, but it came out of his mouth as insults.

The ref threw another flag down on the play.

Y. A. called over. "Hey Mr. Ref, what's that for?"

"I'm not putting up with this. That's fifteen yards for unsportsmanlike conduct on account of your coach over here." Tittle looked over. Johnson was fit to be tied. There was no doubt about it, he thought. Tittle took a quick look at the ball with the name, *George Halas*, on it. And then he looked back at the ref.

"But I've never seen that guy before in my life," said Colonel Slick.

"What? You mean to say that you don't know that man?"

"No sir," Tittle replied. "I don't believe I do."

Then the ref shouted over to the head coach, Frankie Albert, "Is this one of your people?"

"Are you kidding? I've never seen that drunk before in my life. I wish to hell you'd get him out of here."

The ref picked up the flag, and Tiger Johnson was given a police escort out of the stadium. Never mind that George Halas stood like a man who had just swallowed a goldfish. Colonel Slick did what it took to get his 15 yards back. Naturally he assumed that Tiger would understand he wasn't worth a 15-yard penalty, not even a five-yard penalty when you got right down to it. Tiger would understand. And so, in the last 15 seconds of the game, Tittle called "Fifty-one . . . Y right . . . rip . . . Alley Oop!" and threw the Alley Oop.

Tiger heard the collective moan of the crowd just when he figured he could get back to the locker room if he first made a dash
to the dugout. The ball hovered in the air,
and R. C. Owens unleashed his stride. He
leaped. The Niners won. Halas gulped.
And Tiger Johnson from Camp Tonkawa
paid for the goldfish one more time.

In 1957, believe it or not, Dad, or Colonel
Slick, was the first recipient of the Len
Ashmont Award, an award in which the
football players themselves chose the most
inspirational player on the team. He was
also selected as the National Football
League's Player of the Year, the highest
award a football player can achieve in
a single season. He also beat Slinging
Sammy Baugh when the 49ers played the
Washington Redskins. According to my
father, "It didn't feel right" to beat his
hero, "the one who killed robots." And it
didn't feel right to lose the championship.
But it did feel good to nail Detroit with
yet another "Fifty-one . . . Y right . . . rip . . . Alley Oop!"

R. C. "Alley
Oop" Owens.

The score? Detroit 31, Frisco 28. At Kezar Stadium, there was 1
minute and 28 seconds left on the clock, and the fans were leaving. Joe Arenas returned Detroit's kickoff to the 49ers' 28-yard
line. The fans were still leaving. But on Detroit's 41-yard line
with 19 seconds left in the game, the fans were standing still.
Tittle had retreated to the 50-yard line, then crossed to the sidelines.

With one second on the clock, Y. A.'s wrist cocked forward and
the referee's mouth fell open. When Tittle first saw daylight after
the play, the ref was still gaping.

"Why, that was beautiful," said the referee, staring at the
crumpled quarterback. "Just beautiful."

Meanwhile, R.C. Owens was headed for the catch of his career, indeed the greatest catch in Kezar Stadium. R.C. made it to the one yard line and was standing there surrounded by Lions Carl Karilivacz, Jim David, and Jack Christiansen, with the ball still on the rise.

Tittle dusted himself off as everyone else on the field waited for the ball to come down. R. C. on the one, the fans in the aisles, everyone standing still. Then R. C. leaped or levitated. For one second, Karilivacz displayed teeth. But it made no difference. "Fifty-one ... Y right ... Rip ... Alley Oop!"

R. C. Owens was Rip. And it was thanks to him and the others who made up San Francisco's Million Dollar Backfield that I remember game time as a time out from the English language, and the games themselves as exotic trips to the enchanted zoo of wild male emotion.

Hut 1! Hut 2! Tittle sang the count. And in 1957, every single player had a lead in what amounted to Everyman's opera. Every man had to take his turn with Lady Luck in a dance to glory, and in those days, before they gave her an agent, she was young and wild enough to make anyone nervous.

Hut 3! Before the games passed into the hands of the media emperors, football was a stage set for the American Dream. Where else in town did the best man win most of the time? And where else did connections count for beans? Where else would the boss's son be mincemeat in a minute? At Kezar, the ancient god of war became a democrat, and we delighted in the myth which appeared before our eyes. By the thousands we were glued to this spectacle of Life where there was no such thing as winning without sacrifice, or without the help of others. And when something spectacular happened, we the people shared in the common knowledge. Could it really be that we the people hadn't come as much for the show as we had come for justice, or for the Dream?

Besides Hardy and Rip, there was Hugh the King McElhenny and Joe the Jet Perry, who moved downfield like a patient first-grade teacher writing on the blackboard: LOOK! LOOK AT THE BLACK MAN WIN! As for the King, no matter how people cheered, the King once told me that he always ran scared. When he was little he was just more frightened than most by the shadows in the alleys of the slums. First he dodged those, and then when he was six, he finagled his way into a pickup game on a vacant lot in what was not an exclusive part of town. The King was scared when the owner of the property showed up with a shotgun, and even more scared when his britches were filled with buckshot. The King ran all the way home. And for the rest of his life, he ran faster and faster just to spite that mean old man.

The King had black hair, a square jaw, full lips, and cheeks scarred as if by driveway gravel by the time I knew him. He had a low voice, high hips, and he ran for the San Francisco 49ers like a crazy colt with an old soul. On Sundays, he proceeded downfield in full majesty, knighting just about every defender there was along the way. He passed them. They dropped to their knees. Of course! He was the King. And at seven years of age, I was proud to be his devoted subject. If only I could run from fear like that. But Hugh made me think that I should run toward fear like that. Full steam ahead! Throw forward my chest to the enemy! Be bold! Juke! Accelerate!

In 1957 the newspapers, like a box of chocolates, were full of stories about our team. 49ERS NIP LIONS; 49ERS UNDO BEARS; CRIPPLED TITTLE SAVES 49ER HOPES; TITTLE HAD BROKEN TOE AGAINST RAMS, LIONS; OWENS CATCH A MIRACLE . . . ALBERT EXCITED.

The team that Morabito founded had not only established itself, but it was a winning team, maybe even a championship team. Joe the Jet, the King, John Henry Johnson, everybody was on fire when Tony Morabito died at Kezar Stadium during the game against the Chicago Bears, the fifth of the season. Mr. Morabito simply passed away in the second quarter. The team did not find out until halftime, and then they came from behind to defeat the Bears in an almost ravenous display of human sorrow and football virtuousity.

I have to admit that the game changed for me on October 27, in 1957. Until then, all I knew was that Bobby Layne was out with a broken leg, and though it seemed like people everywhere were being chewed to pieces besides, it was a great luxury to know that my father and our friends were only talked about in the green section of the paper, where it was safe.

Second best was getting to know and like black people who knew and liked you too. Under the card table, I'd watch my father pass a card to Joe Perry with his toes. And it was something to see that card bringing together a white foot with a black foot.

The third great luxury was getting to see big men laugh and cry. But if they cried, one expected it to be for joy. But that changed too. When Mr. Morabito died, Joe Perry cried in front of everyone and Nomellini cried and couldn't stop. That's when I knew it didn't really matter if the 49ers lost the championship to Detroit, which they did that year. It was more important that they beat the Chicago Bears. The Chicago Bears had not done anything wrong. It was just important that our team show that being the best was not impossible. And it had to be our turn, that day.

So, I watched my first real football game in 1957. I watched carefully because Tony Morabito had passed away, and nobody called time out. Nobody. Everything just kept going like a game without a referee, like a game without a whistle. And in those few seconds when I expected the world to stop, everything that moved amazed me. If the world was not going to stop, it seemed like the least I could do was try to hop on and be with everybody else at the same pace and with the right attitude.

I observed that, with or without the face mask, there was an entirely new mountain range of human expression. Leo Nomellini never did stop crying, but that didn't stop him. The score was 17–7. To come from behind, Leo the Lion became Nagurski so that Joe Perry could hammer to the 11-yard line just like John Henry, the steel driving man from the storybook. Meanwhile, Billy Wilson caught the winning pass.

It *was* the championship of 1957, according to me. The 49ers had shown respect for something and turned it from the ordinary into the extraordinary. That was human magic. And in the end, I had respected something too, although I found I had no words for what I felt. But I was lucky, considering every other daughter of a warrior I had heard about. In books, those daughters were always paying the ultimate price. Jephthah's daughter was sacrificed when her father slew the Gileadites, and Agamemnon's daughter died that the wind might blow and the ships set sail for Troy. Losing my voice at the game against the Chicago Bears was a very small price to pay for victory.

At our house, Mom does all the work and nobody claps, nobody cares or gives her a dime. One day a week, she gets a baby-sitter and leaves us to go watch other kids who can't run, or old soldiers who are shell-shocked and must sit out under the trees. I have noticed that when Dad is away there is never enough food in the kitchen. There is no music and no dancing, no Dad to dance with or say 1-2-3-Dip. It's like the minor key when Dad goes away and the major key when he comes back.

In 1958 the problem was that we were not very lucky. Not only was my father constantly getting injured but I, too, discovered physical pain.

I thought I knew pain when I argued with Richard, my next door neighbor. Richard hated dirt more than anyone I knew and thought he could make up for it by sounding reasonable and speaking in a voice that sounded like it had been born in a teacup. At the same time, Richard had freckles that put the Milky Way to shame and hair so red you had to take him seriously.

Once, Richard said that people could not change shape and that they had to grow up and be human no matter what. At the time, my only revenge was to climb to the roof of the Oldsmobile parked in the driveway and shout: "Flake off, buckwheat!"

"And people can't fly either," chirped poor Richard. One look at his shiny shoes from the car roof made me know that I had never seen or heard anything worse from a monster in a nightmare. There just had to be some way to wipe that expression off

Richard's face and prove to him once and forever that man was not just some rotting peach made into a creature, but a pinch of every lion and star made into a miracle. I *would* fly! Change shape with the will of my mind and take flight. "Watch!" I yelled at poor Richard.

It was a short flight. After I dove into the asphalt, my father wiped the blood off my face as gently as sunshine. I remember thinking that he was an old hand at pain, and I was grateful that he forbade my brothers and their friends to laugh. But the pain of flying was nothing compared to the pain brought on by the the elm seed. The elm seed disaster started as a simple throwing contest with Steffie, the Peck boys, Tommy Winters, Mark O'Donoghue, Jeff Ferrar, and the handsome Tommy Carter. We picked oranges from the Crebbs' tree and threw them higher and higher over our heads. We had to catch them with one hand. And the person who could throw the orange the highest and still catch it was the champion.

My orange was unbelievable. We were practically born for each other the way it fit my hand so perfectly. Higher and higher it went. Meanwhile, my left hand flew to the right spot and grasped it. There was a power in my hand that was greater than me. Concentrate, it said. And keep your mouth shut.

Spinning around, again I threw the orange up through the branches of an elm tree. And as it ripped through the tender leaves, countless elm seeds floated down into my eyes. When I rubbed them, the fragile seeds broke under my lids. So I took a hose and tried to wash them out. Then Steffie, breathing like a doctor, peered into my eyes. When her fingertips went away again, the pain was excruciating.

I was blinded like Polyphemus the Cyclops! My friend Steffie led me home.

There, my father stood at the front door. He pinned back my eyelid with a thumb and touched a finger to my eye. Because the seed he removed was fragile, he touched his finger to mine, and there, I had it—one unbroken elm seed that looked just like a dove. My father saw it, too, with its nub for a head and its flying wings in miniature.

After that, he took me to the doctor. And then my parents put me in their bedroom under the big bedspread as green as grasslands. Blinking hurt. My eyes were scratched. But I remembered in the darkened room, how my father put the dove on my finger and said, "Well, some people come by good things the hard way." This was true for the both of us.

Dad is not sympathetic when it comes to the boos. He is used to them. Ignoring the boos is practically his whole life. But why does Mom have to be punished because she can't ignore everything? Mom is not emotional. I think she is more alive than anyone I know. When I see her crying, I can always say, "Are you happy or sad?" And she will always tell me.

I imagine she hears the boos all the time. I think about it. Where does the boo come from? It is not just a sound, it is a mentality. It means to me that people are fat in their thoughts and they don't exercise. They are not athletes. The boo is a virus and it is spreading through the human race.

1958 was the year that the fans booed. They booed till it seemed that a tidal wave of jeering noise crashed over us. As for my father, 1958 was the year that Tittle lost his knack of sensing the hit. This happened only twice in his career, and the first time was in a 49er game against the Baltimore Colts.

So that my father could bend rather than shatter, he always braced for the hit by relaxing in time for contact. For a split-second in 1958, his instinct failed him. And when he could not get up, it was like watching a newborn foal trying to stand, except that Gino Marchetti and Baltimore's other defensive tackles were standing around with their hands on their hips and smiling ugly. The picture in the newspaper was called "Tittle and His Friends."

When Bobby Layne retired he said, "There ought to be laws against guys like Marchetti. . . . He's the worst thing that ever happened to any quarterback. Just thinking about him makes me shudder. I'm going to miss football, but believe me, I'm not going to miss Gino Marchetti."[6] And Red Hickey said, "I've been in this league 22 years and never seen anybody so emotional. To

Marchetti, any guy who raises his arm to throw or any ball carrier is like a thug about to bomb his house with his wife and kids in it."[7]

Even though Dad said that Gino "didn't mean it," I really don't think that helped him walk any better. In 1958 my father limped around the house, and the fans booed. As the NFL's most valuable player from the previous year, Tittle had some negotiating power when it came to signing his contract. Assuming that the 49er organization would be fair, he signed his contract before the amount of his salary was even specified. As it turned out, $15,000 was fair. But some of the fans apparently weren't getting their money's worth.

"Sun On The Beach! Sun On The Beach!" I sat next to a man at the games who bellowed like an opera star. At first it was fascinating because there wasn't any beach. But next thing you know, we were left at home on Sunday afternoons to eat plums in the ivy. Our mother felt obliged to spare us unnecessary violence. And that is also why, prior to meeting up with the opera singer, we were so often dragged off to that most humorless place on earth —the stadium bathroom—when we wanted to stay right where we were and fight it out with the spectators.

Week after week, we had to be careful that a wave of human emotion didn't take us with it. If it did, we could be left wondering who would be the first to go, Mom in the stands, or Dad with a collapsed lung. Many were the times we were prepared to run onto the field and save a 49er, but the thought of leaving her alone prevented us.

At the time, we were living at 86 Rosewood Lane in Atherton, a suburb of San Francisco. Sometimes I thought we lived happily in a house built on the shoulder of a giant—so it did not seem fair to be afraid of an acorn rolling on the roof and have to think it was a football fan. But that was the way it was in 1958.

Dad never blames or explains himself and he expects Mom to do the same. He expects her to be tough. But you know, I don't think it is fair. Like last week, the man in the Duca Hanley market. He rushed up to my mother like he was some sort of saint. He could hardly wait to say how terrible my father was. It was like the best thing that had ever happened to him in his whole life. I noticed the spit at the corners of his mouth. And at home after she put the groceries down in the kitchen, my mom dropped to the floor like a rock. The fruit rolled out of the bag and I didn't know what to do.

1959. From the *San Francisco Examiner*, by Curley Grieve:

> By jet, crutch and wheel chair, the injured Y. A. Tittle came home from Baltimore last night vowing that he'd be "ready for the Colts" a week from Saturday at Kezar Stadium.
>
> Even in the face of pessimistic predictions of his doctors, the thin-faced 49er quarterback insisted that his ailing right knee was "not seriously hurt" and would regain its strength quickly with treatment. . . . Tittle, clobbered by Baltimore while trying to get off a pass, enjoyed his first elation in 10 days when his family met him at the foot of the TWA plane ramp.
>
> His wife, Minnette, greeted him with a kiss and the three children, Dianne, 9, Mike, 7, and Pat, 6, tried to clamber all over him when he took his seat in the wheel chair.[8]

That year, the 49ers snuffed out Detroit 34–13, and played ring-around-the-goalpost with the Chicago Bears. With 1 minute and 27 seconds left, Tittle rolled out to the right and faked a run. Then he arched the ball to R. C. for the 20–17 win. The next week, my father landed back in the hospital for a game-related injury and Brodie took over as quarterback for a 24–16 victory against the Rams. Though plagued by injuries, the 49ers were back in the running and leading the league, until they lost the last battle of the season, 34–14, to the Baltimore Colts—who went on to earn the world title under the firepower of quarterback crackerjack, Johnny Unitas.

By 1960, Tittle had earned a reputation as a military strategist on the playing field, and San Francisco had finished in second place for four straight years. But overnight, it seemed that Y. A. Tittle became a ball player with one foot in a lost civilization. Humor simply left our universe, with the exception of my father's coach, whose name was a real treasure in an uncertain world—

"Life in the
Fast Lane."
Kezar Stadium,
1960.

RED HICKEY. It was as though the football immortal could not become mortal without becoming the object in kick-the-can. My brothers were approached by classmates who tore up our father's picture in their faces, as if an athlete's injuries and poor performance could somehow threaten our national security. No doubt their parents took the state of my father's joints personally. But it was strangely reminiscent of the gladiators who performed poorly and therefore died on the command of the Roman masses, with the word, *"Jugla!"* or "Throat!" ringing in their ears. Lucky for us, it was 1960. Only the word, "Trade!" rang in ours.

Frankly, in 1960 there was so little sympathy at our house for aches and pains that, by comparison, it seemed like all the other kids who went home with jammed knuckles were carried through the streets on a litter of bay leaves flanked by murmuring dwarves. There was also a time problem. While every one else seemed to be growing older gradually, day by day, the Tittles were like gnats swarming in an invisible bag. We were old from the start, and it seemed that we lived and died in the course of a few hours.

Old. Old. Old. Benched. Booed. Old. I got so sick of everyone talking about my father's age, I wondered: was this any way to show respect for such a rare fossil? Life was complicated enough when the 49ers were winning. Take the first time my father was chosen MVP in 1957. I did not know what an MVP was, but the new trophy in the house was no red Impala, and my parents both lit up like Christmas trees when a new baby grand piano was rolled into the living room. How did I know its little gold plaque spelled doom? In this room I practiced daily my running, jumping, diving, in the hope that I could be the savior out on the football field if things really got tough. I had it all figured out. And now, poof! I had to practice the piano?

Until that one trophy arrived, I practiced my balance on our grape stake fence, while my brothers made the little fat boy play Y. A. Tittle and argued over who was going to be R. C. Owens. As a wild multi-colored horse I ran around the block with my best friend, Steffie Hopkins. We set fire to the leaves that filled the pit in her orchard and practiced jumping over the flames. To develop strength in our arms, we walked on our hands down Lupin Lane. At night, in our nightgowns, we ran the dark streets in braids created from blue wool, and we lived by drinking from the breath of friends and biting at the air. We even found other girls who would run through the streets in their nightgowns, steal flowers for the bathtub, and climb the oak trees with bare feet. But Steffie could climb higher than I. And no one ever broke her record for climbing the oak on her property and plucking the farthest leaf. Up she went into the night sky, scaling the finer branches like an inchworm on a rope. Steffie was simply inspired, whereas my motive was football. Practice. Practice. Practice. Who knows? I thought. Maybe one day, the players would actually need me. If my father had not earned a baby grand piano as the Most Valuable Player in the National Football League, I might have continued to practice throwing a block or making mincemeat out of Marchetti by jumping over oleanders and breaking dirt clods with my fists. . . . But as it was, poof!

And then, for three straight years, 1958 through 1960, it was bad even when it was good. For one thing, I didn't feel as sorry when our players went to the hospital as I did when they came over in swimsuits. Our team members did not look very good once those Titan outfits came off. Their black and blue bodies were grotesquely splotched, scarred, and lumpy. My father and Hugh McElhenny looked the worst, with nicks, cuts, and scratches even on their stomachs, and bruises everywhere. At swim parties, and at the beach, I felt so sorry for them. But the feeling didn't last. Each morning, my father went around the house singing, "Rise and Shine!" And worse—"When the Going Gets Tough, the Tough Get Going!" Although he charged a phrase like this with all of his electricity, it always sounded to me like a dry hamburger with nothing on it. It was almost unforgivable.

And then there was inspiration. When the Niners won, it was like catching a strange disease. What was a person supposed to do with this inspiration? And what was the matter with mine that it didn't know how to come in the silences of my life, when I would climb to the tops of trees looking for it or bury the potato bugs as if they were popes. Why did it never know how to come in the smell of broken sticks or crushed leaves, in the ordinary disguise, and instead came all too often in the smell of beer breath at ball games, in the worst of all possible moments, between boos, for example, or when my father was carried off the field and I was cold. Why was it always there big as life, big as Big Daddy Lipscomb?

In some ways I think it was harder when the Niners were winning, because then I and my brothers felt that our father was in some way responsible for a stranger's joy. On those days when the Niners won, my younger brothers would be in a frenzy of competition to see who could collect the most garbage under the seat, and I had to sit alone bribing God Almighty with fingers, ears, and toes for touchdowns, field goals, and touchbacks. Then after the game, when it should have been over, that's when my brothers pitched in, and we became the gadflies of the hero's conscience, kicking our father under restaurant tables in a puny if noble effort to remind him to smile at those strangers smiling at him.

Personally, I felt very lucky when Red Hickey decided to go with the shotgun formation and a younger quarterback, because in 1960 I had had a hero in Perseus for nearly half of my life. It happened in kindergarten that I had opened a book before I could read and found a picture of a man holding a ghastly trophy. Like sports, the picture had its share of violence. But the severed head of the Gorgon was only a part of the picture, and what was even more amazing than the head of snakes was the peace and contentment of the man leaning on one hip as if to say that he was not surprised in the least by what had to be the most bizarre and fantastic moment of his life, because victory, in spite of its strange and sometimes startling shapes, was not only his, but humanity's true element.

And so it was that I began to wonder about the hero. And it was a good thing, too, because when the going got tough for my father in 1960, there were a multitude of Greek heroes I had come across in books who had it a lot tougher than he did. These people who faced nine-headed hydras, clashing rocks, three-headed dogs, were like exotic candles being lit, one by one, inside my own dark and brutal world. My mother sometimes read to us from Homer. And no matter what happened in real life, you could always count on Menelaus getting sideswiped in a chariot race. *Damn you!* he screamed, *We Achaians lied when we said you had good sense!*[9] Then there was Epeios the boxer. Because my mother was always trying to skip over these parts, I had to go back and read for myself, *I claim I am the champion.... For I tell you this straight out and it will be a thing accomplished. I will smash his skin apart and break his bones....* [10] One day, the very same words would fly out of the mouth of Cassius Clay. Until then, what a delight it was to think of real heroes acting like children.

I used to believe that the game of football was like a myth not only to me, but to anyone who really loved the game. Was not the story of war the oldest story in the book? Whereas I only watched my father, the real fan might have seen Hector, Hannibal, Alexander, or even Ajax out there instead. And it *was* lovely how they kept getting up instead of dying. How they were even helped up by the enemy, sometimes hugged. And then, everyone trotted off to the sidelines. It was the most beautiful story of war anyone could hope to see. No matter what team won or lost, it really did not matter as long as Life beat Death. And Life always won!

"*Jugla!*"

For me, the rumors about *the trade* were a signal to wonder, but then everyone wondered what was going on. My father was getting ready to go to Portland to play against the New York Giants. Sam Huff. Andy Robustelli. Their defensive line was legendary, and against this line Hickey had promised to give Tittle and young John Brodie equal time. Against New York, my father would have his last chance to vindicate the T formation on the turf of his first and most beautiful professional pass, and Brodie would strut his stuff with the shotgun.

"*Jugla! Jugla!*"

I must say that in 1960, *trade* was not a neutral word in our vocabulary; it was a bad word. A trade was like a divorce from the community. As a player, it meant that you were leaving and letting strangers from another place fall in love with you. And even if everybody booed, you were not supposed to leave in the middle of a family argument, because that was weak.

Before the exhibition game against New York in 1961, my grandmother, Minnie Anne DeLoach, arrived to stay with us for the weekend at our home on Rosewood Lane. I overheard my father telling her that if he was traded to the Rams he might go, but if he was traded to New York he would hang it up, because New York was just too far away and it would uproot the family. Then I heard my mother tell him that if he was traded to Timbuktu what difference did it make? We would just pack our toothbrushes and go. He couldn't quit now. If he "bombed" out of New York, couldn't he always come home and "peddle" insurance? Besides, there was the "championship" and something about a "jinx" in Mom's speech. I gathered that my father had been battling that jinx for years as he dropped back into the pocket. As Rookie of the Year in 1948, he had lost his first championship against the Buffalo Bills. In Frisco, the Niners had come close but had finished second for four straight years. Then he said that "pride" made him play. But could "that pride" make him play too long? "Give it a year," she said. "Why not shoot the moon!"

With the phone ringing off the hook and my parents kissing in the back yard, I retired, somewhat exhausted, to my oak tree where I lived as the great spy, and I waited for my hands to hurry up and show themselves as old as oak bark. I was sorry that my family could not keep step to the beat of ordinary time. Old. Old. And I wondered about panther-time or hawk-time. But by this time, I had to go in. My father was leaving.

I can't believe I swept out my brothers' new playhouse for them. They have started The Woman Haters Club and all the boys around are joining. It is like they have come down with a thought virus.

And now the pipsqueak of the century, Victor Ferrari, has it. It's not Victor's fault that he is a shrimp and even if he has muscles, it just looks like the fruit bowl tipped over under his skin. But I won't ever forgive what he said about Steffie Hopkins. I will never repeat it either. He was yelling at us from across the street and he said about me, "Dianne Tittle is flat." So what? I don't want to wear a bra like some girls in our class have to already.

But now the problem is that even the boys who don't hate girls have to hate them. Like Mike. I know that Mike doesn't hate girls because he loves me. He is my brother.

He is the only person in our family who doesn't want to win as much as he wants to know things. He even leaves the encyclopedia in the bathroom, and he can actually sit still. He just sits and reads like a baby bird mouth.

But he has sports qualities too. Dad says that Mike is a better athlete than him in grade school, and he talks about passion *and hand-eye coordination—I know that Mike is really good, but what about me and Pat?*

And now Mike has joined the club. So far, it is the only mistake he ever made. I still love him anyway, but did he forget I'm a girl or something? I can't believe he's going to throw rocks like the other boys.

. . . He never did.

RED RIGHT POWER 29 B LIKE BOY ON 3!

At Multnomah Stadium in Portland, Oregon, young John Brodie was riding shotgun, playing with the zeal of the convert, yet not exactly rattling the old archbishops of the Giant defensive line. Who but the mighty New York defense had been known to remark to their own offense upon leaving the field, "Just hold 'em?" Brodie soon found himself at their feet, his "revolutionary new" shotgun offense laid to rest by the likes of Huff, Robustelli and Modzelewski—Giants who shifted their weight on the line of scrimmage as a way to say "ho-hum."

For the entire first half, Tittle watched from the bench. If Norman Rockwell could have painted the picture, it would have been called: "Churchboy in Hell." It was tough.

How he wanted another chance to put the ball in the air and let the world revolve. Red admitted that Tittle was throwing better than ever, and this apparently made him the fly in Hickey's ointment—the quarterback who would not break mentally in this war of nerves. Thirty minutes left in the game, and the Giants led, 21–13. Finally Hickey sent Tittle in, switching to the T formation. Now it was all or nothing. Fading back, with his first professional pass in his mind, Y. A. let loose with another. But this one did not spell pretty words across the sky. This one spelled bullet.

Tittle came uncorked. He missed a short pass to Stickles, then hit six straight. He completed six of seven passes for 84 yards and scored within 3 minutes and 30 seconds. When the 49ers got the ball next, Tittle marched the team 75 yards in four plays, then hit Monte Stickles in the end zone in the final minutes.[11]

"Why, excuse me," said Sam Huff when he knocked my father down after the bullet. Sam helped him up and dusted him off.

"Sorry, Y. A.," he said over his shoulder as he trotted off.

Strange, thought Tittle. Very strange. But then it happened again. My father did not want to think he was getting special treatment. That had certainly never happened before. But then, it was not like Sam Huff to say "Excuse me" when he tackled you, either.

Tittle proceeded to vindicate the T formation. As a seasoned veteran, he felt like a kid in a candy shop. It seemed he could do anything. Nobody rushed him. The game in Portland against New York was the easiest game of his whole career.

When the game was over, man, was he happy. He ran off the field and leaped in the air. Sam Huff ran alongside and said, "Y. A., I want to be the first to congratulate you."

"Why's that Sam? What do you mean?"

"Well, you are a New York Giant now. And we are damn happy you are going to be one of us."

"What? Sam . . . tell me one thing. When did you find this out?"

"Yesterday. Allie Sherman told the team that if any one of us laid a finger on you, it would cost 'em one hundred dollars. Congratulations, Yat. And welcome aboard."

Lindenwood. We lived among sprawling ranch homes dwarfed by a canopy of oaks and bay laurels in whose shade azaleas, oleanders, and ferns bloomed around large puzzle-pieces of ivy for hiding and even larger puzzle-pieces of grass for somersaults. It was a place where the sun went down on kids, chamomile, mint, mustard, poppies, nettles, tiger swallowtails, cabbage butterflies, monarchs, buckeyes, California sisters, mourning cloaks, bees, tree moths, slugs, snails, worms, robins, quail on the run, pincher bugs and black widows in a jar. Luckily, the house did not get in the way of the wisest tree in the neighborhood, which happened to live in our front yard, right outside the kitchen window. Its base formed a cave from which three massive trunks grew, and its branches laced the air from one end of the property to the other.

After the game between San Francisco and New York, day dawned on a house under siege, where film crews with gleaming instruments of torture filled the driveway and newsmen with hungry faces appeared at every window. Maybe the quarterback was used to that. But he was not used to us shrinking from his touch or screaming in fear that the man in their midst was an imposter, not their real father. That's when my father felt his age.

The newspaper headlines read, YAT BOOTED OUT OF FRISCO. It was like reading that one of our parents had been put to sleep—until we discovered that our father had only been traded for a rookie lineman named Lou Cordileone. Red Hickey had made up his mind to go with the new offense and a young quarterback because the classical T formation, in his opinion, would soon become a thing of the past.

Y. A. was called into Red's office next morning. It was a bit of an insult for a veteran and member of the Million Dollar Backfield to be traded for a rookie lineman. But Tittle told him he understood that a professional decision had been made for the good of the team, and he asked if he could say goodbye to his teammates. The Niners knew something was up when they saw my father crossing the parking lot in his street clothes, and they gathered round.

The San Francisco paper said:

> Y. A. received the word more calmly than many of the old teammates he must leave behind. With some of them weeping openly, the "Bald Eagle" told them in a farewell speech that "these things are all part of professional sport . . ."[12]

Y. A. told the 49ers that he respected Hickey's decision in light of the coach's belief in the shotgun, and that he did not want the trade to disrupt the team. He thanked his receivers for being so slow that they preserved his arm. "I wish you all the luck. Wish me luck," he said. Then quickly, he got into his car, honked the horn twice and was gone. When the coach clapped his hands and said, "Let's go fellas!" nobody budged. Practice was called off and Tittle hit the road with memories.

HALFTIME

Yelberton Abraham Tittle

Born: 24 October 1926, Marshall, Texas
Mother: Alma Allen Tittle
Father: Abraham Tittle
Sister: Huline
Brothers: Jack, Don, and Stafford

Played Football In Junior High: 1938, 1939, 1940
Played For Marshall Mavericks At Marshall High School: 1941,
    1942, 1943
Most Valuable Back: 1941, 1942, 1943
All District: 1942, 1943
Louisiana State University: 1944–1947
Most Minutes Played Award: 1945, 1946, 1947
Selected to Blue and Grey: 1946, 1947

Drafted #1 Detroit Lion NFL 1948
Drafted #1 Cleveland Browns 1948, but traded prior to season.
Played for Baltimore Colts: 1948–1950
Quarterbacked San Francisco 49ers: 1951–1960
Quarterbacked New York Giants: 1961–1964

Rookie of the Year: All American Conference: 1948
Selected to Pro Bowl: 1953, 1954, 1957, 1959, 1961, 1962, 1963
Most Valuable Player Hula Bowl: 1955
All NFL Quarterback: 1957, 1961, 1962, 1963
Played in NFL Title Games: 1961, 1962, 1963

NFL Most Valuable Player: 1957, 1961, 1962, 1963
Played Professional Football 17 Years
Held Most Passing Records upon Retirement
Still Tied for Most Touchdown Passes in One Game

Member of Texas High School Hall of Fame, Louisiana Hall of
    Fame, Texas Sports Hall of Fame, San Francisco Bay Area Hall
    of Fame
Elected to New York Sports Hall of Fame: 1990
Elected to Pro Football Hall of Fame: 1971

Y. A., 1961.

BOOTLEG
NEW YORK GIANTS

New York Giants (*l. to r.*)
Hugh McElhenny,
Alex Webster,
Y. A. Tittle,
Del Shofner,
Frank Gifford, 1963.

In the stadium, Phrastor it was who hit the mark,
and Nikeus, who, with a circling sweep of his hand,
excelled all others in flinging afar the weight of stone.
And all the friendly host raised a mighty cheer,
while the lovely light of the fair-faced moon burned on . . .

—Pindar, *Olympian* 10

Father: *There was something in the air in New York and winning there was like winning nowhere else. It was expected, for one thing. And the high level of expectation was a freeing experience, if you can believe it. Winning was supposed to be a statement of what we as individuals are capable of. And winning was the one thing we could give to ourselves, each other, and to the fans who gave us everything in the way of support. It doesn't make sense, but certainly for me it was an honor to come in contact with the great pride and long-held traditions of the Giant organization, to play for greater stakes and to partake in, well, that kind of optimism.*

... But even in the good years, I always felt that any day someone was going to take my job. I never let myself be convinced they really wanted me. And I worked "hungry" until the day I quit playing ball.

In San Francisco, I sat on the bench clapping for Albert and Brodie with my fingers crossed, all the while hoping their next pass would be intercepted, so that I could get into the game. But in New York it was different. I couldn't clap that way for Charlie Conerly. He had tremendous presence as a leader. Athough it must have hurt his pride to see me there, there were times that he'd come over in practice and say, "Well, you're looking pretty good, Y. A."

Daughter: *Tell me about Big Daddy Lipscomb.*

Father: *For obvious reasons, it's rare that a quarterback ever feels sorry for a defensive player, because you don't really get a chance to retaliate, and they are always unloading on you. But once I felt sorry for Big Daddy Lipscomb.*

As I've said before, I've always enjoyed the bootleg, where everybody goes one way and you go the other. To run the bootleg, however, you have to make sure that everything is right. You have to make sure that everybody's following their key.

This particular play I thought was well set up, and so I ran the bootleg play. There I was in mid-field and there was Big Daddy. Didn't fool him a bit. And Big Daddy was headed my way.

So I ran toward the sideline, but Big Daddy was catching up. That's when I put out my arm to try to stiff-arm this 335-pound man. "I'm going to break your neck," whispered Big Daddy.

"That's not very nice," I said, and then I grabbed his face mask for one second. I was about to turn loose when he hollered, "You know, when you turn loose of my helmet, I'm gonna kill you."

"My gosh," I said to myself, "I'm not going to turn loose of his head!" Because you know, I don't care how big you are, you have to follow your head. When you grab that face mask, of course, you have got the biggest man in your power, in a disadvantaged and dangerous position. And that is why there is a 15-yard penalty against this sort of thing.

So now I am in front of the Baltimore bench about to turn him loose again. But Big Daddy says, "Now I got you! And now you're gonna die!" Well, sh—oot a monkey! Forget it! I was not in the mood to take any unnecessary chances. So I jump over the bench, and Big Daddy, he jumps over the bench because he has to follow his head. We're heading out now, out toward the Babe Ruth Memorial Plaque. Big Daddy, well, he is following his head, and finally, I sort of sling him into the first row of seats. These fans, in particular the ladies out there in Yankee Stadium, take their purses and their high heel shoes and they just beat the living tar out of him. I mean they were really giving it to him. And I figured, well, when I turned around and saw flags, yellow flags all over the field, I knew they couldn't penalize me for more than one 15 yards. And I didn't care anyway. Just one time, I had saved myself. And so, as I headed back to accept my 15 yards, these officals start running right past me and shaking their finger at Big Daddy Limbscomb. "Big Daddy!" they said. "If you ever chase a man off a football field like that again, you're suspended for the season!" I felt terrible for Big Daddy, I admit. I guess they thought he had been chasing me!

Daughter: *Dad, that's a lie.*

Father: *Not really, not a total lie. Actually, I was stiff-arming him at first. And then when he threatened me I did grab hold as we went over the bench. Then I turned loose really quick and ran. The way I tell the story, I just flung him over the seats.*

Daughter: *YEAH! (And if only Big Daddy could have been there with us, I would have shot my fist in the air and given him the high five, because Big Daddy was one of the pillars of my childhood, and from this defensive end the Tittle kids had learned compassion for their father and the world!)*

Childhood Heroes, 1961

Fall afternoon. Atherton, California.

"I want to be Big Daddy."

"Tough buns. I want to be Big Daddy."

"No, you be Johnny Unitas and I'll be Big Daddy."

"But what about me? Who's going to be Y. A. Tittle?"

"Can't I be Big Daddy too?"

"No, you be Jimmy Brown. And you, you be . . ."

"Hardy The Hatchet?"

"Forget it. You can't play."

"I can catch."

"She can catch. Oh crumb."

"I can run."

"Halleluiah, she can run."

"Well . . ."

"But I'm better than him."

"Is that right? Tiddliwinks here thinks she's better than you."

"Did you hear that?!"

"Uh huh."

"But I am. I know some plays."

"Uh huh."

"Uh huh."

"Get her!"

And when the spirit of Big Daddy Lipscomb came upon the boys in the neighborhood, only then did I know for sure that my parents did not bring the wrong baby home from the hospital. I was theirs. And there was some satisfaction in knowing, despite my father's habit of throwing back his head as if to ask the ceiling where I came from, as if it cared that he thought his real daughter was picking cotton somewhere in Georgia. He was sorely mistaken if he thought I had dropped out of a light fixture. If that was so, then why with Big Daddy Lipscomb hot on my trail did I feel my father's and mother's genes all over the place flashing and beeping like sirens?

Obviously, I had inherited the gene from my father that *knew* to run and the gene from my mother that knew *how*. From her came the ability to spurt, to go beyond myself and run faster. And from my father the fox came the brute—that gallumphing gene for fear—the great gene of survival without which no Tittle would have ever made it to Yankee Stadium to run out of bounds in the first place. . . . Don't get caught—BIG DADDY LIPSCOMB!

One of the ten commandments in pro football in 1961 was that nobody fooled Big Daddy Lipscomb ever. Maybe that once, he was unlucky and the refs gave him hell for chasing my father into the stands. But what I remember was the tackle when Big Daddy took my father by one arm and swung him 360 degrees before letting him go in a belly flop. And the play before when he helped him up after twice stepping on his throwing hand. The nicest thing about Big Daddy Lipscomb was that he did not have thumb tacks taped to his fingertips. But then there was always the chance that he was saving something special for next week.

Eugene Lipscomb was the Samson of the age. The scariest thing about Big Daddy was that you loved him regardless, as he was the champion of passion, zest, and ferocity. There was nothing ho-hum about this man, who possessed the greatness of the darkened sky before a catastrophe. Lipscomb was a wake-up call. He was the aurora borealis of the game. As a force of nature that came along but once in a lifetime, Big Daddy was either hated or loved. But to hate Big Daddy Lipscomb, you had to be the kind of person to hate the lightning just because it struck your house and burned the trees.

We loved him. My mother loved him. My brothers loved him. I loved Big Daddy. My father could never understand why we loved Big Daddy so much, but I believe he loved Big Daddy too. Eugene was a man who could have been famous had he not lived at the dawning of the drug age. Two weeks after his greatest game he died from a drug overdose, and three little kids wanted to know the names of the killers. It was scary to live at a time when the drug world was getting its face lift and the thugs began going after heroes as part of their marketing scheme. It was scary because it worked. The thugs won.

If Big Daddy Lipscomb had not died before I had a chance to grow up, I had planned to marry this volcano who was also an earthquake when he chose. He was my heart weighing in at just under 400 pounds. He was my soul with a number.

When he died, the axis of the world snapped and what heroes we had started dropping like flies. Drugs were in. Picnics, bird baths, and Big Daddy Lipscomb were out. In the new age that was dawning, Lipscomb was just another human sacrifice taking place at dawn. And in that early morning light, it would not be long before the games would pass into the hands of the media emperors and the altar was spread out like the blue sky.

Gooo Giaaaants!

Winter...

Because I was a girl, I didn't count. Because I was a girl, I was "no fun to beat." Because I was a girl, nobody listened when I spoke. And it was great. Because I was a girl, I was left alone. And I did not have to play Monopoly. I had hated Monopoly ever since my father wished I was dead for not selling anything. And why would I sell my green properties, when green was my favorite color?

Instead, I went as far away from arguments and games as I could. I got under the car when it was night outside, and I opened my window and got under my bed any time I felt like it. I was free. And I was an American. Just because I was a girl, I wasn't dumb. I knew I was born on American soil. I was born in Marshall, Texas.

I was never alone, because I believed in God, in railroad tracks and cherries, tall blue flowers and pomegranates, oak branches, and the human sneeze. And guess what? God liked begonia petals, willow branches, and shade, just like me.

In 1961, God came over every day. He had a way of sneaking up on me when I was peeling open seed pods or eating a snack. Then We played. God never beat me. We made forts. He never said anything insulting or rude.

We played hiding games and then We buried every dead squirrel, robin, and blue jay we could find. There were rules of course. We couldn't just kick the creatures out of sight. We dug real holes in the ground. We supported the little flopping heads and sometimes We cried. We made sure that they were covered completely with soft leaves so that they could be protected from the insults of clunky shoes and indifferent eyes. I didn't care that I was one of zillions. God was my best friend. And I could always count on Him to believe in me, that I was a real person.

Summer...

One day, God and me were walking in front of David Weber's house when a car drove past. Then it stopped in the road and slowly, like a shark, it moved alongside. The voice from inside the car said, "Does Miss Tittle want a ride?" I looked at the salami face of the stranger and stared at his stare that was dull and blank as a Kleenex box. A bad feeling glued me to the ground because the man had doll's eyes and he knew my name. He didn't ask it like a normal person. He knew it.

When he reached over to open the door, my feet came unglued. I had never run like this, where my legs did all of the thinking, and my feet knew just where to step! But he had no right to say my name! It was mine!

While running, I breathed like a horse at the track, and I could see my own fear. My very own. It was not about ordinary kidnappers, it was about extraordinary strangers, who were angry because my father had thrown an interception and did not get the right squeeze on the ball. It was the fear of strangers who were not cheering the beautiful chaos, but who might steal from us our names and maybe even our hearts, if ever they found out our address.

In 1961, I was eleven years old. I knew better. Real heroes were supposed to be dead or buried under book covers that read: Myth. And then up in the left hand corner—$2.00. And yet, just as I worked at my 500-piece puzzle of Ludwig's Castle, I worked at creating a hero, too. I started with Bernadette's patience because from the looks of her in my story book, I could imagine her kneeling in that grotto for a thousand years. Another main ingredient was Joan of Arc's wit and her ability to ride. This was a must. And Demeter? *Dread goddess. Noble mistress of fruits in their season?* I didn't care if she was a goddess or not. She let out a piercing cry when her daughter was abducted to the underworld. *Brandishing shining torches she circled the earth for nine days . . .*[1] Demeter could have worn a muumuu and left her hair in spoolies. My hero would have to love that much, and be able to cry out like Demeter, when need be.

On a fall day, inside my den of leaves I gave the hero hands. Finger number one—Enkidu, a sad Sumerian with a funny name. Hero for his loyalty to a friend and his ability to remember dreams. Finger number two—Sappho. She sang for an audience: *If you are squeamish, don't prod the beach rubble!*[2] Finger number three was the nuts and bolts type with good hand-eye coordination. The great survivor—Perseus. Who could forget the sheer grace with which he lopped off the Gorgon's head his first time at bat? The ring finger was Beowulf. Though old, he fought the terrible Grendel to show the path between honor and male pride. Finally, Joseph—was the nominee from my Bible book. One hand was complete with this great adapter who also respected dreams, and what is more, forgave those creeps who were his kin.

I burst from the leaves. And from then on I, too, was like a leaf, caught and carried away in the flow of my secret.

Go!

In 1961, with a magnolia flower from the yard squashed between asthma sprays, at first I felt certain that my father could handle anything that New York had to offer. Unfortunately, on the night that he left for New York City, *King Kong* was playing on TV. It was late when we returned from the airport, but my mother let us stay up. Oak branches scraped against the roof, our beagle dog howled, and Kong arrived in New York City about the same time as Y. A. Tittle did. It was hard not to jump to conclusions: from the looks of the situation on TV, it seemed that maybe my father had made a big mistake in leaving. What kind of place was New York City, anyhow? And what if my father did not know that gorillas hung out on the tops of the skyscrapers there? This place was different.

This was New York. This was KING KONG!

Gooo Giaaants!

According to Giant Emlen Tunnel, "it was pretty low budget for everybody at Giant training camp in 1961. Torn jerseys were patched up. Players bought their own shoes and the Giants had a team cobbler who fixed broken shoes."[3] Giant Kyle Rote told William Wallace of the *New York Times*, that "the Giants locker room was like some Middle Eastern bazaar with goods being sold to help the players make ends meet. Jimmy Patton had shoes, another guy had something else, and they were forever trying to sell each other something."[4]

Among those who showed up at camp in 1961 was singer and musician, Roosevelt Grier. He brought with him a lot of high-tech audio equipment. Says Coach Sherman:

> We'd stick him up in the top floor of one of the Fairfield University dorms so he wouldn't disturb so many people. The first ten days or so all you'd hear from his room was lowdown blues. Sad, sad, stuff, you know. But then, Rosey would start to pick it up a bit. And that's when we knew he was getting in shape, because he was feeling better. The coaches used to say, "We can go to one-a-days now cause Rosey's in shape."[5]

And then perhaps the most battered and abused player in the league's 36-year history arrived. Quarterback Charlie Conerly had been "bounced so much," Giants physician Dr. J. Francis Sweeney couldn't tell you how many spinal concussions he'd had. "Charlie would come in as a mass of bruises, black and blue on his elbows, his arms, his shoulders, his back, chest and ribs. But he resented it whenever I asked him where it hurts."

A man of few words, Conerly admits that "the mental beating is as much as the physical." When the Giants had struggled through a losing season five years before, "the fans displayed banners reading, "Goodbye Charley," "Back To The Farm, Charley" and booed him so vociferously that after the game against the Chicago Cardinals, he sat out the following game." Now he arrived at camp wondering, "what quarterback they've got who thinks he's going to take my job."[6]

In 1961 the New York Giants were not one big happy family. There were deep divisions between the Giants offense and defense squads and there was also considerable loyalty to Conerly. Given all of this, Charlie might have ripped the Giants apart over the question of his successor had he not been what is called "a real pro." But Conerly stepped aside with dignity, realizing that no youngster or hot shot had come to beat him out, but another who knew the "feeling" and would carry on after him, and Tittle felt honored to assume leadership behind the veteran.

That first season with the Giants, my father was away from home from August until December. In December of 1961, Y. A. Tittle did not win the national championship. What he won was an image as a sports hero. And in 1961, you could turn off the TV set, and our father was still a famous man. By that I mean that when people asked for his autograph, they blushed when they asked. That blush added weight to our lives. And we were good at protecting a father who was no longer like the others. Ours was fragile and breakable. So, naturally, we were on guard against the *image*, because we did not want this monster to trick the people or to disappoint them. Nor did we want it to take our father away.

When he was a 49er football star, life had been relatively simple. Once, I remember, my father, like some King Farouk, arrived late to pick us up at the airport in San Francisco. He had been delayed, apparently, by an entourage of autograph seekers. And when he showed up finally, prancing down the airport aisle, my mother gave my father a look. The look said that when my brother Pat was born in Austin, Texas, my father was playing a football game in San Francisco; that when Pat was 10 days old and suffering from an earache, my mother had made the move from Texas to California by herself. (I know because I was one of three competing for her lap, and I remember because she sang the dreaded Muffin Man Song for the duration of the plane trip.) The look also made clear that while our mother was very capable when it came to managing a wide variety of catastrophes, she could not handle the short end of the stick for one minute. And then, just as calmly and gracefully as Odysseus once took aim with his great bow in the hall of suitors, my mother took the tray of formula she held in her one free hand, and threw it like a bowling ball right down the airport aisle at King Farouk.

But in 1961 my father's image was changing shape. And that colossal image of something human but not quite right was heading our way like Frankenstein. Profoundly lovable and deeply misunderstood, no matter how good he was he was still a monster, and his fame was a monster, and some of the attention it attracted was monstrous too.

Before that year, the phony phone calls mostly came on Saturday nights during football season, because that's when my father had a sleep-over with the team. And if I picked up the telephone, it was like entering a dark cave filled with bats inside. First there was silence. And then the words just flew. Some people shouted, "Your father is a bum!" and there was no way to get a word in edgewise. But when people called up 20 times in a row and said nothing, then I could shout like an Old Testament screamer, "Creep!" right into the void. Once, I even outlistened a phony phone caller while gathering hate from the four corners of the globe. "Mosquito bite!" I screeched. And it felt better than getting an A on my report card.

But on the night my father left for New York City, the telephone rang and my mother's hands trembled on the receiver. Apparently, the monster knew what we wore when we took my father to the airport, and *it* knew what we said, when *it* watched us say good-bye. The monster thought it was very funny every time my mother hung up, because *it* called back, as if we cared to hear *it* laughing. Sad to say, what called on the night that my father left for New York was not so dumb. And just as New York City was different, so was the monster. Every day of the week it called. And whereas most of our Saturday night phony phone callers sounded angry and like they had just been stuck with a pin, the monster's voice was very polite. It said very calmly that "we are watching you," (as if we were some boring TV program) and "we will come over when we feel like it."

For once, nobody knew what to say. Not my mother. And not the police.

At first it was only the telephone that scared us. And then it was the car that was parked across the street. A car with men in it watched our house and sometimes watched my brothers and me when we walked home from Encinal Elementary School. One day, that zombie car followed me home from the bus stop, moving as slowly as a giant stink bug. I was a big fan of silence in those days. Silence, I felt, held the key. And the dread quiet of that car was the first silence that ever made me want to spit with fury. The police thought it best that we move out of our house for several weeks. So we moved to a motel in nearby Menlo Park. It was like a bootleg. We pretended to move away. We got an unlisted telephone number. And then we came back home again, and it seemed like the bootleg worked. Everything was just like before, except that the San Francisco 49ers were losing and the New York Giants were winning. Everthing was the same except for the new silence, which, like the blush, had added weight to our lives.

And then one night the monster came over. And I ran my own private bootleg. I was wide awake and listening to the house creak, trying to separate the good silence from the bad. Until then, nothing in my life had ever seemed indifferent to me, not the weather, not the plums on the trees or the birds that were dead in the driveway, not the houses on our street even when they were empty, not the dew, not the acorns, not the dirt. The world was my friend. And if anybody had asked me if I knew the facts of life I would have answered, of course—*the silence cared.* But that zombie car—a grey Ford Fairlane convertible with fins—had rolled into my childhood, infecting the body of a living, breathing landscape with a cancerous silence, and it was an insult to the entire universe.

On that night, everything in my bedroom was traced in shadows by guardian angels with marking pens. There was my bed table and the lamp. There was the present my parents gave me when they came home from a trip. As I lay awake, listening to the heat go on and off, I could see their gift, a folded card with the paper face of Jesus on it and prayers around him like a fence. Even though everything was in its place, it felt like two kinds of silence were doing battle in my room. Then, quite unexpectedly, this battle was interrupted when I heard the front door open and steps sound on the tile in our entryway.

To the right of this entry was the kitchen. Dead ahead was the living room with the baby grand piano. On the left and down the hall was my bedroom, the first room you came to. My room was blue with a great heat duct, a windowsill jammed with plastic horses, including one appaloosa, a music box over the four-poster bed, and my brother's teeth marks in one of the posts. And I slept with the same books in bed with me every night: D'Aulaire's *Myths* and the *Story of St. Bernadette*. Next was my brothers' bedroom. Their walls were knotty pine, and they slept in big bunk beds under navy blue bedspreads. Turning right, there was the thermostat, the towel closet, and a door leading into my parents' room where everything was pale green and the bedspread was very large and soft with a silver sheen to it, and what looked like newborn baby ferns stitched into it. There, the house came to an end, and beyond was a row of gardenia bushes, then a patch of grass, a petunia mound, and a fence which marked the beginning of Weirdsville because it belonged to Richard, the boy who preferred his room to a fort, and always went to bed when he was told to.

But tonight I could not believe my ears. Those footsteps were not going away. And when compared to the sounds from Night's own music box, crickets, rolling acorns, the occasional train in the distance, they sounded as loud and clumsy as a tuba blast. Yet sure enough, slowly and deliberately, somebody was coming down the hall and interrupting the night song, interrupting the battle between the good silence and the bad. Of course, it had to be a joke. And by the time that somebody got to my room, I heard breathing which sounded like a joke although it was not funny. Somebody was imitating a fish out of water, if it could gasp out loud.

One part of me wanted to help, get up and get the person a glass a water. But that didn't happen, because what silence there was in my room collapsed on my eyes and would not let me open them. My eyes squenched down and my face too, just like an automobile being crushed into a cube.

For a dream, I felt very much like a live wire. Thoughts were no longer floating by like clouds, they struck like lightning. *Yes. Bootleg. Pretend.* If only I could be dead already, then nobody would have to kill me. So I held my breath and breathed in sips so that my death would be more convincing. The only problem was that my heart would not shut up. And what happened was more like a shouting match, with my heart becoming as loud as the strange breathing.

While my mind was telling me quietly and practically: "Be dead!" my heart would not give up, it would not even let me pretend. "You are not dead!" my heart beat back. And finally, like lifting two very heavy garage doors, my eyes opened.

At first, the darkness was like fuzz, but then I could see my lamp, coming into view like Steffie Hopkins, my best friend, coming over to my house. There was my table and my picture too: Friends. And to the left of my picture, in my peripheral vision, legs.

It was funny. The breathing, the presence in my room did not scare me anymore. I think that my fear was like a bridge, a rickety bridge that I was running across high above the world. And, at some point, I made it across. My books were still in bed with me, and there in plain view was my picture. I watched that calm paper face, and discovered it like Cortez who found the Pacific Ocean. I journeyed to the center of the world and gazed upon its molten core—not in the tiny picture of Jesus, but in his two closed eyes.

And then, when I was no longer afraid to die or to live, when it was OK—everything—and we could all be in the same room together (something beautiful, something ugly, and me), the paper eyes opened. It did not surprise me. And it didn't make any difference because I liked my picture either way. What surprised me was that my own heart paid attention for once and stopped pounding. And so it seemed the breathing grew gentler and finally subsided. The stranger turned and left the room.

With my eyes still focused on my picture, I saw him leave out of the corner of my eye and heard the house creak under his footsteps going down the hall and stepping onto the tile. Then carefully, very carefully, the front door was shut. Clitch.

I never told anybody. But I did turn on the light, because I wanted to look *behind* my picture. The eyes were closed again. And it was only a piece of paper, folded on the sides so it would stand. Then I turned out the light and went to sleep. Or maybe, I just fell into sleep more deeply than before. A dream. It was not news to anyone but me. It was not like winning the championship. But that night, I did feel that I had won something, if only because the face had protected me, if only because I fell asleep in the belief that the night was a black rose at my shoulder. And *my* silence was still the queen!

On the night that my father left for New York, when the monster called and I watched my mother's hands trembling on the telephone, I wasn't sure who would win. And at the moment my mother's hands trembled, they struck me as much smaller than ever before and very beautiful. When I saw her hands that way, I knew it was my job to stand in the doorway and breathe with dignity, the way an Indian chief was supposed to smoke a peace pipe. In the end, I did not care about the monster anymore, because finally somebody had told the truth about fame. And though my mother's hands did not express what fame was, they did express what it *felt* like. And it seemed to me that the people who knew that feeling must be vulnerable to the world in exactly the same way as my mother's hands were, in that instant, vulnerable to me.

And so, from then on, I turned my attention to my mother's *image*, which was communicated to us mostly in stories that trailed off like butterflies disappearing overhead. Her dreams and stories were her way of making the sky seem higher for us, especially when the monster came around. But then she also had a temper, which did not let the good get out of hand, and which most certainly accounted for a whole lot of crop failures and hurricanes off the coast of Brazil.

During my father's four months of mud and glory in New York City in 1961, I think that I fell in love with my mother. Yes, this is all that I mean to say. Other than that (and if we don't count Jesus opening his eyes), nothing out of the ordinary happened at our house. It seemed like all we did was stare at a recurring piece of meatloaf and wait for the same geography lesson. We heard about the starving peoples from every nation, and what was truly depressing was that we knew whose fault it was. (Mom's.) Nevertheless, she did everything in her power to make it clear that we were tough, we could take it. And not only that, she kept us posted about Y. A. Tittle, the great Bald Eagle. She let us know New York was different.

NEW YORK WAS KING KONG!

Safeco Insurance Company of America
Home Office—Seattle 5, Washington

Tittle-Iverson & Company   October 18, 1961
P.O. Box 1041
Tel: DAvenport 5–4433
Palo Alto, California

Dear Dad,
      You'll never guess what happened. I got a hair cut, it's cut real short and when grandmother comes out again she is going to give me a permanent.
      Dad do you like New York? I hope you do. Have you seen the Statue of Liberty and the Empire State Building? (Tell me in your letter.)
      Jeff Hesselmeyer broke his collarbone playing tackle football. Billy Moore made Jeff lose his balance and then Mark Steven tackled Jeff, and that's how Jeff broke his collarbone.
      By the way, when the 49ers played the Vikings, they didn't do so hot.

Daddy, please play your very very best so that Hickey will get mad.

I *miss you* very much.

Love,
Dianne
xxxxxxxxxx
P.S. I went to a horse show. I love you. xxxx

The countdown began. "10 . . . 9 . . . 8 . . ."

At Yankee Stadium in 1961, it was the Giants versus the Cleveland Browns, and for Y. A. Tittle the greatest thrill of his football career. The New York Giants were ten seconds away from winning the Eastern Division championship, and he was standing in New York City's Yankee Stadium under a darkening sky as the countdown in the stands began.

The voices of the New York fans echoed like East Texas thunder, drowning out the doubt that had tormented him since before the season began. The voice of doubt was but the voice of reason in August of 1961. Tittle was old and injured. 49er coach Hickey had dumped him because he was through. Yet within 24 hours after Hickey gave him the word, Tittle arrived at the Willamette campus in Salem, Oregon, and was directed to the girls' dorm where the New York Giants were staying.

In front of the dormitory Y. A. paused for a moment, maybe for many moments. He didn't know how long he stood holding his luggage and daydreaming, still trying to add it up. What was he after then, by going to New York? Money? No. More fame? Hell no. What was it then? In the mirror of his life, suddenly a man whose confidence was shaken blocked the view. The question wasn't whether he was too old to play. Was he too old to believe anymore in that glimmer of excellence that lay buried in the cool dark of his mind? That belief had glowed in him ever since he and H. L. Blocker had shot marbles together. But if he still believed, it meant breaking into the closed corporation of the New York Giants. It meant more injuries, humiliation, and doubt. More aloneness.

When Minnette and Y. A. left Marshall in 1948, Blocker had said "I hope you make a million bucks. I wish you all the luck." For the most part, the luck had come through for Y. A., and H. L. was working toward that million. Y. A. had heard somewhere that H. L. Blocker had moved to Los Angeles and become the successful proprietor of several pressing shops. He would find out later that Blocker had watched every game that Tittle played, no matter where he was. He had the TV in the pressing shop and watched the camera zero in on a tackle the day that Tittle's jaw broke. Then, out of the blue, he showed up at the Rams game in 1960. With arthritis in his hips, he stood up and cheered as others began the chant: *old old old, benched booed old.* The game ended. And H. L. hollered to his old friend as he left the field. He was almost close enough to touch him. But Tittle was in his own world, bruised but not broken by the tackles or the boos.

"You wanna have some lunch or are you going to stand out there all day?" said Coach Allie Sherman.

Embarrassed, Tittle fumbled with his luggage. At lunch, except for Billy Stits who said hello, he was ignored—naturally. As an older team, the Giants were a closed fraternity. Tittle was too old to go out with the rookies, and the veterans were too loyal to Conerly to go out of their way for his backup. And that was fine. All Tittle wanted was a shot at earning their respect.

His shot did not come easily. The manner of calling plays, the cadence, as well as the system of using automatics at the line of scrimmage, everything was different in New York. "In S.F., for example, the numbering system was the same. The odd and even numbering of the holes on the offensive line was the same; the pass terminology was the same, X and Y instead of L and R as with the Giants. In San Francisco, halfbacks were odd and even; with the Giants there were A and B. The flare pass in New York was known as a circle pass in S.F.; the flare pass in Giant terminology was a swing pass to the 49ers."[7]

With the Giants, every call was snapped off in the same crisp rhythm:

"Hut one . . . hut two . . . hut three." No matter what, the rhythm was always the same. Sherman wanted to achieve an over all team rhythm where every man would be prepared to move at the same instant with no hesitation or indecision. In San Francisco, however, each play was called with a varied cadence in a non-rhythm count. In S.F. the tempo of the quarterback's call was always changing, speeding up, slowing down. And this allowed the quarterback to change his timing if the defense started to move around. If, for instance, the snap number was two, he might start the call by saying, "Ready, set . . . go . . ." Then, if he saw the defense starting to shift around, he could hesitate before calling the second "go."[8]

To add to Y. A.'s confusion there were the automatics. While in S.F., "automatics were called occasionally and designated with 'live' colors—red, green, blue, white etc., the Giants used numbers instead of colors and called automatics on every play." Y. A. would later confess that "he found himself guessing more than the defensives he was trying to fool . . . found himself suddenly with numbers spinning around in his helmet as he tried to change a lifetime of habits and absorb a completely new system."[9] Not only was Tittle's lack of confidence beginning to snowball but everything had to be memorized. And the real problem, in addition to his preexisting injuries, was that Tittle "did not memorize a play step by step, he 'felt' it. A slant-34 was WHAM! the fullback over this tackle and through the hole . . . And now he found that he was trying too hard. Trying too hard not to make mistakes."[10]

After just one week in which to prepare himself, Y. A. flew with the Giants to Los Angeles. A preseason game against the Rams was scheduled, and the new quarterback would be put in for a few plays. The night before the game, Tittle desperately needed to break the ice with his teammates, if only for the sake of the game next day.

On the pretence of waiting for a friend, Y. A. stood in front of the hotel as the players filed past. When he overheard several players mention the Bull and Bush, he made a bee-line to the restaurant and then nonchalantly strolled into the room, still on the lookout for his imaginary buddy. The Bald Eagle passed six Giants seated at a table and spied one empty chair.

Lee Riley, Billy Stits, and Eddie Sutton looked up.

"Who are you looking for, Tittle?" asked Riley

"Oh, somebody. But I guess he isn't here."

"Well, sit down and eat with us, why don't you?" said Riley, looking sideways.

Y. A. forced himself to count, Hut 1 . . . Hut 2. Then "Might as well," Y. A. sighed, and he sat down.

The next day, on 19 August 1961, Tittle broke his back on a 37-slant. One minute Lee Grossup was saying, "Go get 'em, Yat." And the next, Tittle, all thumbs, fumbled the hand-off on the three count, recovered the ball, scooped it up and tried to run. More like a butterfly, he fluttered and seemed to go nowhere. Then suddenly he went down. Immobile, with his nose pressed into the dirt and pain leaping up his back, he thought, "My God. How embarassing! One stinking 37-slant!"[11]

Doc Sweeney gave him five weeks in which to recover. During those five weeks Y. A. was forced to realize that he might never play again. Moreover, Tittle was still light years away from becoming one of the guys. His teammates knew the score. Lou Cordilone had been traded for a bespectacled, homesick, punched out bag of an athlete. So he studied. He memorized that Giant playbook (which I remember being as hefty as *War and Peace*). He made friends with his crutches and with great humility entered those whirlpool baths. In effect, he reached some kind of truce with his body because, more than anything else, his home-sickness was driving him nuts.

After their late-summer sojourn on the West Coast, the Giants returned to the Northeast. En route from Salem to training camp at Fairfield University in Connecticut, most of Yat's teammates were met by their families at Idlewild Airport. In Stamford, the team bus made a stop where Andy Robustelli, an avalanche of a man, was swarmed by his eight children, passed around from one to the other as though he were a little feather pillow, his big bruised face splashed with kisses. For Yat, this was just about the last straw. And yet—he was ready to stay, because Andy also epitomized what it meant to be a New York Giant. Robustelli considered the Giants to be "the people's team" and at every opportunity he showed himself to be a man of integrity as well as tenacity. To him the word *athlete* designated merely the process whereby he could become a real citizen and a real man. This was his challenge.

At Loyola Hall, the Giants' dorm at Fairfield University, the team bus pulled out of the parking lot and left Yat standing alone in a cloud of hot exhaust. The younger players had already disappeared into the dormitory as Y. A. struggled up the steps with his luggage. The first floor, he discovered, was sewn up by the veterans. On the second floor he found that all of the doors were locked. And that's when he plunked his bags down and sat on them in the dimly lit corridor like a troll. That's when Y. A. Tittle sank into doubt as deep as quicksand. Would he ever play again? Would he ever be able to get up, for that matter? With difficulty, he stood and started twisting doorknobs again, slowly making his way around to a dank, empty wing where at last he found a room in which to spend the night. And a long night it was—without blankets or sheets.

That was Tittle's first record as a Giant. He was the first veteran in history to spend Sunday afternoon in camp. But the next day, the Giants resumed practice. And Yat welcomed the prospect of watching the drills and dummy scrimmage at his first practice in Connecticut. Coach Allie Sherman, however, informed him early that morning that he was not to show up at practice even in sweat clothes. For that matter, he was not even allowed on the football field. "And one thing more," Sherman said. "Come to my room this afternoon because we need to talk." Naturally, Y. A.'s mind raced back to his meeting with Red Hickey, and he figured that this time he was done for. There wasn't going to be another shot. Sherman would hit the switch.

Coach Sherman motioned for the injured Tittle to come in and sit on the bed. Then he asked, "What do you think of Delbert Shofner?"

The words fell on Y. A.'s ears like the numbers "7 . . . 6 . . . 5 . . ." And the countdown in Yankee Stadium continued as the voices swelled to a magnificent roar.

" . . . A walking scarecrow?" "A clarinet player after a hard one-night stand?"[12] These were descriptions of Delbert Shofner, traded to the Giants from the Los Angeles Rams. Known as "the Blade," Shofner would become Y. A. Tittle's roommate as well as his partner in shining moments, but at first Tittle's back was so sore he could not even get up off the bench to shake Shofner's hand after a stupendous catch.

In the weeks that followed Shofner's arrival at the Giants' camp, Y. A. often found himself leaning on crutches in Yankee Stadium's locker room, alone but for the invisible past heroes who once wiped their sweat in the place where he stood. My father knew that although Ruth and Gehrig were gone, ghostly patterns of success continued to ripple in the stillness. And he felt their luck, their superstitions, breathing in the room. It was a presence to wonder at as he stood there in New York City, standing as if at the bottom of a Grand Canyon of humanity and looking up. The Yankees were winning at the time, and America was going to the moon.

One afternoon in the Giants' locker room, middle linebacker Sam Huff asked Y. A. about his Christmas plans. When Tittle replied that he was anxious to get home to his family, Huff shot back that the Giants would be in the playoffs over the holidays. "Welcome to the champions," snapped Huff. And with those words, Y. A. was almost knocked off his crutches by New York's swift and thrilling undertow.

Tittle felt like a rookie again, trying to make it as a pro, and his enthusiasm helped kindle the rebirth of the Giant offense and the reuniting of the Giant team. Tittle and Shofner became the first offensive players invited to parties given by the Giant defense. The masters of the air and the masters of the earth now moved in unison. Previously, the great Giant defense practically did the scoring. And Tittle would never forget the first time he heard the fighting words, "C'mon, baldy. Punt. And let us get back in and score a few points."

Action commenced. And with Shofner in the equation, the 37-slant was a winner this time around. In the time it took for Y. A.'s back to mend, his old groin injury healed too. In the second game of the season, Conerly was injured and had to leave the game. The Giants were trailing Pittsburgh 14–10 when Tittle ran out on the field with the prayer that his body would hold. He wasted no time. Ten out of 12 passes were completed for 143 yards, 42 of them in the winning touchdown drive. He pulled out the stops, and everyone felt the magic. "It seemed he always waited too long, but he never did. At just the right moment he lofted the pass to one of his backs, often taking his punishment from those onrushing linemen."[13] He showed his teammates that his play calling was "akin to having a coach on the field. Jim Lee Howell once said that he found it almost impossible to chart Y. A.'s tendencies while watching him during a game. "The closest I came was to believe he simply did exactly the opposite of what was expected."[14] According to Robustelli:

> his enthusiasm and competitiveness affected everyone. . . . He inspired everyone to play to his utmost for the overall good of the team. He brought the team together with his spirit, viable because he formed no cliques and ran with none. He had as much time for the defensive players as he had for his offensive teammates; and he treated the stars of the team no differently from the last guy on the bench. After Y. A. became one of our leaders, the split between the offense and defense quickly healed, and we won or lost as a team, not as individual units. . . . [15]

Gooo Giants!
"6 . . . 5 . . . 4 . . ."
The Giants clicked.

In line for the Eastern Championship instead of last place, the "people's team" stood atop the dugout steps listening to the crowd whose emotion was always their proud banner and their hair trigger. Without the New York fans, the Giants could never have done it. Nor could they have done it without the equipment man, Pete

Previte, who came up with the play of the 1961 season—The Giants Special. On a roll with 170 points in four games, the New York Giants had busted the league wide open, beaten Philadelphia, 38–21, Pittsburgh, 42–21, Cleveland, 37–21, and whipped the Redskins, 53–0. The Giants were tied for first place when they met the Eagles. They needed an edge against the Eagles and the Pete Previte Giants Special was it. It was crazy.

> Tittle lined up in the *shotgun* as Patton and Barnes streaked onto the field and took their positions. Before the Eagles even had a chance to see what was happening, five guys were running downfield. Y. A. looked first at Patton, who with Walton and Rote had run underneath patterns, but Jimmy was covered. Shofner took off down the sidelines and got double coverage. But Barnes, who never had played one down of offense in the NFL, headed diagonally across the field, and he was open. Yat and Erich were always on the same side during our Tuesday touch football game, so this hook-up was a natural. Tittle sent the ball to him, and Erich caught it on the run and scored.[16]

And there it was, the Pete Previte Giants Special. Pete, meanwhile, was sweeping out the locker room and listening to the radio. He smiled. And everybody smiled. Even those who hated the game, were forced to admit that outside their childrens' *Anderson's Fairy Tales Book* there was nothing else around so violent and yet so shining. For Tittle, there was nothing like it at all. 1948, 1953, 1957 had been better years from a technical standpoint as an athlete. But nothing compared to those few seconds that signaled the beginning of a legend.

"3 . . . 2 . . . 1 . . ."

From that first day of training camp to this December night in the Bronx, it had been a haul. And if the Bald Eagle had only returned from the underworld of pro football to earn Pete Previte the team ball, I say it was worth the doubt, the two broken transverse processes, the cracked cheekbones, and every phony phone call that ever was. As if to hear from Life itself that he was still in the game, the bald-headed man took off his helmet like one putting on a hearing aid. And at zero seconds, Y. A. Tittle danced like the juggler of Notre Dame amid the pandemonium.

To one and all a winner. And to himself, a winner for the very first time.

When the phone rang in our Atherton kitchen I answered it, and we learned from my father that the Giants had won the Eastern Championship. The news was like rain falling in the desert, but as to the details and specifics there is only one stat that I am able to report. My parents cried for three straight minutes. I had never heard my father cry before, and so I timed him with my new watch. (Somebody in the family had to be practical). One minute. Two minutes. Three minutes.

It was like a song in a scale not found on my piano.

I am also able to report that another trophy arrived for the shelf. We now had an entire civilization and a room full of gleaming bodies made of steel holding up wreaths and worlds. Posture perfect. Indestructible. Not a girl among them. As I grew up, those gold and silver figures stayed the same. And while every other room in the house could be a merry-go-round, that room was inhabited by another race, where only steel eyes fixed upon eternity were allowed.

. . . They took position in the blossoming meadow . . . thousands of them as leaves and flowers appear in their season. . . .
He put over his head a helmet of bull's hide . . . known as the skull cap . . .
He steered his way through the ranks of the front fighters like a fly-ing hawk
who scatters into flight the daws and the starlings.
He stalked through the ranks of the champions . . . with a shrill scream . . .[1]

—Homer

Snow, 1962

The key to the Giants defense was, according to Andy Robustelli, "the ability of middle linebacker Sam Huff to slide into the gaps and make the play."[2]

"In the 1961 title game, played in Green Bay," according to the journalist Barry Gotterher, "the Packers humiliated the Giants in general and Huff in particular. Just about every time Jim Taylor or Paul Hornung carried, the play came right at—and over—Huff. The Packer blocking was superb and Sam Huff had played one of his weakest games as a professional. With this memory, Huff was not out to make friends in the 1962 playoff . . .

"Sure I feel good when I hit someone. That's what I'm getting paid to do. But playing dirty football is something else. If you want to play dirty, it will cost you a $50 fine from the league. I don't have that kind of money to throw around."[3]

When Dad was home from New York, he broke the ice by wearing a toupé. He played Ping-Pong with my brothers, even one game with me. Talk about blood sports. It was a compliment I suppose that I was being treated like a true competitor. Rally, rally, dink—slam! Dad never gives me a break. He calls me a "monkey on a string" when it comes down to a close point.

But you could not pay me to play croquet with him again. If I did, I might have run away from home. The way he sent me to kingdom come, just so he could go through the wicket. And then he would come over, jiggle my shoulder and say, "Isn't this fun?" I think the competitive spirit is more like the big bad wolf!

In the fall of 1962 we moved east, and in Tuckahoe, New York, we raced through the streets at night with cloth braids pinned on for power, and my brothers came after us with broomsticks. There was Pat, singer of songs. Horrible, humming, mocking songs which no adult could hear since they went straight from under the skin to shatter the gates of hell and send every monster screaming. And Mike, who raised the butter knife high in the air and wore choochoo train pajamas.

Basically, they were boys who marched to the drumbeat of a single word, *trespass*, and respected only dirt, scary stories, and equals. By day, they leaped over fire pits and made clay eyeballs. By night, they were the Sioux warriors who scoffed at houses and telephone lines—rode roughshod, churned the flowers, smelled of bay leaves, and spoke no English. Occasionally, they might resurrect a stricken parakeet or Easter duck, but then they would thunder off to a far country, decapitating every single rose bush on the way.

But for a time, one could not ask for more. Life was as good as clouds. And the great Giants defense was making mincemeat out of Jimmy Brown. After their turn would come ours, as thousands poured onto the field at twilight to let their dreams play on the darkening grass. Once, we saw people laughing and rolling in the mud after a victory. The lucky ones tore down the wooden goalposts, while we waved pennants or held warm chestnuts. Never were we in a hurry to separate ourselves from the chaos of our lives, because it was our ritual, for better or worse. We were the displaced wavers of wands and pine cones from out of the ancient world. And the Giants were our guys, and New York was our town.

I think Dad is getting too used to calling his own plays because he is expecting us to listen at home and even to obey his orders. I think he should be getting this out of his system on the football field. We are not his receivers and we go our own way even if he threatens to get a switch. Great-Aunt Dorothy goes in for hairbrushes and she uses them on my brothers whenever she babysits. If Mom and Dad are out, she makes them stand out in the dark hallways and wait their turn for punishment. "I'm gonna blister your hide," she says. And she means it. To me she just says, "Stop running around or your uterus will fall out!" What do I want with a uterus? But sometimes I think this word is all that stands between me and Dorothy's hairbrush.

But Dad, on the other hand, could not hurt a flea. Sometimes when we drive him to the end of his rope, he will slap his own hand, as if the sound would scare us. And I've only a couple of times seen him stomp out to the tree in front and rip a switch from my bookshelf branch. Even then he just switched the ground like Zorro does his whip.

Now I lay me down to sleep . . . As my parents hummed the words, I sank into them and caught a glimpse of the bald eagle making wide arcs and flying high above the sparrows, taking his own good time, just like a solitary creature should. To be sure, the creature would not condescend to flap his wings, but would swoop, or stay where he was, indifferent, as if it were the most natural thing in the world to be beautiful.

God bless, God bless so and so . . . My mother smoothed my brow and swept aside the curtain of my imagination so that I could pretend to be a potato growing inside the earth or an ear of yellow corn bursting at high noon. Then, sinking deeper, I would end up at the bottom of all the arenas that ever were. The dust was very fine there, and before the lions came I could listen to the human roar and practice making stars with my finger.

If my parents only knew that when they tucked me into bed at night I was practicing as a potato or playing cheerleader to Athena fighting the Gorgon with Perseus, I know that I would have been in big trouble. But there is nothing like living in what others think is a fairy tale to make a person appreciate the value of myth, which deals more often than not with an unhappy ending and a good struggle, as opposed to the fairy tale, which honors the happy ending above all else. I was drawn to myth, because unhappy endings and good struggles made sense. Besides, I was the daughter of someone who did not even know that he was in the business of mythmaking.

Childhood then marked the least innocent days of my life. Those were the days when I believed that all cheerleaders should be put to death for acting like ballerinas at a bullfight. To me the game was a once-a-week opportunity where it was good to cross the lines. I could freely play any part of a person or a thing. Like a dream, I could be a pass, a fumble, the rain and the torn green grass all at once. I could be the air. It was fun to tumble in that tidal wave of hope.

During this time many thought I was lucky because I knew a hero. But all I knew was a somebody no bigger than my thumb fighting a big clock and being beaten up. My real luck came from being a girl, because I was free to think that we were supposed to love what kept on trying. Since no-body bothered to tell me any different, over the course of many Sundays, I grew up despising Tinkerbells, fairies, and all little-girl cuteness. I liked the Vikings and the Rams because they taught me to set my mind as a trap for wild gods. Andy Robustelli mopping sweat from his brow, and high-stepping Gifford on the run. Real heroes because they gave the gift of inspiration.

Frank Gifford.

Today Mike and Pat washed Mr. Jay's new car in the driveway with Brillo pads. The car was all covered with soap, so at first no-body noticed the scratches. Mr. Jay was going to hand Mike two quarters, and then Pat turned on the hose. I don't think Mr. Jay was such a football fan after that.

It is for this reason that I will now be forever grateful that I don't have to learn the value of a dollar. Dad says that my brothers have to make money but I will most likely marry a shoesalesman and live in Bakersfield. I don't think I'll do that because Bakersfield is a terrible place. It is like an egg that just fries in the middle of a skillet. We are always throwing up by the time we pass the sign to Bakersfield. I have explained that I am going to be a writer and a missionary and an archaeologist. Of course, Dad says that writers mostly write home for money, and that I should just learn shorthand.

Sunday afternoons at Yankee Stadium in 1962 always began with 80,000 screaming fans and my prayer: *Dear Lord, give me two heads but please don't make me a cheerleader.*

For the players there was Father Dudley.

"We give thanks for this opportunity to be together . . ."

Mean Sam Huff and Rosey Grier—their heads are bowed, only they are thinking (How are we going to get back at Concrete Charley?)

"Heavenly Father, help us to do our best . . ."

Uh oh, thinks Yat, *that means win by three touchdowns.*

"And may the best man win."

"Yeah!" shrieks Rosey Grier. "I'm gonna kill that sonofabitch the first play of the ball game!"

After the away games, the coaches usually sat back on the airplane and sipped two beers slowly. If they lost:

"Well, they didn't do a damn thing we told them to."

"Why on earth do you think Yat would throw the ball when we were on the one-yard line, coach? I just don't understand it."

"No, if they had just executed what we practiced, it should have been a snap. The other team didn't show us a thing we didn't prepare them for."

If they won:

"What a day! Can you believe that double reverse I put in?"

"Yeah, but what about that safety blitz? That was just the way I planned it."

"I do believe that was the best game plan we have ever had."

"Yep. Just like on the drawing board. I knew it was going to work. What did I tell ya?"

Meanwhile, among the players, little was said. Typically, there was only the stewardess speaking in low whispers to Yelberton.

"I'm sorry sir, but this section is reserved for the athletes."

"But I am a player," says the quarterback in bifocals.

"I'm sorry, sir. I mean for the active players."

Yankee Stadium was home to the New York Giants. From my seat in the mezzanine I watched men come together peacefully and temporarily seem to know where they were going, even if it was only to their seats. The people smelled good in the glaring emptiness of the concrete stadium, making it come alive with their cigarettes and their hurrying, their elbows and their anticipation. At Yankee Stadium, we wound our way past the sweet smell of lipstick and beer breath to that inner sanctum of mayhem. Yankee Stadium was where we settled into our seats and felt happy. It was where men showed emotion, and where we were able to feel proud in the end for having smelled a whiff of courage.

While some might point a finger at those who allowed themselves to act like animals, there at least were everyday people coming together in droves to celebrate the achievements of somebody else. It did not happen that way at the bank. Nobody got drunk with joy over the accomplishments of a loan officer. The sky usually glowered, but in 1962, I'll eat one raunchy helmet if I lie—we were *where the wild things were*. Chanted obscenities, the blond in the tacky outfit, and the man who was most welcome in your life because he would sell you peanuts. Yankee Stadium. Greater than the Acropolis or the Taj Majal! Where the seas actually parted. You felt peaceful, and it was kind of nice that there was no mercy or compassion for the loser—because frankly he was the bum. He was the reminder that you were human.

We have made a commercial, an oatmeal commercial. We were put up at a hotel in New York City and we went to the studio next morning. They gave us outfits, they combed our hair and put makeup on our faces and on top of Dad's head. This was the first time in my life I wore lipstick and put on nylons. Then we went into a room filled with lightbulbs and sat down at a kitchen table. My father faced the camera. My brothers were on both sides of him. My back was to the camera and my mother stood at the sink.

"Hai," said my mother in a Southern accent. "That's my husband Y. A. Tittle. He needs plenty of energy and that's why I give him H-O Oatmeal." Then the cameraman came down near my father and my brothers. Their cereal bowls were in front of them. Dad did need some energy. His eyes were half-closed and his voice stayed on one note. He looked like a drug addict.

Dad looked down at his bowl (of slop), then he looked up. "Yes, I do need plenty of energy," says my father, "and H-O Oatmeal tastes great." Then he turned to Mike and Pat who were chewing as fast as they could. He said, "How 'bout it, boys?" They both choked down their last clump of oatmeal and shouted, "Tastes great, Pop!"

This took about *twelve hours.*

I cannot believe there are jobs like this. Of course we never ate H-O Oatmeal before that day. And I *promise* I would rather eat a mushed eyeball! At least with football they're not just pretending to play.

Having lost two of three opening games in 1962, the real battle for the New York Giants was the game played on October 21 against the Detroit Lions. This game marked the turning point after which the Giants took nine straight wins and their division title. And at the same time, *Spartacus* was playing. On one of our Wednesday family nights we had dinner at Albanezi's Diner and went to see the film. There were the slave gladiators, in the arena and in revolt. There was Kirk Douglas, with his dimple, saying, "Verennia! Verennia!" as if destiny was in the word. Of course, he was just pretending, too.

Hut 1! Hut 2! I'd seen it all before on a nature program that showed a wildebeest in trouble. Tittle at the center for the snap count. Tittle fading back, and me and my family sitting on the edge of our seats with Kirk Douglas fighting in our bellies. Fortunately, our defense *wanted* that win desperately, and our offensive line had more moves than funnel clouds.

Detroit. Allie Sherman told his players, "Nobody runs straight at Karras and Brown and the rest of those big boys. They are always trying to run slants and sweeps with fancy angle blocking. But that is not the way. You've got to beat those front four guys head to head. You can't pussyfoot around them. That is what we will do Sunday. We will take the ball and run it straight at them. We will not look for the easy way. We will beat them right up front, man to man, and we will win the game."[4]

Sherman told me years later: "At that time, of course, you played each team in your division twice. Pro football had a much stronger identity then, because there weren't that many teams, so you got to know your guys and those of the opposition. The emotional fabric was different. Some of the rules were different.

"I can tell you," said Coach Sherman, "We had any number of great games, great beautiful games in '62. We'd go out there and those teams would get that glazed look in their eyes because our ball moved around. He'd [Y. A.] throw it here and throw it there and then would come that little dinky screen. . . . Let me tell you," he said, "about a leader. Is there anything with more variables than the human element? Therefore, if you are the chief officer it is up to you to feel, to understand, to sense and see as many of the variables in as much depth as you can in the service of excellence."

He sat back. "I'll tell you a little something about your dad. In 1962, I'm watching the traditional Thanksgiving Day game between Detroit and Green Bay. With Detroit there was Alex Karras and he had sacked Bart Starr 10 times. I start laughing as my wife Joannie walks by. 'What's so funny?' she says. 'Well,' I say, 'here's the greatest team. And what the hell are we going to do?'

"On Monday morning, the coaches met at 8:00 in the Essex Hotel overlooking Central Park. They got into their jammies, because they wouldn't come out until Tuesday. We'd look at film of the games. Ken Kavenaugh said, 'Look at those holes in the secondary. We can throw the ball there.'

"'Only one problem, Ken.'

"'What's that?'

"'I've never in all my years ever learned how to teach a quarterback to throw when he's lying flat on his back. Hell, those holes are open, but we've got to have Y. A. standing up to throw. Look what they did to Green Bay! They're tough. They're good.'

"We went back and forth like that. To make a long story short, on Wednesday morning at 1:00 I tell 'em I think there is only one way we can go with these people.

"'What's that?'

"I said, 'Run the ball.'

"Well, they all fell down laughing. They figured I was out of my mind. (It was always a standing joke with the coaches, 'How many of the running plays do you think Y. A. is going to use?') So I said, 'I'll tell you what. We go to our regular offense—they get to Y. A. . . . . Let's put a running game in there. I tell ya that I don't want him to throw a ball over eight yards the first half until he gets word from us, and this way we'll make sure that Karras, Brown, Joe Schmidt charge full steam ahead with blitzes and all. We will lessen the pass rush and then we'll see where we go.'

"Oh, it was so simple. We double-teamed both of them. Oh, I won't get into all of that. Y. A. would remember. We got through with it, we got ready to present it to the team. And Pops (line coach Ed Kolman) said, 'Tell me how you make out with the old man.'

"So, okay. I sat down with Y. A. and said, 'Look. I'm going to tell you something now I've never told you before, and I hope I don't ever have to tell you again. This is going to be the one major percentage shot we have at getting this team.' And he looked at me.

"'I say we've got to run. Also, you must not throw a ball over eight yards.' Yat's eyes opened up!

"'But,' he said.

"'Y. A., the reason I want eight yards, look, I don't care if you don't complete one of them just so long as they don't sack you. It creates a pressure and mentality for them, and for us, and for the other teams they play. Just as long as they don't sack you. Well, think about it.'

"Next day we went to work. By Thursday, he was working and practicing. We wanted to make those defensive linemen dig in there and start worrying about running. And then Kavanaugh says to me, 'Well? You think he's going to hold up to it?'

"'Who?'

"'Y. A. You think he's going to stay with that damn run.'

"I said, 'What's the matter? You wanna bet?'

"'Yeah, I wanna bet.'

"'I believe he is, Ken. But I won't betcha. Let's see what happens.'

"We went out, I'll never forget, against the Detroit Lions. We took the opening kickoff and we were running double dives. We started going upfield three yards, three and a half yards. We made it to mid-field and crossed mid-field. Oh, the hum in the stands! People could not believe this was their team! Their great, beautiful, exciting, passing team hadn't thrown a ball yet and we usually opened a game with a pass.

"Well, we stayed all the way on the ground, chewing it up all the way into the end zone for a touchdown. Phil King and Alex Webster chewing it up like that. It turned into a most beautiful ball game—a real traditional ball game, where both lines on both teams played beautiful football up the front. The game was 17–14, and we won. It was a great day. And your dad, he told me later that night at a late supper at Toot Shor's, 'Well, I gotta tell ya, ya made a believer out of me. I couldn't believe it, but I guess we can do it running once in a while.' He had discipline that day. I was asking him to be something that wasn't a part of his nature."

What Allie did not tell was that my father suffered from amnesia during the first half of that game against the Lions. Early on, Dick "Night Train" Lane nailed Tittle on a bootleg. When Yat stood up, for a second the earth bent on its axis before his mind went blank. Pain evaporated then, and every play, every formation disappeared into a black hole. But he felt great.

Having scored on his bootleg, my father trotted to the sidelines. Sherman began talking to him and mentioned the 34 automatic, a standard play in the Giant repertoire. Yat had never heard of it before. And it wasn't until halftime that his mind cleared and he shouted over to Coach Sherman, "You're right Coach! I do know that play!" They carried the day against the Detroit Lions, but Tittle suffered another injury. He took a bad blow to his right elbow which caused him to bleed, bruise, stiffen, and swell. He was forbidden to practice or to play in the upcoming game against the Washington Redskins. On Saturday, however, his elbow bent, miraculously.

And on the next day, Sunday, October 28, Tittle conducted a football sonata. Lady Luck pasted a smacker on my father in front of the multitudes that afternoon and left a record for him, seven touchdown passes, and a fellowship of jubilation that those in heaven itself would die for. Team. Fans. They called it championship fever.

Said Frank Gifford:

I've never seen anyone like him. Y. A. is like a high school kid with a Univac brain and a great passing arm. . . . His biggest—and best—afternoon came against the Washington Redskins, who led the Eastern division, at Yankee Stadium on October 28. In one of the most amazing afternoons in NFL history, Tittle completed 27 of 39 passes for 505 yards and tied the league record for seven touchdowns in one game. Afterwards Tittle was his quietly restrained self. "My job is to direct the team over the goal line in some way," he explained. "It doesn't make a heck of a lot of difference whether it's 100 yards passing and 300 yards running or 300 yards passing and 100 running. We throw a lot because we have the players to catch them."[5]

Frank Gifford (*l.*) and Y. A. Tittle at Yankee Stadium.

I have decided never to marry or have children. No punishment will ever bother me as long as nobody touches my books. I am happy to go to bed with the sun still up. I make the Land of Counterpane, and I have my music box and my books, whatever happens in my life.

TITTLE SKALPS SKINS! THROWS SEVEN TD PASSES! On Broadway, the Planter's Peanut sign had announced the news. Broad daylight. People standing on a city street in earmuffs and overcoats, clapping. All my father could say to me was, "How could you spend twenty dollars on a flute instead of a pair of shoes?"

The Giant team was on the move. And just as Tittle once ran in front of Miss Poole's boarding house against the seventeen-year-old Bobby Layne, he was running now, all out, and reaching for that flashing sports baton once more.

Layne, like many of Tittles contemporaries, had retired by this point. Naturally, Bobby, who retired from professional football as the most productive passer of all time, did not go quietly. He expressed some pointed cynicism about the direction in which game was going and the players who were more interested in money and investing in the stockmarket than the meaning of teamwork. In an age of waning patriotism, the game of football seemed to be just the caboose. Layne did not miss the glory, did not miss the glamor image and the toll it took on his family, and he did not miss the sportswriters. In fact, he said that "being a pro football player was a lot like being a used car dealer, sooner or later, you're a son of a bitch . . . But I'll tell you what I miss," he said. "I miss the guys. That's what I miss more than anything. I miss the road trips and the card games. I miss the fellowship. The practice sessions. I miss the ball games. . . . We had that perfect thing for a while. What I miss now is my teammates."6

Tittle had his teammates. What he wanted was that perfect thing. And in 1962 he got it.

A few weeks after the game against Washington, the Giants faced Dallas. Says Andy Robustelli:

> When we got down to the four yardline, Tittle wanted to call a running play against the Dallas Cowboys, but as had happened in his seven-TD game against the Redskins, he met with some firm opposition inside the huddle.
>
> "Forget it, Y. A.," Webster told him. "Go for the record. Throw the damn ball."
>
> "We could probably run it in just as easy," Yat argued. "They have to know we're thinking about a pass."

"We didn't bring you this far to have you run it," Shofner said. "Throw it. We only have a three-point lead, and you never can tell what might happen."

So Tittle threw the record-breaking pass to Walton (33 touchdowns in a season) and it was a terrific way to end the season . . . it sent us into the title against against the Packers fully confident that we could win. We also felt that playing in Yankee Stadium and away from the frozen condition of Green Bay would also be to our advantage. After all, New York can be cold at the end of December, but it has to be better than Green Bay, right?[7]

Wrong. December 30. On game day, championship number two, the sky over Yankee Stadium was blue and the winds like razor blades. I read somewhere that the Giants were creamed on the ice once, and in 1962 they were beaten by the wind. "It's sour grapes. We just plain lost," my father tells me.

In 1962 the Packers won a second consecutive NFL championship, and Green Bay's Jimmy Taylor broke Jimmy Brown's record for most yardage gained in a season, 1,474 yards.

At "wind-blown, frozen Yankee Stadium," wrote Barry Gottehrer:

> Jimmy Taylor demonstrated the animal courage and strength that have made him one of the most remarkable ball-carriers in football history. Keyed to stop Taylor, the Giants, led by middle-linebacker Sam Huff, started pounding and piling on the Packer fullback from the opening minutes. His right elbow stiffened by pain and five stitches, his tongue splintered and pouring blood down his throat, and his head and ribs numbed from countless elbows and knees, Taylor continued to carry the ball and continued to fight back. He elbowed several Giants, kneed a few others, and even bit defensive tackle, Dick Modzelewski. In all he carried 31 times for 85 yards, gaining the yardage vital in Green Bay's 16–7 victory. "I don't remember ever being hit so hard," said Taylor, running his split tongue over his bloodied lips. "I bled all game."[8]

I am happy to report that my own experience was slightly different. At championship number two, my own belief in the fairness of the world was loosed in my deepest and darkest, pagan child-self like a helium balloon attached to a thread of blood. Naturally, I wanted the world to be fair. As a child, I saw that as one of my main jobs—to say "it wasn't fair" when it wasn't.

At the championship, however, those many thousands of people in the stadium presented an overwhelming challenge to my eyes. And I confess that I could not always rise wholeheartedly to the occasion when presented with the spectacle of all those people trying to pin the tail on the donkey—my dad, Jimmy Taylor, or anybody else. But in 1962 I discovered that if the world could not be fair, and if I was ever tempted to stop wanting or want less because it did not made sense to try, then I would just have to remember Rosey Grier, and how the Giants wanted and kept wanting harder, no matter how silly it seemed and no matter how desperate the silliness got.

The example of the New York football Giants left me with a determination to believe in the possibility of fairness when it no longer made sense to believe. And like them, I would never give up.

Guess what! A little girl who was kidnapped was dropped off in front of our house when I was playing in my tree. Her dress was torn and she was crying in the middle of the street. I invited her into my tree and told her to sit in the living room. My parents and the neighbors came outdoors and looked at the little girl. One neighbor told my parents they should not get involved even though he goes to church every week. He said it could be dangerous. "I don't care!" is all I heard my father say. They ran into the house to make phone calls. The little girl stayed with me and I gave her imaginary food from the cubby holes in the tree trunk. I fed her on plates of leaves.

GO! GO!

"Simplicity," said Coach Sherman, "was the key in 1963.

"In 1963, as you know, everyone was thinking that we couldn't repeat. They say that you soften up the next year because everyone enjoys greater riches. And it was difficult in New York to maintain the mental and emotional commitment when there was more of that puff and that pfaff of glory surrounding you. I'm just saying that a man could soften up a lot quicker because you've got more people gladhanding you and backpatting. But indeed, winning starts from that invisible point with the individual. And it's like anything you strive to achieve. As soon as you achieve the first leg of whatever it is, you cannot allow yourself one ounce of self-satisfaction. This is what real winners have and you don't qualify that by one game. That's unreal.

"Hey," said Coach Sherman. "There's an art form, you know, to throwing the screen. Everyone thinks in terms of the linemen. That's not what makes it go. It's the quarterback. The quarterback makes the screen pass go, because he's a great actor. He must look like he's in trouble, panicking in effect, so he can draw those defensive linemen into him with smoke coming out of their noses, thinking they are going to sack the quarterback. Yat made it go. But you know what? It's not just your steps, it's the body English. The look in the guy's eyes, the way he holds his head. Y. A. would get that look in his eye, and man, we had screens, different kinds, drawing straight back. We used a little rollout, but your dad would roll out 25 yards. They'd chase him out to the side and he'd throw back to the center. It would help us crack a game open, but how different can you look? Everyone knew to watch out for that rollout screen. But it was a tribute to his acting. There he was in the crucible. So sure. So precise. So confident.

"Against Baltimore your dad ran the best bootleg I ever saw. Just like that rollout screen they knew he was going to run. He faked a handoff to Alex Webster and circled out. He was not an Olympic sprint champion you know, but he ran it, got a score on it and someone fell on him and collapsed his lung. I asked the doctor, 'Is he in danger? What's the time frame?'

"'You have to give Mother Nature a chance. It could be three weeks,' Dr. Tony told me.

"The third day after the injury your father started throwing again, and I'll be damned if he didn't look better than ever.

"'Yeah, I'm a little sore,' he admitted. 'But come on, Allie, did you see me throw that ball today?'"

Sherman went home and told his wife Joannie that the old Bald Eagle was talking about that lung the way somebody else would talk about an earache. And she told him that if he dared play that old man against the Steelers, she would leave him. Not to worry, Allie told her. But it wasn't going to be easy. He would have to fight him.

"Well, I called him into my room the day before the game and he said, 'I feel great. We can take these babies.'

"'Yeah, but I'm not going to play you. If we win it, fine. If we don't, we'll get it back. The percentage isn't there, Y. A. Tony Pizano says the lung is coming back into shape but it's got to come back the whole way.' I showed him the diagram. It was very slight that it could be life-endangering, but it could happen. Well, he didn't play. And we got skunked. 31–zip!"

September 1963. At dawn, Coach Allie Sherman heard the chant and looked out of his small window at the Giants training camp in Fairfield, Connecticut. In the haze, at least 10,000 fans were sitting on the sloping hill, having come some 60 miles from the city to watch the inner squad scrimmage. Some were holding bed-sheets covered with the encouraging words:

GO! GO! GO!

In some ways I think that everyone is like most football players everywhere. Everything hits them and they just take it because they have to.

In 1963, Y. A. Tittle became a full blown sports phenomenon. According to one TV program, he was "the oldest pro quarterback in football and the most productive."[9] And though weather had conspired with fate in 1961 and 1962, "once again his battle cry for a world championship was heard and the Giants charged to the top with new records of achievement."[10] In 1963 the NFL started keeping records for sacked QBs. The Giants' defense led the league with 57. In that year, Tittle broke his own league record from the year before and threw 36 touchdowns. His passing records, which superseded those of Sammy Baugh, Sid Luckman, and Bobby Layne, also invited vicious tackles. This, I was told, is a compliment for a great quarterback.

For us children, the 1963 season began with our name like a toy in the hands of the world. But that's when we had to buckle down and concentrate. Nothing could stand in the way of the pretend sacrifice and the ritual crossing of fingers, arms, legs, and feet in exchange for field goals and touchdowns. That was the deal you struck with destiny until the pinch. Then you crossed your eyes for luck. Maybe to a casual spectator we looked like pretzel-kids, but really, we were as fine-tuned as yogi masters. As children of our parents we became children of the game. In the end, we were destiny brokers, we struck deals with the angels and we bartered with the wind. And, we could spit nails with humans twice our size and enjoy it. We were wicked, mean, nasty, and bad.

On the home front, however, it was difficult. There, in Tuckahoe, we were like moons. We thought we were beautiful. We didn't know that we shone by reflected lights. And then, it was confusing to be always treated like the emissary of a barbarian king when you were coming of age in the 1960s. Strangers ablaze with questions seemed to know more than we did. And they always made our father seem as far away as the stars.

My brothers and I also received a small share of compliments and lingering glances relative to our station in life as the children of somebody. I will never forget the day my brothers discovered to their shock and dismay that quarterback Y. A. Tittle did not play for the Harlem Globetrotters. But worse, my brother's Pop Warner coach made such a point of who Y. A. Tittle was that Mike came home after practice with his arm prodigiously wrapped up and trailing bandages behind. It was broken, he claimed. He couldn't play anymore. We would not have been half as sad if his arm had actually been broken. It was sad because not since my brother had last run away to Alaska in his pajamas had he worn the same lost look. Typically, Mike got as far as the mailbox and stood there, armed with a butter knife and holding a plum, for about five minutes before the look came on. And if he couldn't go to Alaska, it always happened that Alaska came to him, and its white-cold terrain stole my brother's face right down to his lips. And so, there it was. Rather than try and fail, Mike's own brilliant hand-eye coordination was put to rest in his mind and shipped off to the snow country.

As for me, on my first day as an eighth grader at Ursuline School, I rummaged through my mother's dresser drawer for some good luck magic and came up with a maternity top and a girdle. I chose the girdle. No stockings. Perfectly white, unshaved legs. But the girdle made me feel like I had a secret weapon, and with it I could probably find my way to the right class and have everyone be nice to me. In spite of its magic, however, the school day began, and there I was walking down the halls in cardboard underwear, feeling as conspicuous as a triceratops. Everywhere there were chattering goddesses with perfectly formed calf muscles and artichoke hairdos, hanging out in low-cut flats that showed the cleavage between their toes. How they swam through halls filled with laughter and secrets!

In science class, our teacher made each of us say our name. When I said mine,—"You!" he said. "Just don't think for a moment that you are anything special." I looked up, wishing my eyes were magic wands. Ashamed, I looked down again, when I found that they weren't. Such was the power of a name that suddenly my girdle was turning to concrete and my eyes were boring through the floor toward China. And that's where the difference between the good of the hero and the evil of hero worship first showed itself to me—in science.

When the bell rang, I could not keep myself from tiptoeing across the linoleum like a nun on a tightrope. But when Mr. Mele actually reached out as if to touch my shoulder and catch me with his smile, I moved. Determined to make it into the hall before my tears broke out full blown, I shot past the chattering goddesses, zoomed through the clusters of artichoke hairdos, and swore that I would never cry like that again unless I was happy.

I felt better immediately when I got home after school. For one thing, a woman by the name of Barbara Walters was coming to the house to interview my mother, which meant extra food in the icebox. For another, my brother Pat was crying. After only one day at the Immaculate Conception Elementary school, he was going to be excommunicated. I tried telling him that he wasn't Catholic, but somehow that was beside the point.

"I'm a *lostsheepfromtheonetruefold*," he said with feeling.

"Me too," I said. Yet when my English teacher had called me the same *lostsheepfromtheonetruefold*, I had assumed it was nothing but an ancient swear word and decided not to worry.

"Shut up!" my brother said. He was a sinner. And that's why he had lost his appetite. He was so full of sin.

And then, between sniffs, Pat explained how the lady dressed up like the man in the moon had stood in front of the class and insinuated that God had dirty hands when he made the world. And wimps. He told about the wimps on the playground who made fun of our father and who laughed at him when it was his turn at bat. Luckily, he cracked that ball a country mile. (No more sniffs.) Yet when they found out that he was good, that, he discovered, was the biggest sin of all! Then Mike lumbered in through the door, wearing invisible handcuffs. From him we learned that the man three doors down had said that our father was a dumb jock who had married a Korean.

Dumb jock. Remember? Before football players were all millionaires, the phrase was very popular. On some days, it seemed that every house on our street was inhabited by people who accused our father of stupidity, of blowing a bootleg, of marrying a woman with Indian blood. Not to his face, of course. To ours.

Hero-worshipers of this sort did not honor their heroes. Instead, they became jealous of the image their devotion had created. When this happened, cowards were born, who only liked a person for his mistakes, so that they could worship failure. Certainly, hero-worshipers like these were in the minority. But in their own way they, too, were true competitors, who not only wallowed in my father's numerous football failures but gloried in them. They pecked at the sons and daughters with gusto. And their revenge packed a punch.

In my own personal quest for a hero, it didn't take me long to discover that hero worship was like a hurricane. It was the one place you could be sure the hero was not, because, like anybody else with sense, he would have fled for cover. I began to wonder not only where, but what the hero was, apart from this hurricane. And I started to notice that those people who felt a certain gratitude to the one who let them worship were the last to care if the hero even existed.

If nothing else, I felt confident that I could sharpen my wits by learning what the hero was not and staying the course as a football player's daughter. At the very least, I knew a sports hero who sat calmly in the eye of his hurricane, and, at the height of his career, took pride in his banana pancakes. (On weekends when he was home he delighted in cooking us five-course breakfasts, always expecting our suburban appetites to expand to those of a Texas farmhand.) But of course this was not what anyone cared about. They did not want gladiators in the kitchen.

When we peeked into the living room that afternoon, it was to hear the voices of women speaking in words like swallows and to see Barbara Walters meet the murderous distraction of our baby brother, Rookie, the infant totem of the legendary Yat. Despite the cameras and the action, it was the intelligence of women that slowly filled the room, while that tiniest of Tittle faces kept trying to tell my father's tale with only a look of grim determination. Barbara Walters was asking our mother about us. She referred to these so-called vicious tackles that my father seemed to invite and she wondered how the family felt, seeing Tittle constantly so bloody and bowed.

"Do you become used to it?" she asked.

"Never," came my mother's reply.

And then the TV cameras zeroed in as if to film the fact that nothing ever promised to be easy. Our infant brother began turning every color of the color chart. As our mother lifted him from his wretched mechanical swing, perspiration poured off her forehead, and a thrilling, telltale thread of spit no less than four feet long came out of our brother's mouth and made it all the way to the floor. For us, this lone startling detail was like a life buoy thrown out in the hallway.

And so it was that we survived childhood in spite of a steady stream of forehand and backhand compliments. My brothers, Mike and Pat, were sometimes ashamed of living in a nice house or afraid to bring their friends home. And my very first blind date blew past me like a jet plane at the front door, disappeared with my father to the shuffleboard court out back, and became before my very eyes—as a mosquito—lost to the bright halo and swoosh of glory. But perhaps you survive any childhood, really, with the sense that, like Jonah, you have suddenly been belched up from the belly of the whale; and though you may feel a thousand things, you know you are grateful.

> "Sure it hurts when I throw, it hurts all the time."
>
> —Johnny Unitas, quarterback Baltimore Colts[11]

> "I used to be for the underdog. But now I agree with coach Lombardi. I'm for the upperdog. I was for the underdog because I was one. Now I see the pressures that are on the upperdog. When you get to be an upperdog, you know the scratching, clawing and grabbing that everybody underneath does to knock you off your perch. The average fan cannot appreciate the pressure and the emotional peak you must reach each week to keep from getting knocked off your perch at the top."
>
> —Bart Starr, quarterback, Green Bay Packers[12]

October. People had some odd notions about football games. A psychologist on the airplane told me that "football has everything to do with the position of the egg." Girls used to waltz up to me and announce that football was *violent*. Then they would swish off like Telulah Bankhead. (A subset of the group of girls who knew they weren't supposed to *get* math—and didn't—likewise, these girls didn't get football because they weren't supposed to, or because it was violent, or because girls were supposed to keep dirt out of their fingernails and their souls out of the mud.) I didn't get football either, I admit. But it was not the violence on the field that bothered me. It was the assumption that we were not all a part of it—the violence, I mean. At least Big Daddy Lipscomb

had the honesty to step on my father's hand openly and forth-
rightly, which is more than I can say for those sportswriters who
trampled and stomped from daylight until dark, but pretended
that they were stepping on nobody. Off the field, in language, on
TV, everywhere, there was violence without end. And it wasn't all
bad. At the dinner table, our meals and even our Buster Brown
shoes told the tale of winners and losers. My father gave thanks
for our blessings. And I said to myself, *God bless the losers.* Because
that's one thing sports could teach you—who the winners and
losers were.

Having encountered strong opinions on violence in sports, I
was sometimes forced to think about it even when I didn't want
to. And this brings me to the one aspect of football violence that
concerned me the most in 1963—the ritual aspect, as it was
termed. Some people were fond of commenting about the *ritual*
in which my father took part. They didn't boo. They simply ab-
horred the violence inherent in the form. They didn't cheer, but
were nonetheless fascinated and drawn in by the human sacrifice
implied in the action. Comparisons were constantly being made,
for instance, between football players and the gladiators of ancient Rome. But I began to wonder if the violence in sport did
not obscure the question of sacrifice, a question that our society
had ignored. As a word, *sacrifice* was even more unpopular than
Hester Prynne. And the question I had was this: What, in 1963,
had sacrifice come to mean? Both on TV and in the news, it
seemed as if society sang a continual song of human sacrifice,
with no ritual to attend it, and only sport gave us back that ritual.

Fascinated, repulsed, yet drawn to games as we were, one had
to wonder if the place of sport in our culture and the issue of violence did not suggest that human sacrifice was still with us, still
a part of our lives, still a part of the human experience. Maybe I
could have come up with an answer to the violence if I had understood the meaning of this word. But I did not understand the
meaning of sacrifice, because the word only came up at Sunday
school. The rest of the time it hung unregarded, like an old calen-
dar in a locker room.

I will say this, however. That even when my father came home covered with blood-soaked bandages, I wasn't fazed. And had the stands become a sea of Neros where fat thumbs by the legion pointed down, we were never in Rome, because out there on the field the players were enacting the story of Isaac, and his father, Abraham, with that perplexed look on his face. Just as those two came along in our history and let it be known that to make sacrifice one did not have to die, one just had to know its *meaning*, so those players enacted for me the modern version of this Sunday story by coming onto the field with their double dives and their zigouts. Perhaps we had not learned from our other institutions what sacrifice really means, or how it could be useful to us all, how it could inspire us to go beyond ourselves, or how it might sometimes ensure the survival of our species. And how were we to learn this meaning, the good meaning of sacrifice, and to value it in a culture that practices human sacrifice on every front but refuses to call it by name? To what altar in our suburbs did we go? At least on the playing field, the riddle presented itself as honestly as a Sunday school parable.

November. Where were the heroes? Like the gods of old, were they still coming to our doorsteps in disguise? If so, then the time had come for the giftgiver to span the centuries and knock on some doors on our street. The time had come, in my opinion, for a real hero to show his face. And that, I suppose, was the way it really was by 1963.

The nun at the head of the class caught me struggling like a seagull on my bony knees as I prayed for the dying president. What did she expect? We locked eyes. But instead of shrinking under her unwavering gaze, I grew, because I could imagine the kind Norse god, Baldur, not only from the steady gentleness in her expression but from the stoop of the old woman. The president was shot. And that was bad news for everybody. But in the aftermath, I found out something more about the hero.

On the Sunday after Kennedy died, the Giants played the Dallas Cowboys. I made it to my seat in time for the national anthem, and even though I heard it every week, I had never heard that song before. Everybody sang. And together, we hit that high note.

Then the wind blew. Nobody moved and everybody listened. In silence, we bore witness. It was just like church, except Yankee Stadium was a place where everyone wanted to be. I was proud of all those people who had shown their emotion. At least 80,000 people stood silently with heads bowed to the wind. The players also stood very still, with their helmets over their hearts and their heads bent, fragile as poppies. Because I was young, I didn't want to bow my head. I was wanting to see the human faces all around as was my habit. And luckily, what was expressed on the faces of so many was everywhere expressed exactly the same. For a New York minute, I was luckier than Yelberton Abraham Tittle, who again was MVP that year, and luckier than Perseus who had slain the Gorgon Medusa. Like everybody else hunched up in the cold, I was humbled, yet stunned by a hope that I had never before even thought to imagine. And it was splendid to be that—together— the hope seemed to flicker, and then, like mean Sam Huff, settle down to business.

At the time, it seemed to me obvious that heroes were meant to die so that hope did not have to. But just how long that hope would flicker in the face of a brutal world—I had no sense of that. I was just glad that once in my life I had hit the high note in the national anthem. I knew that I would probably never get to that pitch again, or understand even half of what it signified.

What followed after that was a scream and a roar. Joy built to a crescendo. And then the game began. . . .

You can't imagine what I have been putting up with. Everybody keeps calling me Y. A. Tittle. "Hey, they say, "there goes Y. A.!" And now, guess what? The lady who cuts my hair says I am developing a bald spot. Can girls get bald? I don't want my hair to go bald because my neck is too skinny. Dad says, it's a turkey neck. (Mom says it is a swan's neck.)

And then today in Social Studies, I became embarassed about my wrists when I was next to Grant Gowdy. They look like bamboo! So I put my wrists inside my book so that Grant couldn't see them if he tried. But Grant Gowdy likes Barbie Thompson. He doesn't care about my wrists, anyway.

Mike has hurt his arm, too, I think he did it deliberately. And Mom and Dad go around arguing like two opera stars about to die onstage. I would like life to be a little less passionate around here and a lot more boring.

Just for one day, and then I swear I will be the first person asleep at the slumber parties. I will save Kristen Meub's underwear from being dropped in water and placed in the freezer before I fall asleep. And I promise never to stay up all night again.

Floating from the unconscious to the conscious mind of the New York football public, came the phrase, *Gooo Giaaants!* Except for Robustelli, Grier and Katcavage, there was nobody else for miles around to teach us about wild instinct and frenzy.

The Giants were on the move with the bruising clarity of a vision. Yet more important than the wins and losses was 4:00 on Sundays—that time of afternoon when the light was the only kindness, when the scoreboard gleamed down on the endless game. Bound to each other by nothing more than the odd familiarity of hats and coats and random exclamations, at last we were comfortable, we were breathing in unison. 1961. 1962. 1963. Win or lose it was always the same. 4:00 was mine and everybody's.

In 1963:

> Yat was truly amazing from his first game that year, when he brought the Giants back from an 18-point deficit in the second half, a first victory ever against a Unitas-led Baltimore team. Against the Colts he ran a nine-yard keeper for the go-ahead score and paid for it with rib injuries that forced him to miss the rest of that game and the next one as well. But he snapped back, and now so in synch with Shofner, produced offense in giant gobs throughout the season, allowing the defense time to get their new people settled in and working efficiently . . . [13]

GOGOGO!

So the Giants were headed for the playoffs again, and from the first we assumed the battle would be against Green Bay. 1963, however, was not to be the Packers' year. As if from out of a bog and a nightmare came those mighty terrors of the grass—the Chicago Bears. According to *Time* magazine, "The experts picked the Chicago Bears to finish no better than second in the National Football League's Western Conference. . . . The Bears just laughed. Their ferocious defense held opponents to an average ten points in 14 games, clawed the champion Green Bay Packers so mercilessly that the Packers scored one touchdown, one field goal in two tries."[14]

In my storybook view, it was just another way of saying that Grendel was tops in the Western Division and the Eastern Division had their old graybeard King Beowulf back one more time to go out and face the latest hellish fiend of the gridiron.

Go!

All my life my favorite place to be is in my bed waking up. But now when I wake up my brother Mike is standing in the hall. Last week, Mike had a nightmare. He woke up and screamed, "Mom! Dad! Are you winning or losing?" I heard him because I was awake and because Mike and Pat's room is next to mine. I ran in and said nobody won. It was just us.

But now when he is awake in the night, I can't say anything. It is a trip for one. And it begins at our end of the hallway. Mike is only 10, and I know he would like to get to the safest place in the world, the place where nothing bad can ever happen—the back bedroom where my parents sleep in the night.

Down at our end of the hallway we swim through our dreams and sometimes when we wake up, the fear comes. The fear is a foreign object that makes you want to go down the hall to the back bedroom. You won't wake anybody up. You will just sleep on the floor. You will just be there inside the doorway and no one will know.

I can feel my brother's fear of the dark. I know that he is petrified. Good! If our parents were awake, Mom would say there's nothing to be afraid of, and Dad says you just have to have confidence. But the fear is real, like a dark ravine or river with something in it, when you stand in the hallway. And the monster is all the people watching us and looking for the hero. I think Mike should try to feel the Earth's heart beating in his feet, and he should run! But last night he walked *up and down the hall at least 15 times, and then I heard him talking.*

"Dad? I don't think you approve of me."

At first, I didn't think anybody heard him but me. But then I heard "Of course I do, Mike, of course I do," coming from the sanctuary.

The championship game of 1963 was scheduled for the end of December, and this meant that we would not go home to California for Christmas. That year, the attention was magnified from previous years, and overnight New York City was turned into an East Texas town where strangers treated us as long-lost relatives, and everywhere my father went he was like the golden goose. There was so little privacy at home that a friend offered to let us stay at his inn in Vermont for the holiday. We drove to upstate Vermont, and upon our arrival, a caretaker led us through an empty house to a room bright with fruit, flowers and packages. (Beat The Bears!) We all stood around the decorated tree. In the quiet, we were as separate as ornaments. We were as separate as flakes of snow. Even though we stood around the same tree, there was no language anymore. And that was the gift on the first white Christmas of our lives.

On the night before Christmas, my mother told us her dream about the blue bull. The bull opened its mouth and when everyone ran away, my mother walked right up to the creature. She stood on tiptoe, and when she looked inside the bull's mouth she found a world where water was poured from urns. Baskets were piled with pomegranates and lemons. Off in the corner, figures of men and women were being hammered into shape. A woman tended a fire. Another stirred the soup. The scene was filled with chaos, yet there was no sound.

This sort of silence was uncharacteristic of our family. At this point in their marriage, my parents were on the Laurel and Hardy trail to marital bliss. Arguing was their style. And despite the tumult of life among words, like bombs, bursting in air, I must admit that when our parents let the bad blood out, most of the time we loved it. When my mother quoted the old proverb, "We fight to keep warm," that was a good fighting day, because I could know that theirs was not a match made in heaven but along the great California fault, where the pressure had to be released little by little, otherwise the state might fall into the sea. I came to distinguish between two kinds of arguments just as I did for my dreams. Just as there were my true dreams and then there were dreams which emptied the garbage, I think that my parents were true fighters most of the time. However, on a weekly basis, the garbage might need to be emptied and that's when the word which bounced around the house like a pinball was *money*. I just couldn't get excited about a word so like an incomplete pass, over and over, time after time.

The problem was that my father the quarterback clashed with my mother, the descendant of a Cherokee War Chief, over territory that was invisible to me. I don't know what general positions they took, because they were both too busy whooping it up like Andrew Jackson and Junaluska behind the cotton bales in New Orleans. But I believe their true fights were about power and a sacred landscape; that is, theirs was the same old dramatization of the cowboy-and-Indian conflict, with an ending that was up for grabs. I say this because their fights started innocently enough with Dad, just like a settler, bumping along in the old covered wagon into somebody else's territory. Slowly but surely, you could see Mom's Indian blood begin to boil. Not about to put up with another land grab, she put on expressions like war paint, and with any language at hand, let that settler know that some land could not be owned. It could not be bought. So get off! That was the gist of it. There was no end to their quest for equality and individual freedom. And this, I take it, was marriage. My parents loved each other. But the fact was that being a wife to a famous athlete was not a task for the fainthearted.

Quite often in public places my parents were separated by crowds of well-wishers trying to get to my father. I remember once in 1963 when my mother was not simply shunted aside and ignored. The crowd lifted her right off her feet, pregnant stomach and all, so that she bobbed on the surface of this bubbling human cauldron—wearing her very nicest cut-velvet maternity top—until finally she was smashed into the wall—crunched by the mob like a gum wrapper.

No less than Y. A. Tittle stood in the pocket, did she also stand her ground in the unreal limelight of the pro football world, and get up when she was knocked down. Passionate and volatile as he, my mother fought for her self-image beside a hero and let my father know that the adulation he received in public did not entitle him always to get his own way at home.

Through it all, she simply refused to shine by reflected light, even if it meant that she didn't shine at all. Even if it meant that she wasn't heard a lot of the time, and her voice was a broken arrow. When, for instance, the good luck and the good press were with us, she wore the beautiful fame as a veil and never an overcoat. She never expected any warmth from it. Rather she was the protector of what really was our family.

"So you can throw a football. Is that such a big deal?"

(I wasn't going to enter into the argument, but the answer was clearly yes. People treated her very differently when they found out about Dad's throwing arm. They gave him a table in a busy restaurant when they told her there was nothing available. They filled up with yeses and smiles when they saw my father. And suddenly she herself was treated not like Cinderella in the kitchen but Cinderella at the ball! The change was so sudden, so obvious and so scary—how could she even ask the question? She, who was constantly being flattered and insulted in the same instant, and who waited out innumerable speeches, banquets, and events in bathrooms from coast to coast. I remember once she said to my father loud and clear that she "could have written the All-American Book of Bathrooms and it would have sold!" Had she forgotten?)

In the end, I guess, Mom was a true defender of the bottom line. Not an adoring, worshipping female. Not a potted palm or a doormat—contrary to what some might think about football wives. Just a fearful reminder of the real world, a fighter for love and her sacred landscape amid the pandemonium of fame.

And so it was that on Christmas morning we forgave our parents for the arguments of the previous year. We clapped for the gifts as they were unwrapped—and revealed more of those astonishing creations of red sequins, which my father so delighted in buying, and which my mother could so seldom be persuaded to wear. (There were bathrobes that might have belonged to Liberace and blouses like abstract renderings of Napoleon's defeat at Waterloo!) Our own fantasies would have clothed both parents even more magically in 1963—but sadly neither one ever turned green, or appeared with palm branches, or bowed down as slaves. Useless as artichoke hearts, both of them, they mostly fed us chicken pot pies and then sent us to bed. But on Christmas we forgave even that, and we knew that their arguments were no big deal. Despite their constant fighting, our parents were still together, and we loved them even as dragons.

After the giftgiving, our father disappeared like clockwork into the kitchen, and our mother searched the page of the Christmas story and breathed: *gold, myrrh, frankincense.* And how we loved and never tired of hearing about being born, and that even God couldn't help when and where it happened. It was something that just had to be.

Then we ate.

But on this Christmas in 1963, I bit into an apple and knew that something had changed. No one talked about the game, but I was filled with a tension of waiting. At the window, I could not take pride in the snow busts of Andy Robustelli dotting the landscape, because just as the snow that was falling, so was I.

At that moment the winds of Chicago began to blow. And from the place where all the Bugsys die, its whistle was heard in the shutters of our room. I flew downstairs, and what is more, I had sense enough to pick up some of the white stuff and rub it in my brother's face before charging the far horizon. War. I was myself again. But not for long.

By the stone wall I took my stand. With clenched fists, I gritted my teeth and said bad things. Then I lay down in the snow in an effort to be a part of the perfect, snowy sound. The quiet. (Four days to the game.)

I remembered 1957, the year that the 49ers lost the championship to Detroit. That was also the year in which my father said, "C'mon!" one night, and we marched out of the house between my brothers, out to the streetlight to practice. And it was quiet there, too, in that glow where I stood ready, perched for takeoff.

"There now," he said. "Pretend. Pretend to touch what you are aiming for." And every time the ball rolled off the side of my hand and my body alone tried to fly forward, it was like *Christmas* and I was getting ankles and elbows that bent. A right shoulder and a left one.

"Perfect!" he would say, and I would freeze to feel that perfection. And then another and another.

And so out of that quiet on Christmas Day at the inn in Vermont, *others* came. Perseus came out of the quiet of a library book I had read in first grade. The picture showed him holding up the Gorgon's head of snakes, and yet touching the great quiet at the same time. He was an announcement of strength and weakness, good and evil, victory and defeat. And yet for all that, Perseus seemed to wait for more.

But I could not think about him for long. There was Nini, too, the wild horse from our grammar school game, who with her touch set all the rest of the captured horses free. Nini would snort. She would punctuate the wild quiet of her world with a wild whinny. Then she would turn and run. She was magic and unconquerable.

There was even time while burrowing in the Vermont snow to remember our trip to the Alamo, after the 49ers lost the 1957 playoffs. As we approached the outskirts of town, I listened to the blissful hum of wheels, watched my father's jaw making its spectacular line and the quiet of my mother's profile, looking as eternal as a coastline looks from an airplane window. I assumed that they knew I was to be dropped off at the Alamo to join in the fight for independence. I had worn my Indian dress for the occasion. In that dress with a silver braid, I would tell Crockett and Bowie and all the people to run, because in kindergarten everybody knew that you did not just run to run. You ran to inspire yourself or to find the particular feeling you wanted to find. We would not fail. The dress was the color of a pomegranate seed.

When the sun went down on Christmas Day in 1963, I thought that the whirling snow in Ridgefield, Vermont, was all the moments in our lives coming down at once. The time left before the championship was running like sand through a giant hourglass, and now every grain counted. As my mother put cold cream on her face and my father brought out the Monopoly board, I wanted to go outside in the dark but couldn't. The Tittle males settled down to their Monopoly, but I could not forget *the* game. I went to bed, where I flailed around in the sheets until the wind blew through the shutters suddenly and then died away. This is it, I thought. The apocalyptic quiet came for one last time, like the silence that often followed my mother's telling of a dream. I could not tell exactly what it was. But the falling had stopped. I knew the wind in the shutters would not scare me and I would sleep.

Instead, I fell into a dream and lay awake all night remembering.

. . . When I was four, heroes had been dream horses who ran through abandoned cities, and brought them to life. They did not drag their bodies around like heavy loads. They played and ran and gave green life to the hills.

But my first hero, my very first hero went back to the well. And the well goes so far back into memory that it comes attached to squishing my belly skin together to make old faces. It also comes attached to the figure of my great-aunt Etheldra. It was she who said, "Let's go out to the well." And we went.

The well was out back behind the kennel and the horse stable. I held onto my great-aunt Etheldra's hand which led up to a great brown shining shoulder.

"Look," said my great-aunt Etheldra. "See anything?" And when she lifted me up I waved my hands across the circle of darkness. When she propped her knee under my rear so that I could be comfortable, I tipped my face into the circle of cool.

"No." I saw nothing but the funny birds of my hands. And

Etheldra shifted me to her other knee. Arching my neck, I looked at her face upside down. And she blew her bangs off her forehead, because her hands were not free. Then she looked down and blew in my face, once. A fierce puff. I looked into the well again and saw the black that was blacker than all the rest and made the shoe.

The shoe! Was it God's shoe turned up at the toe and worn out from so much running around? My chest and throat were ablaze. Triumph. The birth of the world.

I could see that out of the shoe would pour more darkness—and snow. There would be snow animals falling through the air, hinds and leopards falling gently as snowflakes. And Etheldra and I and everyone I knew would be falling from God, becoming many things as we fell. And the hero would come walking across this snowy world on his way to climb. And I would say, "Here! Take the shoe and give it back!" But the hero wouldn't listen. He would put it on and he would keep going.

The hero was alive! I had only to find him in bits and broken pieces all over the world.

When Etheldra set me down, it was as if the entire created world rose up to greet me.

The sun was beating down, the light was still flashing like a kitchen knife. But I knew it was trying to say: WELCOME!

BRING ON THE BEARS!

I beseech you lady . . . with good will, accept this garland
   for splendid Midas. . . .
He has beat Hellas at the art that once Athena invented when
   she composed into song
the death wail of the bold Gorgons. . . . The maiden goddess,
   when she saved her friend from distress
created the polyphonal music of flutes, to mimic the wailing clamor
   that closed on her from the mouthing jaws of Euryale.
   The goddess invented it, and inventing, gave it to mortals to use,
naming it the melody many-headed, splendid summoner to games
   where people throng.

—Pindar, *Pythian* 12

Monsters of the Midway

Wrigley Field, 1963

Go! Giaaants!

A Short History of The Monsters of the Midway
adapted from *The New York Giants* by Frank Terzian

1933 was a turning point in the history of the National Football League. To help lessen the frequency of low scoring games and ties, goalposts were placed 10 yards deep in the end zone instead of on the goal line, and a backfield man was permitted to throw a forward pass from anywhere behind the line of scrimmage. This led to the T formation and the development of the multiple offense. The shape of the ball was also modified and the new design streamlined the ball's rounded ends and made it easier to throw . . . .

On a spring morning in that year, Tim Mara strolled over to the midtown offices of Billy Gibson and purchased the New York Giants for $2,500. By 1933, the The National Football League consisted of a rather shaky band of teams, twenty in all, and what little stability the young league had was due to a combative ex-sailor named George Halas, who owned, coached and played for the Chicago Bears. In its genesis, football was on the back burner as one more American melting pot, and teams were manned by former All America football players, aging Olympic stars, out of work baseball players, part-time cowboys, dock hands, wrestlers, factory workers and anybody else who felt he could play. There were teams like the Pottsville Maroons, the Frankford Yellow Jackets and the Rhode Island Steamrollers.

The winners of their divisions, the New York Giants and the Chicago Bears, met on 17 December 1933 in Chicago for the league's first championship game. Still an experiment, it drew only 18,000. It was a wild game won by the Bears. And the losers went home with $150 bucks each.

Go! Go!

In 1934, the championship game at the Polo Grounds matched the same teams on a December day so cold that the gridiron was as hard and slippery as an ice-skating rink. The Chicago Bears had blasted through the 1934 season without a loss or tie to mar their 13–0 record. The Monsters of the Midway, as they were called, outmatched the piddly New York Giants, whose regular quarterback, among others, was sidelined with injuries. Giant coach Steve Owen was in despair. He had no choice but to start his rookie quarterback who was only a few months out of Fordham University.

The second league championship was underway with 35,000 fans present. Monster Bronco Nagurski ran roughshod over the Giants, crossed the goal line twice only to have the scores called back due to penalties. Monster Manders missed two field goals inside the 30 yard line. Even so, the score at the half was 10–3 with the Bears in the lead. Not only were the Giants outweighed man to man, but their cleated shoes got no purchase on the frozen field against the ponderous Bear charge. They were pushed up and down the field until they were bruised and exhausted. But that's when coach Owen dispatched a volunteer to nearby Manhattan College to beg, borrow, or steal anything that looked like sneakers.

When the Giants came out for the second half, they seemed more assured and alert, and certainly more sure of their footing. The radio announcers noticed the sneakers first. And the fans soon chimed in on the chorus: *the Giants are wearing sneakers!*

"Hey," snarled a Monster who happened to be standing on the sidelines next to coach Halas. "Those guys are wearing sneakers."

"Good!" said Halas as he loosed a stream of tobacco juice that promptly froze in the nine-degree air. "Step on their toes!"

And so the second championship game in the National Football League ended with a Giant triumph. And from that day on, no

NFL team ever again took the road in cold weather without rubber-soled shoes as part of their winter gear. . . .[1]

Go! Go! Giants!

The Chicago Bears and the New York Giants were not to meet again in a championship game until 1956. The mood in New York City on that December 30 was at fever pitch. Fans stormed the box office at Yankee Stadium. It was 18 degrees above zero and the stadium resembled a wind-blasted Siberian tundra as coach Jimmy Lee Howell ordered, "Sneakers all around!" And the New York Giants demolished the Chicago Bears with a shocking 47–7 score.[2]

GOGOGO!
GO!

Sunday. 29 December 1963. We wore face caps with red rickrack around the eyes and mouth, and huge pompoms on top. In the taxicab, my brothers argued over our collection of seat- and hand-warmers. A hand reached over and opened the door; my mother got out and moved down the sidewalk like a glacier. It was cold— 11 degrees and falling. And in the cold, everything seemed twice as hard. I pulled my mitten off for a minute, but my hand looked as awkward and exposed as a naked lady, so I put my mitten back on.

Just entering Wrigley Field was like crawling through the remains of an animal whose gargantuan bones were frozen in Chicago's cold. No fun. No fun at all. It was shocking that anything at all could move in that landscape, much less run or jump. When the New York Giants ran onto the field, the boos made my rib cage vibrate, while the sun shrank to the size of a tiny eye and the sky was a terrible whiteness. Chicago.

As we sat in the end zone, the temperature dropped to five below zero, and somebody shook my hand when my father was injured, just seven minutes into the game. As the roar of the crowd gained momentum, a tidal wave of enemy joy dwarfed us three bundles of fury enthroned on our seat-warmers with our arms crossed.

Finally, rather than wait in silence for death, my brothers and I began springing up in our crazy costumes every time the Giants moved an inch. We tore off our hats and our hearts flew out of our mouths in inarticulate shrieks of encouragement and love with every handoff. My face was raw and my naked hands danced in the air.

The New York Giant historian, Frank Terzian, gave this account:

It was a classic matchup.

The Giants had the highest scoring team in the league with 448 points in 14 games. The Bears had the best defensive record in the league with 144 points allowed.

The Giants had Y. A. Tittle who had thrown 36 touchdown passes that season, an NFL record. The Bears had Ed O'Bradovich and Doug Atkins at ends and Larry Morris, Bill George and Joe Fortunato as linebackers in a nutcracker defense, coached by defensive aide George Allen.

The Chicago defense, it was felt, would find it difficult to defend against Tittle's passes because of poor traction on the frozen field. . . . The weather was almost frightening. Both teams started cautiously, waiting for breaks. . . . The Giants got the first one early in the game . . . Tittle, mindful of frozen hands, sent running backs Morrison, King and Hugh McElhenny crashing into the line for short gains. Two, three, and four yards at a time until the ball rested on the Chicago 14.

Now thoroughly warmed up, Tittle switched tactics and went to the air. His first pass was right on target and right into the hands of Gifford who scored the game's first touchdown.

The celebration, however, lasted only a moment. On the play Tittle had been hit by blitzing linebacker Larry Morris. Now he was sitting on the frozen turf, groggy and clutching his left knee. As the kicking team came on for the point-after, he limped slowly off the field.

"It's all right," he insisted to his concerned coach. "I'm okay, Allie . . . just took a whack, is all." He walked up and down the sidelines gingerly testing the knee.

Yat returned to the ball game sooner than expected when cornerback Dick Pesonen recovered a fumble by Bear back Willie Galimore, this one on the Chicago 31. Trotting out with his offensive squad, paler than usual behind the face mask, Tittle showed no signs of a limp. The leg hurt, but he wasn't going to let the Bears know.

As if to emphasize his rapid recovery, Tittle sent Shofner deep on the first play, leading him with a bomb thrown from the Bear 40. The pass was long, arching and Del was open in the end zone. He turned, got a hand on the ball—and dropped it.

Shofner kicked the ground in angry frustration. He'd blown a sure touchdown. Meanwhile linebacker Morris, reading Tittle perfectly, had stepped into a little screen pass thrown for Phil King, intercepted, and was now lumbering down the field with Giants in frantic pursuit . . . After the conversion it was a 7–7 ball game.

The Giants, knowing they were in for a fight, moved with determination after the kickoff. Tittle, patiently probing the Chicago defense, mixed a series of runs with short passes that carried the Giants inside the Bear 10-yard line. Then, when the Bears held on third and short yardage, Chandler came in and kicked a field goal for a 10–7 Giant lead midway in the second quarter.

Then Tittle, dropping back to pass in his own territory, stumbled on the freezing turf. He managed to release the ball but Morris, who again had broken through Yat's protection, fell heavily on him with a crushing tackle. . . .

"That second shot, it really hurt. I felt the pop," Tittle later admitted.

After the hit, Tittle lay on the grass face down, his injured leg drawn up under him. Allie Sherman called time out immediately and gave the signal to sub quarterback Glynn Griffing to get off the bench.

The half ended. New York 10, Chicago 7.

. . . During the half, ice packs reduced the swelling and yards of tape braced his leg at the knee joints. . . .

"Let's give it a try, Allie," he said finally.

It was a grim band of New Yorkers that resumed play in the

second half. In addition to their crippled signal caller, starting linebacker Tom Scott had suffered a broken arm in the first half and would see no more action that day. . . .

The first time Tittle dropped back in the third quarter, everyone could see he was far below the form that made him No. 1 among the league's quarterbacks. He was awkward in setting up, the result of having to pass off his right leg instead of his damaged left, now all but useless.

Later in the quarter, star running back Phil King was injured and the Bears knew the Giant running game would be as crippled as their passing attack. Their defense stepped up the pressure accordingly.

Tittle countered by trying to throw screen passes. . . . But because his movements were hampered and he couldn't act out his play fakes, the Bears read him well. . . . After the conversion, Chicago led, 14–10.

With five minutes left to play, Allie Sherman struggled with a mind-wrenching dilemma. Should he send in a rookie at quarterback or go with his veteran, bad leg and all . . . He decided on Tittle. . . .

Tittle braced for a final effort. He strung two, three, four successful plays in a row for a couple of first downs. The fifth play took his team across midfield.

Chicago fans were uneasy. Players on the Bear bench prowled the sidelines in their enormous greatcoats, like threatening gladiators. The Giants reserves were also on their feet, shouting encouragement to their teammates. . . .

The ball now rested deep in Bear territory. . . . On third and five, Tittle took the snap from center, [then blacked out on a pass to Gifford.]

All the Bears had to do now was hold the ball until the final gun. They almost succeeded. . . .

On fourth down, Bobby Joe Green booted a towering punt downfield that rolled dead on the Giants' 16-yard line. With only a minute and 30 seconds left, New York was 84 tough yards away from victory. The Bald Eagle tried, first by passing to end Aaron

Thomas for 10 yards. Another pass to Thomas picked up eight. Joe Morrison took the next and picked up 12 more. Distance to cover for the TD: 54 yards. Time left: 54 seconds.

A pass to Hugh McElhenny fell incomplete but it stopped the clock at 39 seconds. The crowd implored the Bears to close in— cover, hit, charge—anything to stop the Giant march.

The next play, a down-and-out toss which Gifford took before stepping out of bounds, looked good for an instant, but a sharp-eyed official waved it incomplete. Gifford had caught the ball fair enough, but with only one foot in bounds.

Twenty seconds remained. With one time out left, Tittle knew he'd be able to get off at least two more plays. "Do it again, Frank," he snapped in the huddle. "Only this time, zig in, not out. They won't be looking for that.

He was right. Frank ran out, cut toward the sidelines, then cut back into the center where the pass just did reach him. He grabbed the ball and was dumped immediately on the Bears' 39.

. . . With 15 seconds left, Tittle dragged himself to the sidelines for a final consultation with Sherman. It had to be the bomb, the Tittle specialty. In whose direction?

"Del!" Sherman snapped.

Del Shofner, who had caught 64 passes for the Giants that year, but not a single one so far in this game, had to be the logical choice. He was sure-handed, elusive; he could get down to the end zone faster than any receiver on the team—and he was hungry!

Tittle nodded and walked back to the huddle. The Giants were waiting for him.

So were the Bears. They sent only three men in, flooding the secondary against the bomb they knew was coming.

Tittle took the ball and dropped back, three, four, five yards, every step a painful one. He saw Shofner go down the right sideline, then cut in. He took two more backward steps, then from close to midfield, he let fly.

Oh, he wanted that one back! The moment he released it he knew it had no authority, no direction. It was too high, too wobbly. He only prayed it would fall incomplete.

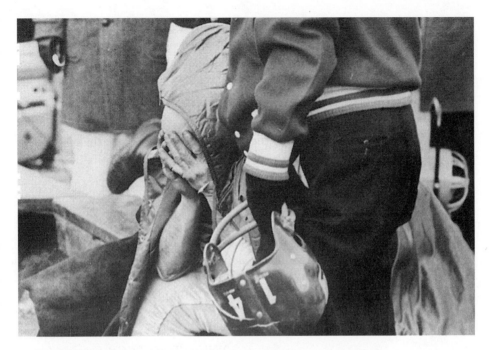

It didn't. The Bears had won, 14–10. Pandemonium broke loose in the stands . . . Tittle jerked off his cracked helmet and smashed it down on the frozen turf.

In the post-game interview with newsmen, Allie Sherman said, "I don't know of any other quarterback who would have gone out there in his condition . . ."

Tittle, meanwhile, had finished showering and dressing. . . .

Bob Marcus of the Chicago Tribune asked, "Other than the knee injury, did the Bears inflict more than the usual punishment?"

Tittle seemed not to hear the question. He was searching feverishly through his billfold. "Oh, here it is," he said, then turned to Marcus.

"No, they didn't hurt me too much. They played a good clean game." With a wave of his hand, he turned, and limped off on crutches.

"What was he looking for?" the reporter asked one of the Giant trainers.

"Who, Yat? His wedding band."[5]

Look again. Y. A. Tittle never dreamed, but on the night of December 28, before the game, he dreamed not once but twice. The first dream he did not remember, although it may have had something to do with football. The second dream he saw clearly. He and his friend, Tiger Johnson, were on a visit to the Alamo. But at this shrine of their childhood heroes, the eroded stone was crumbling and the graffitti told the truth. The two boys read the inscription, though not all the words came clear in Tittle's dream memory.

To the People of Texas And All Americans In The World:

> I am besieged with a thousand or more of the Mexicans under Santa Anna. I have sustained a continual bombardment and cannonade for 24 hours and have not lost a man. The enemy has demanded surrender at discretion, otherwise the garrison is to be put to the sword, if the fort is taken. I have answered the demand with a canon shot, and our flag still waves proudly from the wall. I shall never surrender or retreat. . . .

—Victory Or Death
William Travis, Lt. Col. Commander[4]

The oldest pro ball player in the National Football League tossed and turned in his sleep but got little rest. He dreamed that Miss Selma was reminding everybody in class that the reason you are supposed to grow up and outgrow your childhood heroes is so that you can grow into them.

GOOOOOOOOOO GIAANTS!

On December 29, Tittle awoke. And just like Hog Killing Day back in Marshall, it was another cold day.

GOOOOOOOOOO!

When Tittle opened his eyes, his mind was wiped clean. The dream he remembered was forgotten. He stood and felt his body, his feet touching the ground. His joints were loose, the weight on his legs was balanced evenly.

In his mind, there was only purpose. And in the mirror of his life nothing except the rectangle of grass at dusk, when the quiet smoothed away the chaos.

The drone of the downtown traffic he did not hear. But the walls of the stadium itself seemed to resonate with a sustained low pitch like that of the harp whose strings continually vibrate, whether or not they are played.

Look again. Circles. Two regions: East Coast and Midwest. Two cities: New York and Chicago. The suburbs of Long Island, a midwestern farm. A circle of one: a man or woman alone in a motel room watching a TV screen. Of all circles, most critical is the circle of players. The team's spirit is comprised of the strength of offense and defense, special teams, trainers, coaches, management, wives and families. A team is a complex extended family with its own rivalries, dynamics, factions, and bonds that only men who have gone into battle can feel for one another. They are interdependent as links in a chain.

Each link has a matchup with an opposing player. And the team that wins the most matchups usually wins the game. The team that has a player who loses his matchup badly will almost surely lose the game. This rarely happens, because of another team within the team: the coaches. The coaching staff's job is to exploit the strength of the superior player, who can be counted on to beat his man, and to protect the players who are matched against an opposing star. The coaches also deal with all the intangibles, monitoring the family dynamics of a team. Empathy. The work of a great coach is as hard to grasp as a slithering fish in white water rapids . . .

They say that the man closest to God is the quarterback because he calls the plays and sees the entire field. He assimilates the matchups and picks the right spot at the appropriate time to deliver the ball. The quarterback needs to sense the spirit in the huddle and determine which linemen to run the ball behind, which players are winning or losing.

On game day, the wind howled in 1963. Had the wind been

stilled, the Giants might have heard, might have found their luck in the quiet. Tittle's passes might have brought to fruition a lifetime of tuning mind and body. Working with Shofner and Gifford in precision patterns choreographed to take place within two seconds, a burst upfield of predetermined length, followed by outstretched hands, and a ball delivered to an exact spot. . . . After all, the field was frozen, and that could be expected to favor a passing team.

Look again. Facts. On championship day the winds blew hard off the lake, the gangsters of the sky preparing for another big fight. We sang the national anthem and I missed the high note . . . Then my mother sat down like the ice queen on her mountain. The wives always clapped so timidly, so fearfully, lest they offend some other wife . . . I did not want to be a wife.

As for Y. A. Tittle, his dream of a championship and all the years had merely earned him a ticket to "Shee-ca-go," the place of the skunk. The exultation, the roar, the hunger, the violence—it might have been ancient Greece or Rome. But it was only football.

Facts. Sure, 1961, '62, '63 were great years for Y. A. Tittle. But what greatness usually means is that somebody has been dragged around the walls of his own city and eaten by the dogs. The greatness comes in the remembering and that is the job for us—the spectators. The participant in the action is playing hostage to the collective dream.

But thanks to our outfits, my brothers and I stood like penguins in the end zone at Wrigley Field, our arms like tiny flippers. Mike looked like he was wearing every pillow in the house. Pat was literally buried in his outfit and could hardly peer out of his coffin of clothes. My mother wore the heavy black coat which had been an old 49er trophy. She wore a hat that bore a striking and embarrassing resemblance to an illustration in a Dr. Seuss book. She wore black kid gloves which drowned out the sound of her applause.

Fact. "When a 240-pound lineman capable of running 100 yards in 11 seconds collides with a 240-pound back capable of covering the same distance in 10 seconds, the resultant kinetic energy is 'enough to move 66,000 pounds, or 33 tons, one inch.' When players stagger about the field after a play—'having your bell rung' in football parlance—the likelihood is that they have been hit on the helmet by a blow approaching 1,000 Gs (1,000 times the force of gravity). Astronauts on takeoff experience around 10 Gs and pilots tend to black out at about 20. Tests run on Detroit linebacker Joe Schmidt reportedly showed that he had to cope with blows which registered at 5,780 Gs."[5]

1st quarter.

> The New York Giants pranced onto Chicago's Wrigley Field. . . .
> At 7:22 of the first quarter, Tittle lofted his 37th touchdown pass
> of the year—a soft, 14-yard beauty to Gifford.[5]

7:22. Defensive captain Andy Robustelli watched from the sidelines. He didn't know that a coaching legend was crystallizing on the frozen sidelines of their opponent, George Allen, the Bears' defensive coach; that Allen was later to bend and weave his magic in places like Los Angeles and Washington as head coach; or that his first indelible mark was to be made in the game in Chicago. Robustelli was concerned with matchups. There were matchups and then there were matchups as far as he was concerned. On game day, Sam Huff would butt heads with the great Mike Ditka. Yet no matchup had the ingredients of the one between Roosevelt Brown and Doug Atkins. Rosey Brown was the Giants' mammoth offensive tackle who could always be counted on to pound his opponent into the ground, providing a safe passage to daylight for his running back over the right side. The imbalance this created had to be accounted for by the opposing coaches, who usually brought up reinforcements on that side, which in turn created a soft spot for the Giants to exploit.

The Bears, though, had a monster of their own facing directly opposite Rosey Brown—Doug Atkins, six foot eight inches high. This was a matchup that football fans dreamed of. The immovable object placed in front of the irresistible force. All the while, the other matchups took their progression: receivers against defensive backs, linemen smacking up against each other like sumo wrestlers, runners feinting and juking tacklers.

Zigout! Gifford broke to the outside in his favorite pattern; Tittle passed to him; the Giants scored.

And on that play, too, my father took a lateral blow to the knee. Clutching his left leg, he limped off to the sidelines. As a cheer went up, my mother put her head down, and stupidly, instinctively, we closed in around her.

2nd Quarter.

> One after another, the Giants retired to the bench, with assorted broken arms, concussions and the like ...[7]

Near the end of the second period, my father's knee was hit again.

Every injury in a football game is the result of many breakdowns. It would be impossible to distinguish the strategic opportunity one coach may have missed from the one another may have seized, from the back who missed a block; and the event seems so narrowly circumscribed that it is amazing it happened at all. In a game of inches, or rather centimeters and milliseconds, jeering crowds, swirling winds, and bitter cold, one step shy fluffs the touchdown, and the energy flows to the other side. The crowd turns crazed.

With this hit, Tittle finally found his way to the game's center and was freed from the fires of his dreams. There was only Y. A. Tittle left and he was down. In the cold, his breath was visible. He seemed like a boy curled up under a tree and sleeping. And he slept while the Chicago fans went crackers over the injury.

"Obnoxious boors,"[8] Andy Robustelli said out loud.

The first half ended.

A Bach fugue wafted up from the ground of Wrigley Field. The band served as a way of clearing the palate for the next course, and of saying, so what? to the joys and sorrows of the game. It was the fashion then for the band to transform itself into living pictures, changing from, say, a flag, to a ship, to a typewriter. That's what we saw at Wrigley Field—a typewriter made from real people. As the keys moved, and the typewriter wrote, we cracked peanuts, sipped chocolate, and wondered quietly.

In the Giants' locker room, Doc O'Grady was shaking his head. It was a classic knee injury in which Tittle suffered severe ligament damage. Had the injury occurred at the beginning of the season, Yat would have missed many games as a result. This was serious for a QB who was out only five weeks with a broken back. And the players who had come so far together huddled around their leader. The backup QB, a rookie, turned ashen.

Y. A. thought back to other injuries. The game he'd gone into with two sprained ankles. The time in 1953 he played with a smashed cheekbone and completed 29 passes. Winning a game for S.F. with a broken hand. 1957, a pulled hamstring; but John Brodie went bad in the first half against Green Bay and Hickey asked, "Can you play, Tittle?"

. . . Tittle spoke in a small and distant voice, as if dredged up from the bottom of an antique radio. He would play, he said. And the tape? Where was the tape? He turned an anxious glance on Doc O'Grady. The miles and miles of tape.

Yat closed his eyes until the halftime entertainment ended. He missed out on the music, and could never have imagined the human typewriter, which scattered as if it had never been.

3rd Quarter. Look again.

> . . . Late in the third quarter on a crucial third-down-and-9 from New York's 13-yard line, Halas sent in the Ditka special, known in the Chicago huddle as "78-Y lookee pass." Wade fired over the middle to tight end Mike Ditka. Known as the man "who could make it through Dante's Inferno," Ditka bulled to a first down on the 1. Then Wade sneaked over. As Halas explained later, "It was a play we had worked on for just such a situation, when their defenders were going to the outside."[9]

Although he didn't believe in aspirin, this once Tittle asked Dr. O'Grady to give him something so that he could play. No, said Dr. O'Grady. A man, like a horse, will keep running, keep tearing himself up. They don't do it to horses and O'Grady wouldn't do it to him. So the other doctor shot him up with novocain and cortisone. No feeling—and no balance.

It showed. When the speed is slowed on a record player the melody becomes a moan, and that is how the Giants played in the third quarter. The day was reduced to bare whiteness and my father was reduced to his smallest self, stripped of his gifts, like a tree whose leaves have fallen. But the world split at his fingertips and was growing large.

Knowing that the only chance the Giants had was to go with what got them there, Tittle came back in the second half.

One after another the Giants withered and dropped. And still, what players were left standing, danced—they staggered forward, danced! Y. A. Tittle staggered like an owl with a broken wing.

According to the rules of child's play, that which honored man was beautiful. That which dishonored him was not. But at Wrigley Field I could not tell the difference anymore than I could separate exhilaration and nausea into Dixie cups.

In the morning, they throw men to the lions and bears; at noon, they throw them to the spectators,[10] wrote Seneca.

This was the game to which we had all aspired, and my eyes filled with mixed tears of hope and shame. My mother was sitting very still.

I had grown accustomed, I suppose, to my father's talent and was dismayed to discover that his weakness could be so utterly exposed. Y. A. Tittle was not the great Y. A. Tittle anymore. He was the not-so-great somebody, whose timing was off. He was limited, weak, injured, and inaccurate, and people cheered as the jackals hunted him down.

I listened to the drone of downtown traffic and wished that my father had not let me down. Was it not better, I thought, to be knocked down and stay down? To be weak behind closed doors? With every play, my father could not get back fast enough, and the Bears charged through the line. A loss of a second or two on the dropback made the difference. And with every play, I felt betrayed, enraged, and confused, not only at him for this shameless presentation of his heart, but also because his best effort was not only painful to him, but it was painfully obvious that it was less than adequate.

But then, I thought, what if Y. A. Tittle's football dream had pulled a fast one? When you are talented, lucky or strong, and when there is hope, it is easy. But what happens when there is no hope and you are ordinary, when your luck has run out and only the will is left exposed? How was one still a champion then? If my father was the hero they claimed, then he would have to go out there with nothing, give his all for nothing, be nothing and ask for nothing in return—just like the rest of us!

Shocked and confused, I stood up in my seat. It felt good to welcome the cold onto my face and hands. I took off my coat so I could move more freely.

With that step, I became as tall as an adult. I moved out of a world in which I reacted to circumstances and into one where I anticipated them and created new possibilities. The guilt of childhood fell away, and I discovered a new freedom from both the future and the past. The present space seemed an invitation to me, author of the moment, to give my all. For in the end, what is there besides one's best effort? That is all we have.

And so I began to clap like a metronome. Moments before, the national championship had been at stake, and the order of a child's universe hung in the balance. But what was suddenly most important in all that large canvas was the knee, like a single brush stroke or the smallest dot of gold. I had scanned the world piecing together my jigsaw hero. And suddenly, my eyes fell on something even more useful than the knee. The crack in my father's helmet; even 50 yards away, with my eyes blurred by tears, I could see it clearly.

4th quarter.

> Tittle tried another screen pass. This time "Big Ed" O' Bradovich lumbered into the Giant 14. After that, there was only desperation. Tittle threw . . . once, twice, the last on a frantic heave into the end zone with only five seconds left . . .[11]

And with five minutes left in the game, they were coming. Broken and limping, young and old, the heroes were coming back.

Streaked with roots and wheat and wrapped in a hurricane of beauty. They were coming!

It wasn't the winning or losing anymore. I was clapping for the moment which could bear the weight of the world.

At 14–10, the Chicago fans were going mad with good reason. To the last second, we were the band of Texans in the end zone waiting for Robustelli and his endurance, the shining Gifford and his hands. But most of all, we waited to see the knee which buckled when Y. A. Tittle went down again, and how again he hobbled to his feet to keep trying.

For his part, my father never doubted the game, never deviated from his purpose. Joe Louis and the other heroes were still the reminder to Tittle of who he was. Like Orpheus, his task was to move forward and never look back. With five seconds left in the game, Tittle loosed a bomb. The pass which had spiraled through his life like a note in a Gregorian chant flew up higher, higher, beyond Del Shofner, as the seconds ticked out, beyond the field. It seemed to be headed right for me, and I leaped for it.

AND FIRST DOWN! I lost my balance and fell from childhood during that miserable fourth quarter. There was no harmony. No balance. No beauty. The drone and roar of the crowd, like a bass clef. Like the treble, my own heart striking out with its bizarre melody. And even though I was the first to hate my piano music and that detestable Mr. Middle C, the world without music, without its occasional measure of harmony, balance, and beauty, was not a world. It was in its absence that I discovered music.

30 December 1963. *New York Times*. . .

> The victory also re-established the 68-year-old owner coach of the Bears as a master of winning football after 17 seasons of frustration and of being "too old for the new pro game."[12]

We celebrated my fourteenth birthday in December of that year.

OVERTIME

Minnette and
Y. A. at home
on Caddo Lake,
1994.

There is harmony in the bending back
as in the bow and the lyre . . .

—Heraclitus, fr. 51

Father: *I was fascinated by a ball spinning in the air as far back as I can remember. In fourth grade, I organized a football team. And then I organized the other teams we would play against. The VA Jacks was one. I could name every player on my fourth grade team and my fifth grade team. The fifth grade beat the sixth grade, and we did it on Billy Ware's vacant lot. Early on, I really loved to play football. Why, I don't know. We just made it up as we went along.*

Let's see. I retired from professional football in 1964. I was almost 39. It was a dream that I had had, and it came to an end. Ever since I was a little kid, football had been important in my life. It was difficult. A lot of players say it is easy. But I feel that if you have achieved something, it only comes from tremendous dedication and tremendous, almost one-sided tunnel vision. And that was my case. And maybe it should have been different. But that was the way it was.

As I see it, I have been lucky. I had the opportunity to play with some of the greatest players in the game. And the players I played with as a competitor, I feel, were all friends. I played against some of my boyhood idols, against Slinging Sammy Baugh, who was my hero. I played against Jarring Johnny Kimbrow when he played with the Los Angeles Dons and Chunkin' Charlie O Roarke. . . . By the end of my career, I had come to know people I had been in awe of. I had met John Kennedy and John Glenn. I had become acquainted with Jack Dempsey, Joe DiMaggio, Archie Moore, and Joe Louis. Personally, my greatest thrill was meeting Joe Louis, because as a kid from East Texas in the thirties, we were just beginning to know about sports, and Joe Louis fought about once a month. We listened to these fights on the radio and pictured him in our minds. He went to the left and to the right. And with a left jab—it was a dream.

And now, I've had the chance to go back to East Texas where I have been able to share memories with some of my oldest friends, like Bobby Furrh who's about to die, Billy Dinkle, Puppy Gilry, and Albert Agnor, OK? Let's name them. That's important too. Praising other people. There's nothing wrong with that. And now to tell stories.... I suppose to tell lies at this point in life is more fun than the truth, because well, I've forgotten where the truth stopped and the lies began.

... But look. We've got a problem here. I haven't robbed a bank and I only fell in love once. So what's the big deal? How can you write a book when there's nothing to say. I am just an old ball player, or was one ...

The Trick
ZIGOUT

Greece. I was not an athlete. I had never run a race before. But in 1981, I had recently discovered the victory songs written for Olympic athletes. In my lifetime, the connection between the arts and sports had been severed. Indeed, in my own family, it often seemed as though poetry and sport were at odds. But I was drawn to this form because I had always seen my father the athlete as artist. And I had also wondered if my love of poetry was not the logical function of my upbringing as the daughter of an athlete. It was the victory song which presented me not only with an opportunity to celebrate the original unity, but also an opportunity, on a more personal level, to explore the meaning of athletics.

So it was that I took my first step into my father's world. I found myself running one hundred times around the stadium in Olympia, Greece, where Pindar had his day in the sun once upon a time. A group of nuns gave me the high five as they came and went. After them, there was only the groundskeeper repeating: "You are nice . . . you are nice," as I completed each lap. Finally, he had sense enough to go sit in the shade.

Even though most people did not give a fig anymore for his sports sonata, for me Pindar was another puzzle-piece of the living hero. A child of my times, I still did not know who or what the hero was or is, but the victory song gave me the opportunity at least to learn the words which once had underscored the athlete as timeless, beautiful, and striving. Although I hadn't memorized a poem since "Annabelle Lee" in fourth grade on the command of a teacher with a hairdo like an inspired tarantula, I decided to memorize Pindar's poetry while training for the Greek Marathon.

As race day approached, I returned to Delphi for several days. Unfortunately, the bus door opened onto my foot and I yelped. But the next morning the foot wasn't too bad, and I left town to explore the olive grove below, which slopes for miles to the sea. For several days I ran deeper into the grove and left stone markers to keep from getting lost. As I ran, I found myself beginning to discover all sorts of things. There was a respect for my father's devotion to practice. So that his body would know when his mind forgot, he spent countless hours. And my dream horses came back to me as I trotted along behind the woman leading a mule into the grove. She waved and so did I.

The day I got lost it was hot, and by noon I was following a new road. At a hollow-eyed ram, dead for some time, I made a U-turn. And within the hour, I was in a village inhabited by sleeping cats. There was also a sign which indicated that Delphi was ten kilometers further on.

Setting off, I tried to forget that I was the only Tittle born allergic to exercise. Exercise-induced anaphylaxis was what they called it. In case I should suddenly blow up like a red balloon and my veins collapse, I carried shots at all times. This time, however, I did not have one on me. I felt a wave of panic and guilt. How could I forget? The reaction can be fatal, and it was only because my mouth was turning hard and my hands were beginning to redden and itch that I now remembered the shot on the little blue table back at the hotel. I slowed the pace. To save time and eliminate switchbacks, I also left the road and began to climb hand over fist. My left temple pounded. The worst of it was that I lost track of my address and telephone number. All the poetry I had memorized was gone too. And along with it, the childhood that was just beginning to come back to me.

There was only granite. And the arena of the world of course, becoming large. I bowed my head when the sky ballooned. I breathed deeply and loved it. And then, but for a lemon tree, I forgot the world.

For a long time, the tree was straight ahead like a hand reaching out for more. Then, as I passed through its shade, I remembered the *trick*—the one thing that my father told me. Without thinking I pointed toward my destination and kept one finger aimed. And through it, words began to flow, timid at first as pilgrims. With the trick, my father the athlete had been able to take aim with a football and make distance, even time, disappear. For me, memories of all kinds came back. One by one until they filled my veins and moved even faster than the dream horses. My heart grew quiet. Looking back. Fragments. Puzzle-pieces. Then the moment broke like a string of pearls . . .

In 1963, the Chicago Bears beat the New York Giant in the championship game 14–10. There was some controversy at the time over the violence, but then, isn't there always. It was only a game. But then, for competitor and spectator alike, the meaninglessness of games is too bold for them to be completely meaningless. We watch what we dream, despite the action. Every game is a myth in this respect. As games are a model for life and society, it is for society to choose either fairy tale or myth, either the happy ending or the good struggle.

And the hero must bear witness to the struggle that we all wage, every moment of our lives—in which there are no happy endings because there is no end—and like Prometheus must remind us that the struggle is heroic.

When my father retired from professional sports in 1964, our life began. Like other families, we had our share of luck. And when times were bad, we held on and went for daylight. If I remember correctly, my parents' arguments took a turn, and their faces, without makeup, without helmets, were like clowns in a sad circus. At first my brothers and I played the stunned audience. Then my brothers left the firing range. And I flung myself into the fray like a ref trying to separate, then bring together two boxing champs. Once, I shouted so that I lost my voice. And this shut them up in amazement. In a state of nervous exhaustion, my mother collapsed in the kitchen in 1965. My father lifted her up in his arms and ran to the back bedroom while we were eating hotcakes. Her face was white. His face was red. He kept running.

After a lifetime in the eye of the sports hurricane, retirement occasioned a sudden drop. And the transition from the sports

world was, for all of us, a bit like going from the Himalayas to the parking lot. The air was different. I can think of no other way to describe it. Fortunately, the stresses surfaced. I had learned from my father that the artist must work at his art. And I felt sorry that for the first time since Dad was six years old, he was out on the streets. He worked of course at business, charity, and public speaking. He was never not working. But in most of those secular games for old people, it seemed to me that victory was a matter of dollars and cents and the moment was always in the future or the past, it was never called into the here and now, it was never inspired, there was never quite the same *we* to it.

I wasn't sure what was happening. But as a connoisseur of bad weather, I suspected in my mother's tears a silent storm. And I sensed that as a family, we were used to the lean years, the hungry years of striving. Attainment was foreign to us. And a cornucopia filled with the accomplishments of the past did not satisfy.

I also sensed that my father was alone in ways that only a person who lives his dream can be. The football field had been my father's emotional home and I believe he was homesick for it.

Retirement. Minnette, Y. A., Rookie, Dianne, and Pat. Atherton, California, 1965.

But what did I know really? Nothing. For the most part, in 1965, I could hear my mother and father arguing at night. Like they were mining for gold in the back bedroom, they brought out hammers, pickaxes, shovels, dynamite. They ripped apart an invisible mountain. I imagined gold dust in their hands. A child no longer, I pulled for both teams.

The sixties continued to be a humbling experience for my parents. My brother Mike walked off the football field and hurled himself into activism and the sixties crusade. He was arrested in peace marches and experimented with marijuana that he stashed on occasion inside a bust of Socrates. But wherever he hid it, my father, as clairvoyant as Edgar Cayce, was sure to find it. And Y. A. Tittle was forever chasing my brother down the driveway in his boxer shorts. He fought. He really fought for his family. And it was a little like the Chicago Bears. He never gave up.

In 1966, my grandmother's little sister, Great-Aunt Dorothy, showed up at our house to widen the generation gap. When we arrived home from school, there was her boat-sized Chevy parked across our driveway, blocking the escape route of my brothers' friends, and Dorothy herself, at five feet flat, prepared to take on the teenage kids armed with only her best poker stare, a washcloth and a baseball bat. No Californian had ever seen anything like it. No one else had relatives like this, who cared about what underclothes we might be wearing when the ambulance came to pick up the bodies after we were dead. But Dorothy cared, mightily. She worked in the credit department at Sears and was also one of the toughest gamblers in the state. Bumpy Bob who ran the Shell Station in our town said so. Bumpy Bob added that Dorothy was a tough customer. The teenagers in the nighborhood would have agreed. She cared in a way that was so far out it was practically a hallucination. People came over to the house, I think, just to get chewed out by my great-aunt Dorothy Armstrong.

In 1967, I went to Greece to study for the summer, and my parents fell in love. But it was with increasingly less favorable results that my father continued to live by his instincts. If every athlete has to have a sex or drug story, my father has his.

One warm, California day Y. A. Tittle was getting ready to go to Chicago to accept what he termed the Mr. Clean Award. Prior to his departure, however, his intuition got the upper hand when he found both of my brothers busied in the kitchen, making, oh, about a half dozen mayonnaise sandwiches for two people. The Bald Eagle, wearing a dark blue suit, marched right back to their rooms, and, like a Mongol warrior bent on sacking a shrine, shut his ears to the sweet sitar music of Ravi Shankar, took up the bust of Socrates and shook it. Out came the baggie again. And with this little sack, my father marched through the cloud of incense right back into the kitchen and read my brothers the riot act. Then he flew out the door and in disgust threw the baggie at least 20 yards into the garbage can. (He could still throw). But then he thought, what if the garbage men found it? So he snatched the baggie out of the garbage can and tore out of the driveway.

At the airport, he hurriedly flushed the baggie down the toilet. The baggie gurgled back into the toilet bowl. So he emptied the baggie and flushed, this time observing the toilet handle as if it were some dignitary. No luck. Glup. Hundreds of little marijuana bits floated into view as the last call for his flight was announced.

With no time to spare, the former football great got down on his hands and knees and began wiping marijuana from the sides of the toilet bowl. . . .

"Sir!" said the U.S. Marine to Y. A. Tittle as he dashed out the door. "I am proud to meet you, sir. Aren't you Y. A. Tittle?" he asked with a wide, warm grin. For a moment, perhaps, Tittle wasn't sure. Nothing is easy, he thought with a gulp. And didn't he know it.

In 1968, at a chapel assembly in a nearby town, I trembled my way through the "Moonlight Sonata," seized by fear, shyness, disgust, chest pains, stomach pains, pains in my fingertips, shortness of breath, and twitching all at once. The piece might have ended up as a polka for all I know. The one thing it was not was *legato*. Rather than wait for the applause, if there was any, I skipped my bow and streaked to the exit. And not for the next twenty years did I touch a piano.

At home, since nobody had any interest in throwing lessons, my brothers took time out from their other activities and decided to become defensive linemen whose job it is to squash the quarterback. This was fine. My father had never pushed his sons into sports. And rather than embarrass them by showing up at their sporting events and adding to the pressure, unless he was invited my father watched from a safe distance, and from behind a fence or bush—just like his friend Blocker had done for him when he was young.

A lull before the storm.

In 1969, somehow my parents got it into their heads that an imagination was even more to be feared than a marijuana cigarette and that my mythology books were as subversive as Communism. The crowning catastrophe of my high school career came when my teacher caught me writing a short story about the end of the world in chemistry. I attended Castilleja, a private girls' school in Palo Alto. I cannot remember that teacher's name but I can remember her brisk walk and her splayed feet. I remember the energy of her ponytail and that she smiled when angry. We got along just fine until the class when I accidentally took one look to my right, out the window, and saw the oval of tree branches and the patch of blue sky beyond. I began writing, and although the teacher's figure snagged my peripheral vision in front of my desk, I could not stop writing until I finished my line. Like a bucking bronco rider, I think the main character was hurtling down the wrong birth canal and the world was a bloody mess. And that's when my whole story was ripped into confetti in front of the class.

Later on, she called my parents. I think they would have been happier had I been carried away writing notes to a neighbor and making flower doodles in the margin. They looked upon my unfinished tale as an act of treason.

The last straw broke on the weekend when I disappeared for a day, again carried away while writing. I arrived home late, stone sober and holding a piece of paper folded over many times. In the ensuing disturbance, I declared defiantly that if I was lucky enough to go off to college I had no intention of joining a *sorority*.

Like a javelin to the heart, that one word did it. In alarm, my parents decided to send me to a party school near, but "no farther east than the Mississippi River!" (I did not go silently but I went.) "Are you dating a third baseman yet?" My father called to ask. "Are you in the mainstream?"

Actually, my freshman year I was playing football after class with a group of 12-year-olds who gathered on the university football field. The boys were short a player the day I took a short cut through the stadium back to the dorm. So I tucked my skirt up like a diaper, kicked off my shoes, and cut loose until the darkness scattered us and we called the game. Would I come again tomorrow? they asked. Would I be a regular?

" . . . Y. A. Tittle?" exclaims my advisor. "But you don't mean." (Yes, yes, oh yes I do. But then I nod my head too soon.) "That great Protestant minister from Utah?"

In the end we had a very nice conversation about names and my ancestor, Exxa, who wrote to her brother Yettie (short for Yelberton) after the Civil War about the possibility of pulling up stakes in Georgia and moving to Sulphur Springs, Texas. In 1871 Exxa and her husband William set off by wagon and got as far as Carthage. They built a log house there. And there never was another Yelberton, I told my advisor, until my father was born. After ten seconds in the cradle, his sister sprayed him with eau de cologne in a goodwill gesture that was completely misunderstood. And some had doubts about the long, old name, which nobody had claimed since the Civil War. It was a mouthful. But when my grandmother Alma said it, it became as fine as a hard seed.

The author and her father. Graduating senior, 1968.

In 1970, while attending the wrong French class, I meet a boy who beats me in a running race later in the day. "I have met the man I am going to marry," I tell my father when he calls later that night. "He plays the classical guitar and owns a black dog. Just give me another day. I don't know his name yet."

1971. I return to Greece to study for a year, and my father is inducted into the Hall of Fame in Canton, Ohio, by his good friend Wellington Mara, one of the owners of the New York Giants: "Y. A. Tittle came to New York in the twilight of his career . . ." I do not grasp the significance of this honor. There is a military dictatorship in Greece at the time, and I am followed to and from classes by secret service police, my mail from home is opened, and several of my Greek friends are tortured.

After finishing a year of study in Athens, I meet up with the boy from French class again. This time, I beat him in a running race. We fall in love and get married. The day before, there is a small party for friends and family on the island of Spetses. In front of a small red house on a cliff between two Turkish towers, our Greek friends roast a lamb and the retsina flows. The Hall of Fame athlete, however, is unable to sit on the ground due to old football injuries. The same old left knee injury, his badge of courage on the field, has for once left my father feeling a little helpless. But an old fisherman comes to his rescue and carries a chair all the way from his house, through the orange grove, through the olive grove, and past the yellow church. He sets it against a tree and sits my father down. Though it is late August and hot, the full moon is a pleasing reminder of coolness. The following day, family and close friends attend the ceremony in a small church on Lycabettos.

Upon our return from Greece, my youngest brother, Rookie, turns seven and I find that my other two brothers have become fine student athletes while I have been away. My brother Pat, though very tough on the football field and a scholarship athlete at the time, was not a tough guy anywhere else. Always the Robin Hood of the family, Pat was forever taking from our refrigerator and dresser drawers to give to the homeless who lived down at the railroad tracks. Nobody even knew they were there until he sought them out, and gave to the one known as Jimmy the Bum, the respect owed to Socrates himself. Pat hung the world on his every word. To him, Jimmy was a hero.

Over the holidays, Pat goes to the Fox Theater in Redwood City with a friend. He takes a seat and is surrounded by a gang of Hispanic kids who ask him to step outside. One of them stabs him in the chest. My brother runs into the lobby and shouts, "Arrest that man!" Meanwhile his attackers have sauntered out and are standing on the sidewalk. The young man with the knife turns and sees my brother, wet with blood from his punctured lung to his knees. And he smiles before taking out the knife once more.

What I'm telling now is, in a sense, a football story. For how my brother went down into a lineman's crouch when his attacker lunged and how he keyed off that metal blade is just one of the ways being a football player can come in handy. Though blood was gulping from his chest, Pat dodged his assailant until he humiliated him. Murder apparently was not unacceptable. But having to try too hard at anything, even killing, wasn't cool.

Later that year, his attacker knifed a fellow inmate and was himself killed in prison. And Pat, who was misdiagnosed with leukemia and covered with bruises from head to toe, remained in the hospital fighting a rare blood disease for some time. If it hadn't been for the bums who kept a constant vigil there, it might have been a bore. Instead, they healed him with their jokes and stories. They called him Pat the Cat and told him he had nine lives.

1972. My daughter, Elisa Mera is born. In this year, I wrote my first real poem. I wrote in the middle of the night when the house was quiet, then I practiced my harp and ran at dawn.

My mother was the first person to read it. She read my poem one morning after looking in on her granddaughter, and she said it was as if I had been blessed and then abandoned. And then she cried. Her tears freed me to write, to write even more. But then, my father wanted in on the action.

He wanted to read the poem that made my mother cry, and he wouldn't take no for an answer. "I like poetry," my father said. "Trust me."

Knowing that he never took the time to read the 1,000 pounds of newsprint about him, let alone the book he co-authored, I gave him the poem like a lawyer serving a legal notice. He adjusted his glasses and sat down, settling into his lawn chair like a bear ready to hibernate for the winter. He opened to the first page of a one-page death sentence. *c* was the first letter of the first word.

"But," he said, "*c* isn't capitalized."

"Well," I said, "I guess you've come to the end of the poem."

And when we looked at each other, the truth was pretty funny and we started to laugh. It was a laugh that made a big sky inside my body. And this laughter freed me to write, to write even more.

1973. For our landlord, Charles Niederhauser and his wife Ruth, whose 92nd birthday it is, I play Erik Satie's "Gymnopedies" on the harp. And though the old performance terrors come roaring back, Charles, deaf at 96, lifts his arms and then plucks the string-less air with as much rapture as Nicanor Zabaleta himself, the true harpist. Mrs. Niederhauser's face seems to be made from the wings of many moths. As soon as they leave I call up a nearby convalescent home and make arrangements to play for the patients in the infirmary next day.

Keeping just one small step ahead of fear, my harp and I crash out of the elevator on the hospital's fourth floor. The place is a real hatching ground for God knows what and there is no question that the cure for cancer is to be found growing in the carpet. In a sweat, I am ushered into a room more suffocating than a bad conscience, where the carpet steams like a tropical jungle and a ceiling painted urine yellow lowers like a guillotine. In that heat, every string goes out of tune as soon as I finish tuning, and even while I am tuning it. No matter, barks an old woman who fixes me with one squinty eye like a pirate. "Let's get on with the show!"

This time, no Charles Niederhauser was there to imagine music. Among others, I played for a grand lady who had shrunk into a delicate bird with sharp black eyes. Afterward, as I packed up, the tall concert harp was surrounded by ancients with voices as breakable as Meissen porcelain, one of them hers. When her daughter asked how she liked the music, "What music?" she answered. "Why, the harp music, mother." The black eyes glared. "What harp?"

1975. I build a classical repertoire and team up with a harpist in church for duets. There are times when my hands shake so violently that I cannot get them onto the strings. When I tell my former teacher that I sometimes find myself gasping for breath during practice, she says, "maybe you are repressing the desire to sing."

On March 26, Michael Christian de Laet is born at sunup.

1978. A Chinook wind is blowing. We have moved to Colorado and I am going to the grocery store. Until this time, I have not sung since reaching the high note in the national anthem at the ball game between the Dallas Cowboys and the Giants back in 1963. It always seemed to me that America fell after that high note, and kept falling from the highest pitch of her song.

At Safeway no one sings, and sibling war erupts as I lift my children into the shopping cart in the parking lot. Then, just as suddenly, they are allies and crouching down as if in their very own cave, with the wind blowing into their wide-open mouths and their hair beating about their heads like chopsticks. Howls erupt when we enter the store and pass the candy next to the cash register. People instinctively turn with the look that says one of two things: either *how lucky are you* or *how lucky am I.*

Moving up one aisle and down another like a mouse in a maze, I do not take comfort in thoughts of swift-footed Achilles, I just shop. I do not notice anyone, don't smile, I am not in the mood. I ignore a very old man whom I pass in the aisle. Then I turn up another aisle, and there he is again. And this time I stop. The kids are flat on their backs and doing the cancan with a hint of malice.

The shoe . . . The old man was reaching for something, a box of Band-Aids, who knows? But it had fallen, and when he bent down to the floor, his body bent no farther than halfway. He paused. I paused. It was nothing, really, at first.

The man's old face was that of an eagle. His nose was straight and his mouth was set like a seam in stone. His face, tight to the bone, was crisscrossed with lines. He was a worker, maybe a farmer or an old hand. And his jacket was a little tattered. When he bent down, I noticed that his shoes were old and turned up at the toe.

The man reflects for a second, as if to note the aches, the pains, and to touch the wall of his body's limitations, as if to say OK. I watch this man as if Odysseus in rags has just bent back his mighty bow in the hall of suitors, for I have never seen such human grace and dignity before. And then the man reaches again, exercising his will in movement, in almost painful slow motion. Precisely, he extends his arm. Beautifully, his hand opens.

The giftgiver. The hero. Nothing new, it happens every day. And Odysseus had nothing on this guy.

1979, 1980, 1981—the years go on. One day at my daughter's music lesson I open a book and read at random: "music and poetry were synonymous in ancient Greece." I jot down the names of the "praisesingers" with a lipstick. Pindar, who wrote sports poetry. And Sappho, who sang:

> *Some say infantry, some cavalry corps*
> *and some will maintain that the swift oars of our fleet*
> *are the finest sight on dark earth.*
> *But I say, whatever one loves is.*[1]

Struck by the line, I memorize all of Sappho's surviving lyrics. Hers was the voice of the individual woman, the voice in solitude.

As an instrument of praisesinging, the harp dates back to the Sumerians in the third millenium B.C. And as the Greek poets sang to the lyre praises of their gods and heroes, people listened, even the blood-splattered warriors listened at the end of their fighting day. The warrior Achilles himself played the harp. With the harp, and with the study of ancient poems, I finally found a way to praise what I admired.

In 1981, I compose music to accompany Greek scholar and poet, Nanos Valaoritis, as he chants from Homer's *Iliad* and *Odyssey*. We perform at numerous universities. And I continue to wonder where the women's voices are.

Then, one night my daughter has a dream. After dinner the next day, she decides to dance it for us. I couldn't very well play "Greensleeves" or "Claire de Lune" to accompany the galloping dance and then the breathless, halting story of my daughter's dream. So I decide on an improvised version of Gregorian chants with lots of fourths, fifths, and octaves. With her brother writhing in agony on the carpet at her feet, and her father seated on the couch, she speaks while I play.

Later that year a Sumerian story, "Inanna and the Huluppu Tree" and the *Homeric Hymn to Demeter* are adapted to the harp and performed for children. It is time to expand the repertoire to include women's voices and other oral cultures: "The Song of Deborah," the story of Jepthah's daughter, selections from Euripides' *Trojan Women*.

In 1982 my parents are standing in the driveway. It is raining. During the previous hour I have been trying out my own singing voice with original music composition at the harp. I need criticism at this point and I am searching for people who dislike poetry, so that I can figure out where it is I lose them in performance. I have already removed that part of the program where the professor's wife fell asleep, and if there are any other weak spots I know my parents will lapse into a coma.

But instead they have listened, listened to every note and word. And when they can listen no more but must dash off to catch an airplane, my father turns around in the rain and calls to me, "What Greek was that?"

"That was no Greek," I shout back. "That was me! My voice! My poem! Or part of it was anyway."

"Oh," he says, "alright. But when the time comes, you sure as hell better throw your voice. Because you know, it's out of balance with the music. Just a little. Either the music is too loud and drowns you out, or your voice is too soft, not strong enough. Throw it! I mean, just point that voice at somebody and fire the tar out of the dang thing!"

Why didn't I think of that?

"And never forget," my mother sings out sweetly, "You have nothing to lose."

And so I did indeed prepare to throw my voice. And when the time came, I threw it. Strange to say, a voice was there, materializing out of thin air. It gathered volume, like a long pass completed.

Karnack, Texas. In 1985 we returned to Caddo Lake for a surprise 80th birthday party in honor of my father's high school football coach, Odus Mitchell. The night before the party, we sat on the back porch like tiny knots in a world of lace. Aunt Huline was there, with her husky voice you could dance to, and so was Alma Tittle's brother, Uncle Burtis, who had brought out the family photo album. From the way he cherished that book, you would think ancestors were kicking up diamonds on every page. While everybody else was enjoying a good argument, I sat on the back porch listening to the bobwhites going back and forth with the whippoorwills. The moon shone with its steadfast light on H. L. Blocker's pickup truck. That afternoon, my parents' friend had brought over to the house pieces from a hornet's empty nest, some lily pods, and an armadillo shell, because he knew that I made small sculptures from the day's leftovers. Blocker joined in my treasure hunts for an occasional wing of a swallowtail or mourning cloak blown apart on the roadway. He also knew the name of every bird on Caddo Lake, and delighted in them as if they were rubies and sapphires flung into the sky. He was the richest man I ever knew. By then, he was arthritic and in his seventies, and his truck was bashed in because Blocker had had a stroke and run it off the road. But Blocker could be dead and still get up the next day. And come hell or high water, he was not about to miss the birthday party.

I noticed my mother sitting in a rocker by the back door in a long nightgown with her toes poking out, looking at sixty like the bride of the night landscape. The quiet of the woods once again was filled to the brim with the clear sound of hoots and crickets, the same quiet my mother had heard years before, when she imagined her grandmother trying to pass on the family story, even though it was broken into pieces, lost, flung into the woods. But the story was safe forever in the forest. Its echoes were picked up by all the wild creatures in the Piney Woods, and by all the trees that swayed, defiant and noble. There was a quiet there that took everything we said and did and found the good. I heard it now.

The next day, everyone would gather for the reunion and for

Coach Mitchell's birthday. This meant that early the next morning was the last chance for H. L. Blocker and Y. A. Tittle to argue about fishing. Since my father's brother Jack had passed away, there was nobody else in the family with patience enough to catch a fish. It did not make any sense for us to try, and I would bet my life that in a fishing contest any Tittle could be beaten by the bait. But that did not stop Blocker from saying, "C'mon Hong Kong!" And it certainly did not stop my father from responding to his latest nickname with a dash to the bait box. (They began calling him Hong Kong Charley the day a snake popped out of the debris down by the boat house. My father could not see very well, but he sprang into action with a hoe nevertheless. Thinking it to be a copperhead, Dad, typically, could not give up, and strangely, the snake couldn't either. When finally he gave pause, the snake did the same. Flopped on its back, it read: "Made In Hong Kong.")

"C'mon Hong Kong!" Blocker said. And then the two of them disappeared with their coffee cups and fishing poles across the surface of Caddo Lake.

There had been no Mavericks reunion since high school graduation. And when it happened, never before had I seen such a collection of bewildered wives. Since every Maverick who ever was showed up to surprise their former coach on his birthday, they came from every state in the Union and roared down Farm Road #9 to deck the tables with casseroles and string beans, pecan and sweet potato pies. Former East End Alley Cats, Northside Ninnies, Southside Sissies and West End Winners all took turns at the chili.

We ate dessert by daylight and the children ran wild, and then we danced. Slide—Step Step—Slide. They called it the Texas Two Step, and I marveled again at how the big-bellied cowboys danced, moving as easily as a longhorn turns his head in the sun.

Even before Odus arrived, this bizarre birthday party on Caddo Lake was taking everyone by surprise. White-haired Lloyd Whitehurst took one look at my mother and began to cry. He told her in our presence that she was still the prettiest girl in town. Like many other ex-Mavericks, my parents were grandparents by this time, and children and grandchildren were dragged around the yard like a string of Christmas lights on the pretense of being introduced to old friends. On this day all the Mavericks seemed more surprised by their own progeny than by each other.

The festivities were now in full swing, and Blocker and Scotty Baldwin, the trial attorney whose job it had been to track the old Mavericks down, were probably leaving Hog Wallow just about then with Coach Mitchell. And no doubt Blocker was spinning yarns in that prehistoric landscape as the herons swooped overhead, Blocker who moved on land and rode in a boat the way the prophets of old once walked with their God.

"He's coming!" cried Puppy Gilry.

And grandchildren who did not know Coach Mitchell from a mud fence screamed and waved slender arms as they ran down to the boat dock. I, who didn't know a blitz from a banana peel, was also caught up in the moment.

When Odus arrived at the boat dock, he was met by generations all wearing maroon T-shirts printed with his famous phrase: "For Cramps Sake!" Odus himself was wearing a smile that was Y. A. Tittle's greatest trophy—and Y. A. Tittle knew it. As my father walked toward Odus Mitchell with his hand outstretched, the former Marshall Mavericks stamped out their cigarettes and stood up straight. A cheer went up. And for some mysterious reason, all the old Mavericks leaped in the air.

Thanks to that look of surprise on Coach Odus Mitchell's face, I would no longer be content with heroes who were dead or played it safe on the printed page. Never before had I understood why an audience was once so willing to listen to hero-stories which took days on end to tell. One after another, the praisesingers got up to tell the good news (the hero was alive!) and for hundreds of years nobody bothered to write anything down. And suddenly it dawned on me too. The human face was the best part. And it was a big mistake to think that there was even a story without somebody up there with lips that twitched like Odus Mitchell's.

After the festivities, I walked down to the lake. I had always cherished the story of my grandfather, Arthur Young, who in 1927 waded in the shallows of Caddo Lake looking for fresh water pearls. Then he climbed a hill covered with honeysuckle and sat down on Potter's Point, so utterly exhausted was he by the thought of a girl living over in Palestine, Texas, way beyond Tyler. When Arthur shut his eyes, there were Minnie Anne's eyes, Minnie's stately walk, Minnie's widow's peak.

But wasn't this the East Texas badlands? Where the stomping ground of Franciscan fathers had become the haunt of pirates? Where outlaws and adventurers flocked to a paradise of wild turkeys and nut trees, a wonderland of brothels and cockfights and the last place on earth to find a trial by jury? Where Arthur now sat, the one-time Secretary of the Texas Navy, Colonel Potter, had been shot for merely suggesting a jury trial. Arthur's dreams would have to include the sad exodus of the Caddo Indians from their native land. With his eyes closed he could hear the speeches of Chowabah, Tarshar, and Oat urging the people on after the Treaty of Expulsion.

Arthur blinked awake, but his dreams continued. Now he saw amber waves of grain beneath skies with room enough for eagles. And now from their shaggy beehive homes, the Caddo Indians emerged. They moved about busily, as vermilion was mixed with bear fat to make paint and salt bricks were readied for trade. Arthur cheered the runners with the tattoos of lightning bolts on their faces and contemplated the meaning of a 50-mile race ending up at the dancing grounds. He listened to White Moon[2] and learned about the ways in which a partner can be found in life. White Moon said a partner could be an animal or a natural phenomenon like a cyclone. But Arthur wanted nothing but Minnie.

He hurried to his sister Etheldra's house to tell her they would marry. He knew. Caddo Lake had told him.

This much is true. My mother was born to Arthur Young and Minnie Anne on 15 October of the following year. And Caddo Lake, though not exactly a member of the family, became something like a hearth for the Tittle-DeLoach clan. Many ghosts are there. Many sad stories on my mother's side. But Caddo Lake is where we gather to this day. In the march of our ancestors, we take our turn.

In 1927 it was my grandfather's turn to dream. Before that, it was Abe and Alma Tittle who paddled down the boat rows among the lily pads in Eagle's Nest and Hog's Wallow. And in 1943 my father took a boat out on the lake to dream of a football career after high school graduation.

Now it was my turn. Here at Caddo Lake, I came close to understanding what it means to be a family. It's like a championship game. Once it starts, you're committed. Get knocked down. Get up. Because victory is the birthright. Standing there, I almost thought for a moment that I knew my father. *But I don't.* I think we only share a nostalgia for the fall and perhaps the funny intuition that the forward pass is thrown in the belief that there is something out there to connect with.

It was September. As always, Caddo Lake was like an only sister who greeted me with some new treasure that time had created in her. And now, the lily pads had grown. They reached out of the water and cupped the breeze in their big round faces. In the boathouse, I touched the fragile spider's web again, and thought: so this is the harp from which to sing the words of praise for the athlete.

I would continue my hunt for the living hero. I would not blame the system or the age, those ahead or behind, but go on looking for the image of a well-trained and steadfast heart.

As for my victory song? Yes, that song was written in the wind from Chicago. Because in the end, all we Tittles suffer from the same condition. We don't always win, but we never give up.

The champions . . .

The winner for the rest of his life has the sweetest calm
as far as victory in the games can give it.
Yet the day by day excellence is best that can come to any man.

—Pindar, *Olympian* 1

Who then, was given the young wreath of victory for his hands'
*   work or speed of foot,*
putting before his eyes the game's glory and accomplishing thought
*   in action?*

—Pindar, *Olympian* 10

THE NEW YORK GIANTS
1963

49 Barnes, Erich	39 McElhenny, Hugh
63 Bolin, Bookie	77 Modzelewski, Dick
79 Brown, Roosevelt	40 Morrison, Joe
60 Byers, Ken	26 Pace, Jim
34 Chandler, Don	20 Patton, Jim
62 Dess, Darrel	25 Pesonen, Dick
16 Gifford, Frank	81 Robustelli, Andy
15 Griffing, Glynn	82 Scott, Tom
06 Guglielmi, Ralph	85 Shofner, Del
87 Hillenbrand, Jerry	66 Stroud, Jack
52 Howell, Lane	65 Taylor, Bob
70 Huff, Sam	88 Thomas, Aaron
37 Killet, Charles	14 Tittle, Y. A.
24 King, Phil	64 Walker, Mickey
81 Kirouac, Lou	80 Walton, Joe
53 Larson, Greg	21 Webb, Allan
76 LoVetere, John	29 Webster, Alex
22 Lynch, Dick	31 Winter, Bill

Program Notes & Epilogue

Program! Program!
Can't Tell a Hog From a Frog
Without a Program!

—Y. A. Tittle

The players today:

Minnette and Y. A. Tittle. A few weeks before my parent's 40th wedding anniversary my father gave a talk in Dallas, Texas. Afterward a man in the audience came up and returned to him the gold bracelet my father had given to my mother when she was sixteen years old. My mother had given my father's present to this man, a boyfriend at the time, and he had kept it for all those years. In celebration of their anniversary, my father gave the bracelet to my mother one more time.

Minnette Tittle fulfilled one of her father's dreams and went to Tibet. In 1981 she was among a small group let into the country. Collector of Primitive and Folk Art, on her travels she has slept in yurts on the Russian border and long houses on the Sepic River in New Guinea. Now in her sixties, she is still always first to the top of the sand dune.

A constant companion on my mother's high road to adventure, my father contents himself mostly with the Folk and my mother with the Art. On their most recent trip, to the Highlands of New Guinea, my father took along a can of tennis balls to teach the warriors "stick ball." It began with the ex-football great wondering if he had died and gone to football heaven or football hell as pigs screeched across the playing turf and several hundred warriors surrounded him like the letters of a strange alphabet. The group before him became as serious as English professors when my father removed his hat and sacrificed other articles of clothing like a jacket or a sweater to serve as the bases. But when he shouted, "Hey badabada! Swing!" everyone knew how to do it. And Tittle's bald and white-haired head bobbed into an afternoon light years from the glitz of pro football yet just a nanosecond from home. The anthropologist and archaeologist in the group soon realized that my father had just discovered the entire "umbrella defense" once more. In the faces of strangers were Ripper, Chunkin' Charley and Racehorse, Stormy, the Geek and the Hatchet, Piggy, Zolly and Alnut, Ski Boots, Hurrying Hugh, Lefty, Mad Dog and Hog, Slim, Rosey and Kat, Big Red and Little Moe. The list of brothers was endless. And today, a New Guinea Chief is on the list.

"Colonel Slick" or "the Bald Eagle" is currently known to his grandchildren as "Yaya." He is founder and president of a national insurance company and honorary president of the Penguin Club, an all-women organization founded by his wife in grammar school. Following in his father's bootleg tradition, he teamed up with real estate maverick Raymond Handley, and built the first solar-powered industrial complex in the country. He is currently involved in commercial real estate in Silicon Valley, California, and travels widely on the speaking circuit as a teller of tales. He still dreams that he can't find his helmet.

H. L. Blocker lived with his wife Odessa in Karnack, Texas, until his death in the springtime of 1990. He is buried in Leigh, Texas.

Blocker's accidental reunion with our family came about after his retirement when he moved back to the Piney Woods and took up hunting in the woods and fishing on Caddo Lake. With his wife, he had gone to town to drop off laundry at the Snow White Cleaners. Having just returned to East Texas, Blocker struck up a conversation with a stranger in the parking lot and mentioned that he once worked at the Snow White Cleaners for Abe Tittle.

"Abe Tittle?" said the stranger. "Why he lives down at Caddo Lake."

Then Abe Tittle wasn't dead?

"No way! This is his son, the football player."

And that is how they found each other and took up arguing and finagling again. Blocker became a deacon in the Baptist Church in Mooringsport, Louisiana. Before that he owned a string of pressing shops. He was a mail carrier in Southern California, and he served in the armed forces with distinction. Blocker got out of town, too, and lived to see the atomic bomb go off while stationed in the South China Sea.

Blocker returned to East Texas and moved into a pale green house with a large front yard, five acres at least. Behind his house was the lake and in front of his house Farm Road #9 and the forest. Blocker had forgotten how to tell the weather from looking out his front window after living so many years in California, but the old ways came back. One afternoon while he was sitting against a pine, a squirrel mistook him for a tree and jumped onto his shoulder. After the squirrel jumped off, both creatures looked at each other and both were stunned. With that, Blocker became a bona fide member of the forest. The quiet of the woods moved in and found a home in the holiness of his heart. He didn't mind that the Klan was back in Mooringsport. And he didn't mind that the woods right across the street were fenced and off limits to all but the military, or that under the Johnson administration, this land owned by Mr. Taylor was sold to the U.S. government to provide a safe haven for a large arsenal of middle-range rocket engines. Explosions were, and are still common, as this arsenal is reduced under Russian observation. But if this was progress, that the Russians loved Shady Glade, this was fine. And if it was progress that the Klansmen in front of the high school wore beards under their hats, it was progress not worth mentioning in Blocker's view. The lake was alive. And how much it came to life in him, Odessa, and everyone else engaged in the struggle for survival—that was progress.

Blocker gave up hunting. Normally he killed one deer, which fed the household for a year. But after the squirrel jumped on his shoulder, he said good-bye to a lifetime of squirrel stew and figured he was an old man who just didn't need to eat that much.

Shortly before he died, I returned to the lake for a visit. I was working as a professional harpist at the time. I was also trying to write this book. But I wasn't very lucky. And on one of the unluckier days, I saw Blocker through the window. He was down at the boat house and getting ready to fish. I walked down to the lake to say hello but started crying instead. Blocker's hands were so swollen with arthritis his knuckles were like baseballs. But his hands managed to do the job, any job, and do it well. His hands were my inspiration though he never knew it. I admitted to him as if to the world that my best was not good enough—to which he replied, "Maybe that's right. But you can still do it." Then he put a fishing pole in my hand and took me to his favorite fishing hole where the fish almost laughed in the water, and where I caught my first fish.

In return, I dedicate to him this story, the record of these memories.

Dianne Tittle de Laet. 1993 . . . "Let's go," said Beverly Stern. "Let's get down to the field."

As we climbed through the railing and slipped through the hilarious Babel to the far edge of the green grass, I reminded myself that I had never really liked the game of football. So why did I love it now for the nerve it touched, even though the game wobbled in my understanding and never fell into the hands of the right metaphor? But this time the kids from our local high school were close to the division championship, closer than ever before. And they had gotten farther downfield than the pros, the Hall of Famers, farther downfield than Y. A. Tittle, the San Francisco 49ers and the New York Giants put together. At the melting pot of Menlo-Atherton High School, the kids had crossed the lines of color and broken the second longest losing streak in California history to win their division championship. Three years before, the crowd in the stands had been comprised of a father, a mother, 8–10 drug dealers with beepers and cellular telephones, and five stragglers at most. The local newspaper said that a school with that much graffitti on the goalpost could not possibly win. Yet the Hispanics, Tongans, Samoans, Blacks, Whites, and Asians at the school disagreed and the article was pasted up on the locker-room door. Three years later, we won. Under the leadership of ex-priest Dave Theis, as principal, and ex-Pittsburgh Steeler Henry "Model T" Ford as football coach, the school made a turnaround and the M-A Bears made a comeback. 4,000 people showed up at the game. The band played. And for me, not in seventeen years of watching professional spit, spirit, and striving do the work of victory had anybody brought a triumph home like this. Now it was Ricky Jones, Antonio Tau, Greg Stern, and Michael de Laet with body heat enough to thaw the memory of the lost NFL championship some 30 years before.

As the reader knows, my quarterbacking father threw a pass back in the 1963 championship that was so overthrown that I went for it from my seat in the end zone. But that pass, intended for Del Shofner, finally found its mark on the fingertips of his grandson's teammate, number 25, wide receiver Ricky Jones.

And in 1994, somebody in the family finally won a national championship—Y. A. Tittle's granddaughter on the women's crew team from Princeton University. Elisa and her teammates set a collegiate world record in Cincinnati, Ohio. It was a sunny day with a tail wind. The weather was warm. And they rowed in one smooth and seamless streak to the finish line.

From *The Odes of Pindar* by Richmond Lattimore:

The victory odes commemorate the success of a winner in the games or athletic meets held at regular intervals from very early times down to the Roman period. . . . The form was a favorite of the lyric poet, Pindar, and the modern reader always wonders why. There are several considerations. Among them, success meant a demonstration of wealth and power or of superb physical prowess, shown through peaceful and harmless means. The very useless-ness of these triumphs, which aroused the contemptuous anger of Xenophanes and Euripides, might have attracted Pindar. A victory meant that time, expense, and hard work had been lavished on an achievement which brought no calculable advantage, only honor and beauty. This may sound somewhat romantic, but competition symbolized an idea of nobility which meant much to Pindar; and in the exaltation of victory he seems sometimes to see a kind of transfiguration, briefly making radiant a world which most of the time seemed to him, as to his contemporaries, dark and brutal.

The occasion and circumstances of the ode must have been somewhat as follows: When a victory was won, the victor (or his family, or some wealthy friend) commissioned the poet to write the commemorative ode. When this was complete, a choir of men or boys (probably amateurs and friends of the victor in some cases) was trained to sing it. The true presentation of the ode was, then, a performance given for the victor and his friends some time after the event. . . .

There are also many mythical passages which were doubtless forecast in advance and which are to some extent self-subsistent entities. Yet even in such "pure" myths, Pindar hardly tells a story, for he assumed that the outlines of legend were generally familiar to his listeners; rather, he lights up some intense moment, or series of moments, in a tale already known . . .[3]

ACKNOWLEDGMENTS

My thanks to the men and women of Steerforth Press for being on my team and for letting me be on theirs. I am especially grateful to writer and editor, Alan Lelchuk, for his words of encouragement.

Thanks and love to my fearless agent, Gerry McCauley, and to his partner, Ted Crane. To John and Joan O'Donoghue for their support. To my children who inspired me with their play to write. To my husband because the right words were always the wrong words first, and he listened. To Evelyn M. Draper, Professor of Drama at Stanford University. To the wonderful Karen Gillum, my copyeditor. To Maggie. And to Ricky Jones. Thank you. I am deeply indebted to the many sportswriters of magazines and newspaper articles about the Giants, to Peter Finney from the *Times-Picayune,* to Don Smith with whom my father co-authored *I Pass,* and to Allie Sherman, Andy Robustelli and Frank Gifford. These players were with me—on offense. On defense, there were those who threw a block with their generosity and a willingness to help. Among them, I count the late Robert Riger, his son, Robert Riger Jr., Jerry Pinkus and Daniel Rubin, Pat Hanlon, R. C. Owens, Alexis Fife, Paul Spinelli and Polly Swann, Herb Vincent, Lyn Cunningham, Richard Greiger, Perry Cartwright, Betty Ann Crawford, Mary Holt, William E. Deibler, Rose Cervino, Palmer Bovie, Antony Raubitschek, Lyn "Huline" Hilliard, and my parents.

Sometimes I was forced to go far afield to find out the facts and figures of my father's life as an athlete. Had it been otherwise, I would have finished this story long ago. But then, I would never have discovered just how good he was.

I would also like to acknowledge a nameless shopkeeper in Delphi, Greece, who used to shout at me when he saw me training for my first marathon. He would shout, "Have fun! Have fun! And then you will finish your race!" He was right about *Giants and Heroes* as well. And I thank him.

Note: Some quotations and photographs are from clippings in family scrapbooks. Unfortunately, these were often trimmed so neatly that it is impossible to identify their sources. Some I have been able to track down; for the imperfect references given to the rest, I beg the writers', photographers', and my readers' pardon.

NOTES

Dedication
1. Martial, *Epigrams of Martial* No. 1, Palmer Bovie tr. New York: Plume Books, 1970

Preface
1. *The Odes of Pindar*, Richmond Lattimore, tr. Chicago: The University of Chicago Press, 1976. *Pythian* 10. All quotations from Pindar in this book make use of this translation.

Chapter 1, Ready Break!
1. Koppett, Leonard. "Fans Hear Bach But Cheer Bears." The *New York Times*, 30 December 1963, C Section, page 24, column 5
2. *Archilochus, Sappho, Alkman: Three Lyric Poets of the Late Greek Bronze Age*, Guy Davenport, tr. Berkeley: University of California Press, 1980. Archilochus no. 201
3. Gifford, Frank and Harry Waters, *The Whole Ten Yards*. New York: Random House, 1993. 182
4. Gifford, Frank and Charles Mangel, *Gifford on Courage*. New York: M. Evans and Company Inc., 1976. 155
5. Ibid., 158
6. Robustelli, Andy and Jack Cleary, *Once A Giant, Always*. New York: Quinlan Press, 1987
7. Gifford and Waters, *Ten Yards*, 194
8. Ibid., 200

Chapter 2, East Texas
1. Gleason, Mildred, *Caddo: A Survey of Caddo Indians in Northeast Texas and Marion County 1541–1840*. Marion County Historical Commission, 1981. 2
2. Ibid., 42
3. Tittle, Y. A. and Don Smith, *I Pass*. New York: Franklin Watts, Inc., 1966. 77
4. Tittle, Y. A. Conversation with author, January 1995. *"Along The Banks of the Caddo from the Piney Woods of East Texas Came the Challenging Roar of the Marshall Mavericks!"* Quoted from memory by Y. A. Tittle from the *Dallas Morning News*, Sports Section, 1943.
5. Tittle and Smith, *I Pass*, 81

Chapter 3, LSU Tigers

1. Kope, Myron. "Layne: I Sleep Fast." *Quarterbacks Have All The Fun,* edited by Dick Schaap. Chicago: Playboy Press, 1974. 90

2. Tittle and Smith, *I Pass,* 93

3. Ibid., 92

4. Finney, Peter. *Fighting Tigers II, LSU Football, 1893–1980.* Baton Rouge: LSU Press, 1960. 157

5. Tittle and Smith, *I Pass.* 108

6. Cason, Jimmy. Conversation with the author, January 1995.

7. Tittle and Smith, *I Pass,* 98

8. Ibid., 99

9. Ibid., 97

10. Ibid., 98

11. Ibid., 98, 99

12. Mule, Marty. *Eye of The Tiger: 100 Years of LSU Football.* Atlanta: Longstreet Press, 1993. 106

13. Finney, *Fighting Tigers II,* 157, 165

14. Ibid., 160–163

15. Ibid., 164

16. Mule, *Eye of The Tiger,* 105

17. Ibid., 102

18. Ibid., 104

19. Tittle and Smith, *I Pass,* 99

Chapter 4, Baltimore Colts

1. Tittle and Smith, *I Pass,* 137

2. Ibid., 136

3. Ibid., 135

4. Ibid., 118

5. Ibid., 125

6. Ibid., 127

7. Ibid., 131

8. Ibid., 132

9. Ibid., 147

10. The Book of Matthew, 5.18

Chapter 5, San Francisco 49ers

1. Excerpts from 40th anniversary issue of 49er program.

2. Tittle and Smith, *I Pass,* 151. A paraphrase with respect to Morabito and founding of 49ers.

3. Ibid., 166

4. Ibid., 182

5. Ibid., 198

6. Gottehrer, Barry, *Football Stars of 1963.* New York: Pyramid Publications, 1963. 68

7. Ibid., 69

8. Grieve, Curley, "Y. A.: I'll Face Colts." In *San Francisco Examiner,* 25 November 1957, Sec. III, page 1

9. Homer. *Iliad,* Richmond Lattimore, tr. Chicago: The University of Chicago Press, 1951. *Il.* 23.440

10. Ibid., 23. 669, 672–3

11. Tittle and Smith, *I Pass,* 148

12. Gamage, Walt. "Sport Shots." From family scrapbook. © *San Francisco Chronicle.* Reprinted by permission.

Chapter 6, New York Giants
Childhood Heroes

1. *Hymn to Demeter.* Lines 54, 47–48. *Homeric Hymns* translated by Charles Boer. Chicago: The Swallow Press, 1970. p.91, 95 (Actually, I remember these words from a translation by Penelope Proddow for the children's book, *Demeter and Persephone,* now out of print. Charles Boer's translation is a close second.)

2. Barnard, Mary. *Sappho* Berkeley: University of California Press, 1958. Sappho no. 84. (Barnard's numbering; in standard Oxford numbering, fr. 145)

3. Steinbreder, John. *Giants: 70 Years of Championship Football.* New York: Taylor Publishing Company, 1994. 49

4. Ibid., 84

5. Ibid., 53

6. Heinz, W. C. "Conerly: The Most Beat-Up Man In Pro Football." In *Quarterbacks Have All The Fun,* 90

7. Tittle and Smith, *I Pass,* 35

8. Ibid., 38

9. Ibid., 37

10. Ibid., 41

11. Ibid., 42

12. Ibid., 51

13. Robustelli and Cleary, *Once A Giant,* 81

14. Ibid., 81

15. Ibid., 81

16. Ibid., 90

Snow

1. Homer, *Iliad.* Lattimore, tr. *Il.* 2.467–8; *Il.* 10.257–8; *Il.* 16.582–3; *Il.* 17. 87–8

2. Robustelli and Cleary, *Once A Giant,* 96

3. Gottehrer, *Football Stars,* 60

4. Tittle and Smith, *I Pass,* 226

5. Gifford and Waters, *Ten Yards,* 194

6. Kope, Myron. "Layne: I Sleep Fast" in *Quarterbacks Have All The Fun,* 134–135

7. Robustelli and Cleary, *Once A Giant,* 101

8. Gottehrer, *Football Stars*, 113

9. "The Y. A. Tittle Story," narrated by Pat O'Brien. Produced by the National Football League Hall of Fame in Canton, Ohio, 1971. Videocassette.

10. Ibid.

11. King, Larry L. "Unitas: Sure It Hurts When I Throw, It Hurts All the Time" in *Quarterbacks*, 1

12. Leonard Shecter, "Starr: Pride of the Packers" in *Quarterbacks Have All The Fun*, 89

13. Robustelli and Cleary, *Once A Giant*, 105

14. "Pro Football: Taste for Honey." *Time*, 10 January 1964. p. 57

Monsters of The Midway, 1963

1. Terzian, Jim. *Great Teams' Great Years: New York Giants.* New York: Macmillan, 1973. 7, 162–166. Material adapted and paraphrased from these pages.

2. Terzian, *Great Teams*, 24

3. Ibid., 95–101

4. Gehrenbach, T. R., *A History of Texas And The Texans: Lonestar.* New York: Collier Books, 1968. 208

5. Atyeo, Don. *Violence In Sports*, New York: Van Nostrand Reinhold Company, 1979. 221

6. "Pro Football: 'Taste for Honey." *Time* 10 January 1964, p.57

7. "Pro Football: 'Taste for Honey.' " p.57

8. Robustelli and Cleary, *Once A Giant*, 111

9. "All The Strings." *Newsweek*, 13 January 1964, p. 71

10. Seneca. *ad Lucilium Epistulae Morales*, no. 7, Richard M. Gummere, tr.

11. "Pro Football: 'Taste for Honey' "

12. "Chicago's Papa Bear." The *New York Times*, 30 December 1963, C Section, page 24

Chapter 7. Overtime

1. *Sappho: A New Translation*, Mary Barnard tr. Berkeley, University of California Press, 1958, 41

2. Gleason, Marion. *Caddo*, 24.

3. Lattimore, *The Odes of Pindar*, p. x

PERMISSIONS ACKNOWLEDGMENTS

Grateful acknowledgment is made to the following individuals and institutions for permission to reproduce photographs and text in this book:

Photographs:
Frontispiece of Dianne Tittle, age 4, from author's collection.

pp. 2, 14: Robert Riger photos; Courtesy of Robert Riger, Jr.

p. 18: Top photo courtesy of Marshall High School, Marshall, Texas.

pp. 54, 69: Courtesy of Louisiana State University.

pp. 61, 142, 177, 184: © Daniel Rubin Photos, New York City, New York.

p. 104: Courtesy of the San Francisco 49er archives.

pp. 117, 215: Courtesy of the New York Giants.

p. 123: Collection of R. C. Owens.

p. 132: © Frank Rippon/NFL Photos.

pp. 18 (bottom) 33, 38, 78, 84, 108, 119, 146, 226, 233, 237: Collection of Y. A. Tittle.

Text:

Martial, *Epigrams of Martial*, Palmer Bovie, tr. Reprinted with permission of the translator.

Pindar, *The Odes of Pindar*, Richard Lattimore, tr. Copyright © University of Chicago Press, 1976. Extracts reprinted with permission of the publisher.

"Fans Hear Bach but Cheer Bears." Copyright © by the New York Times Company. Reprinted by permission.

Gifford On Courage, Copyright © 1976 by Frank Gifford. Reprinted by permission of the publisher, M. Evans and Company, Inc.

The Fighting Tigers II, LSU Football, 1893–1990, by Peter Finney, Forward by Paul Dietzel (Revised Edition). Copyright © 1968, 1980 by Louisiana State University Press. Reprinted with permission of the publisher.

Once A Giant, Always, by Andy Robustelli and Jack Cleary. Extracts reprinted with permission of Andy Robustelli.

New York Giants, Frank Terzian. Copyright © 1973 by NFL Properties. Reprinted with permission of the publisher.

A NOTE ON THE AUTHOR

Dianne Tittle de Laet is a poet and harpist dedicated to the re-creation of women's voices from the
Sumerian, Old Testament, and Greek oral traditions. She lives with her husband in Menlo Park,
California.

A NOTE ON THE BOOK

The text for this book was composed by Steerforth
Press using a digital version of Walbaum, a typeface
designed by Justus Erich Walbaum in the early
nineteenth century. The book was printed on acid
free papers and bound by Quebecor Printing~Book
Press Inc. of North Brattleboro, Vermont.